PENTATEUCH

A SPIRITUAL INTERPRETATION

VERY REV. PETER SAMUEL KUCER, MSA

En Route Books and Media, LLC
St. Louis, MO

⊕ENROUTE

Make the time

En Route Books and Media, LLC

5705 Rhodes Avenue

St. Louis, MO 63109

Cover credit: TJ Burdick

Library of Congress Control Number: 2020944880

Copyright © 2020 Very Rev. Peter Samuel Kucer, MSA

All rights reserved.

ISBN-13: 978-1-952464-28-7

Acknowledgments

I would particularly like to acknowledge Very Rev. Edward Przygocki, M.S.A., U.S.A., Province Provincial of the Missionaries of the Holy Apostles, who gave me permission to publish.

Special thanks also to Dr. Sebastian Mahfood, O.P., President of En Route Books and Media, for publishing this work.

Contents

Dogma and Sacred Scripture

1

While listening to both Scott Hahn and Brant Pitre the idea kept reoccurring in my mind to write an overview of the bible as a systematic theologian with the intent of demonstrating how Sacred Scripture is at the heart of Catholic doctrine and supports doctrine. With reference to Vatican II and Pope Benedict XVI, Hahn in affirming the complementary relationship between Scripture and dogma writes:

> Vatican II has stressed in recent times that Scripture must be "the very soul of sacred theology" (*Dei Verbum* 24). As Joseph Cardinal Ratzinger, Pope Benedict XVI echoed this powerful teaching with his own, insisting that, "The normative theologians are the authors of Holy Scripture" ... He reminded us that Scripture and the Church's dogmatic teaching are tied

---

tightly together, to the point of being inseparable: "Dogma is by definition nothing other than an interpretation of Scripture." The defined dogmas of our faith, then, encapsulate the Church's infallible interpretation of Scripture, and theology is a further reflection upon that work.[2]

In a document of the International Theological Commission prepared by Cardinal Kasper and authorized by Cardinal Ratzinger the supposed conflict between Scriptural exegesis and dogma is likewise firmly rejected:

> The conflict between exegesis and dogma is a modern phenomenon. Following on the "age of Enlightenment", the tools of historical criticism were developed with the aim in mind also of favoring emancipation where dogmatic and ecclesiastical authority were concerned. This critical method became more and more radical. Soon it was no longer a question alone of a conflict between Scripture and Dogma: the very text of Scripture itself came under critical scrutiny to discover the so-called "dogmatic second-coatings" in Scripture itself. This line has been continued in the socio-political and psychological critical methods and these have searched the text for socio-political conflicts or for suppressed psychic data. All these approaches are based on the common suspicion that the dogma of the Church and Scripture conceal a primitive reality which can only be uncovered by critical questioning. ...

---

[2] Scott Hahn, and Curtis Mitch, *Ignatius Catholic Study Bible: The Book of Exodus* (San Francisco: Ignatius Press, 2012), 8.

Correct interpretation of Scripture is vital in the matter of the dogma of the Church. In this question of dogmatic interpretation of Scripture and the obligation involved, the Magisterium is not in an inferior position to God's Word, but rather at its service (cf. *DV* 10). The Magisterium does not judge the Word of God but the correctness of its own interpretation of it. No age can go back on what has been formulated dogmatically through the Holy Spirit as a key to the interpretation of Scripture. This does not exclude the fact of new points of view in the future or new formulations. Finally, the judgment of the Church in matters of faith is constantly being enriched thanks to the advance work of the exegetes and their careful studies of what Sacred Scripture intended to say (*DV* 12).[3]

Interpreting Sacred Scripture with reference to the literal, historical meaning while, at the same time, acknowledging that God intervenes in salvation history avoids on the one hand the error of a Scriptural interpretation that belongs, Benedict XVI writes, "only to the past" and on the other hand the error of a Scriptural interpretation that is an excessive spiritualization of Scripture by failing "to respect the historical character of Revelation."[4]

Although this book gives a special emphasis to a spiritual

---

[3] International Theological Commission, "The Interpretation of Dogma," 1989, http://www.vatican.va/roman_curia/ congregations/cfaith/ cti_documents/rc_cti_1989_interpretazione-dogmi_en.html 2-3.

[4] Benedict XVI, "Verbum Domini," 2010, no. 35, w2.vatican.va, http://w2.vatican.va/content/benedict-xvi/en/apost_exhortations/ documents/hf_ben-xvi_exh_20100930_verbum-domini.html

interpretation of the Pentateuch, it does so in a manner that springs forth from and is based on the literal interpretation, in particular the actual words used in Hebrew. Although the presented spiritual interpretation is distinctly Catholic, in which Jesus Christ is the fulfillment of all the types contained in the Old Testament, this does not mean that the ancient Israelite people did not also read the Bible in a spiritual way, and their spiritual interpretation, also, at times, will be presented. As Brant Pitre points out, "For the [ancient] Jews …it is the invisible that is more real than the visible, and if you want to understand what's going on in the visible world in history, pull back the veil of heaven and then you will see."[5]

For example, as will be seen later, marriage in the visible realm is representative of the spiritual marriage between God as Israel, as is particularly evident in the prophetic literature. Another concrete example are the two visible cherubim statues that sat upon the ark of the covenant and there functioned as signs of the greater invisible angelic reality. Similarly, the Tabernacle, and the later Temple were believed to be patterned upon the invisible reality of heaven and were for the Jewish people a place to encounter heaven on earth through visible, material signs.[6]

Section Questions

1. Fill in the blank. Scripture is the "_____ of Sacred Theology (*Dei Verbum* 24)."

---

[5] Brant Pitre, *Genesis and the Books of Moses: Unlocking the Mysteries of the Pentateuch*, MP3, 7.

[6] Pitre, MP 3, 17.

Introduction to the Pentateuch

The Bible differs from all other books because it is divinely inspired. This means, explains the *Catechism of the Catholic Church*, that since God is the primary author of Scripture, Scripture teaches without error "that truth which God, for the sake of our salvation, wished to see confided to the Sacred Scriptures (*CCC* 107)."[2] This excerpt from the *Catechism* cites Vatican II's document *Dei Verbum* paragraph eleven which in turn cites passages from, among others, St. Augustine, St. Thomas Aquinas, The Council of Trent, Leo XIII encyclical *Providentissimus Deus*, and Pius XII's encyclical *Divino Afflante Spiritu*. These cited passages provide the context by which to properly interpret the *Catechism*'s teaching that Scripture teaches without error truth that pertains for our salvation. With respect to truths that do not pertain to our salvation, such as, as explained by St. Augustine the shape of the universe, God may allow these scientific explanations to be described as they appear to the eye:

St. Augustine *Genesis Ad Litteram* 2, 9, 20

> I must say briefly that in the matter of the shape of heaven…the Spirit of God, who spoke through them [the sacred writers of Scripture], did not wish to teach men these facts that would be of no avail for their salvation.[3]

Errors that do appear in the text of Sacred Scripture, further teaches Leo XIII in his encyclical *Providentissimus Deus*, must be seen as due to mistakes made by copyists, by a translator and are not proper

---

[2] "Catechism of the Catholic Church," no. 107, vatican.va, http://www.vatican.va/archive/ENG0015/__PP.HTM.

[3] Johannes Quasten, Walter J. Burghardt, and Thomas Comerford Lawler, *Ancient Christian Writers: The Works of the Fathers in Translation, no. 41* (Mahwah: Paulist Press, 1982), Augustine, Genesi Ad Litteram, book 2, chapter 9, 20, p. 59.

to the text itself since it is impossible for God as "supreme Truth" to "utter that which is not true." Some difficult passages may appear to contain error, but it is forbidden to hold that they actually do since, once again, God does not teach falsehood. Therefore, exhorts the Holy Father, the reader of Sacred Scripture is required to be patient while believing that it is possible with the right methods of interpretation to clear "up the obscurity" and to reconcile texts that appear to be "at variance" with one another.[4]

Often, apparent errors are only perceived as such because the interpreter of Scripture is reading Scripture overly literalistically while not paying attention to the genre through which the author is using to express his words. For example, an overly literalistic interpretation of Hosea's phrase, "I desire mercy, not sacrifice," is that God wants mercy and not sacrifice. However, this interpretation forgets that Hosea is using hyperbolic speech, which contains exaggeration. When Hosea is interpreted literality according to the hyperbolic form the words are in then it becomes clear that what is being taught is that God wants mercy more than sacrifice but still wants sacrifice as long as it is properly ordered by mercy.[5]

The century following the publication of Leo XIII's *Providentissimus Deus*, which affirms the unlimited inerrancy of Scripture, Pius XII affirmed this teaching by forbidding the restriction of Scripture's freedom from error to only that which directly pertains

---

[4] Leo XIII, "*Providentissimus Deus*," Nov. 18th, 1893, no. 20-21, w2.vatican.va, http://w2.vatican.va/content/leo-xiii/en/encyclicals/documents/hf_l-xiii_enc_18111893_providentissimus-deus.html.

[5] Amy-Jill Levine, The Old Testament, Transcript Book (Chantilly: The Teaching Company, 2001), 310; Scott Hahn, *Catholic Bible Dictionary* (New York: Doubleday, 2009), 390.

to faith and morals. As Aquinas, explains, this is because some matters in the physical and social sciences do pertain to salvation.

Pius XII *Divino Afflante Spiritu*

> When, subsequently, some Catholic writers, in spite of this solemn definition of Catholic doctrine, by which such divine authority is claimed for the "entire books with all their parts" as to secure freedom from any error whatsoever, ventured to restrict the truth of Sacred Scripture solely to matters of faith and morals, and to regard other matters, whether in the domain of physical science or history, as "obiter dicta" and - as they contended - in no wise connected with faith. Our Predecessor of immortal memory, Leo XIII in the Encyclical Letter *Providentissimus Deus*, published on November 18 in the year 1893, justly and rightly condemned these errors and safe-guarded the studies of the Divine Books by most wise precepts and rules.[6]

St. Thomas Aquinas

Does Prophecy [Inspiration] Deal with Conclusions Which Can Be Known Scientifically?

Moreover, I say necessary for salvation, whether they are

---

[6] Pius XII, "Divino Afflante Spiritu," 1, Sept. 30, 1943, w2.vatican.va, http://w2.vatican.va/content/pius-xii/en/encyclicals/documents/hf_p-xii_enc_30091943_divino-afflante-spiritu.html.

necessary for instruction in the faith or for the formation of morals. But many things which are proved in the sciences can be useful for this, as, for instance, that our understanding is incorruptible, and also those things which when considered in creatures lead to admiration of the divine wisdom and power. Hence, we find that mention of these is made in Holy Scripture.[7]

Section Questions

1. Discuss how exegesis and Catholic dogma are not essentially in conflict with one another. Do so by carefully defining key terms and including the following: Scripture and history, excessive spiritualization of Scripture, literal interpretation, and spiritual interpretation.

2. Fill in the blank. According to the *Catechism of the Catholic Church*, the primary author of Scripture is _____.

3. According to the *Catechism of the Catholic* Church, what type of essential truth does Scripture teach without error?

4. How does Sacred Scripture teach truth without error? Include the following in your response: scientific explanations, copyists, translators, literal and overly literalistic interpretations, literary forms (provide a few examples).

---

[7] Thomas Aquinas, "Questiones Disputatae de Veritate," q. 12, art. 2, dhspriory.org, http://dhspriory.org/thomas/english/QDdeVer12.htm#2.

5. According to Pius XII's 1943 *Divino Afflante Spiritu* are the truths of Sacred Scripture restricted only to matters pertaining to faith and morals? If so why, and if not why not?

Salvation History

Scriptural history is a presentation of key moments of salvation history. Salvation history, as Benedict XVI explains in his 2010 papal exhortation *Verbum Domini*, "is not mythology, but a true history, and it should thus be studied with the methods of serious historical research."[9] This means that historical claims of Scripture, respecting

---

[8] Julius Schnorr von Carolsfeld, "*The First Day of Creation* (woodcut by Julius Schnorr von Carolsfeld from the 1860 *Die Bibel in Bildern*," 1860, https://commons.wikimedia.org/wiki/File:Schnorr_von_Carolsfeld_Bibel_i n_Bildern_1860_001.png, Julius Schnorr von Carolsfeld [Public domain], via Wikimedia Commons.

[9] Benedict XVI, "Verbum Domini," September 30, 2010, W2.vatican.va, http://w2.vatican.va/content/benedict-

the genre in which they are written, are true. When reading Scripture, we are not, explains Pitre, to approach the Bible like a prosecuting attorney, where the subject, in this case the Bible, "is guilty until proven innocent."[10]

According to this prosecuting approach, historical truths described by Scripture and accepted by faith are subordinated to modern literary analysis. Such an approach not only places faith below reason but pits the two against one another with a priority given to reason. The "Catholic view" asserts Pitre, "has always been you take the truths of Scripture and then reason can support them and can confirm them but never can disconfirm anything that has been revealed by God."[11]

Some historians claim that since their discipline is a science and in order to maintain objectivity it is required to be suspicious of historical claims in Scripture. Pitre counters this claim by pointing out that the study of history is a very "soft" science and highly speculative since history, by its very nature, cannot be repeated to verify a hypothesis. In addition, it is very rare for a historian to be able to give a precise calendar date to an event since even when relying on archaeology the historian often arrives at a relative date by correlating the finding with established historical records, found on pottery, coins etc. The relative date that a historian arrives at is typically presented in popular form with a certainty that does not exist since the dating is based on varying degrees of probability: possible, probable, plausible,

---

xvi/en/apost_exhortations/documents/hf_ben-xvi_exh_20100930_verbum-domini.html

[10] Brant Pitre, *The Old Testament-A Historical and Theological Journey through Jewish Scripture*, MP 3 19.

[11] Pitre, MP 3 19.

demonstrable.[12]

Section Questions

1. According to a Catholic response, represented by Brant Pitre, what is the relationship of Sacred Scripture to history? Include in your response, 2010 *Verbum Domini* on Scripture and history, prosecuting attorney approach, modern literary analysis, probability and history as a science.

Motives of Credibility

According to the *Catechism of the Catholic Church* salvation history presented in the Bible as interpreted by the Magisterium and Tradition is credible, and hence reasonable. The specific motives of credibility that the *Catechism* identifies are, "the miracles of Christ and the saints, prophecies, the Church's growth and holiness, and her fruitfulness and stability (*CCC* 156)."[13] However, explains the Catechism, these "external proofs"[14] of God's Revelation are not what primarily move us to believe, even though the truths of Revelation "appear as true and intelligible in the light of our natural reason."[15] "We believe" asserts the *Catechism* "because of the authority of God himself who reveals them, who can neither deceive nor be deceived."[16]

---

[12] Brant Pitre, MP 3 19.

[13] "Catechism of the Catholic Church," no. 156, vatican.va, http://www.vatican.va/archive/ccc_css/archive/catechism/p1s1c3a1.htm .

[14] "Catechism of the Catholic Church," no. 156.

[15] "Catechism of the Catholic Church," no. 156.

[16] "Catechism of the Catholic Church," no. 156.

Nonetheless, continues the *Catechism*, "So 'that the submission of our faith might nevertheless be in accordance with reason, God willed that external proofs of his Revelation should be joined to the internal helps of the Holy Spirit.'"[17] These external proofs, or motives of credibility "show that the assent of faith is 'by no means a blind impulse of the mind'."[18]

Summarizing the position of the Church Fathers in relation to the motives of credibility, Pitre states, "Early Christians relied on motives of credibility also known as preambles of faith to demonstrate that it is reasonable to believe Divine Revelation. In defending Jesus' divinity, they appealed to miracles and prophecies. Jesus was prophesied about and fulfilled these prophecies." One important way to help our intellect and other people's intellect to be embrace the truths of faith with greater "accordance with reason" is by knowing, insists Pitre, "both the articles of faith and the basis for these articles of faith."[19]

When reading the Old Testament, therefore, Catholics are both to, explains Pitre, quoting the *Catechism*, to "read the Old Testament in the light of Christ crucified and risen (*CCC* 129)."[20] This faith filled interpretation of Scripture which recognizes that the Old Testament prophecies are fulfilled in the New Testament should not, though, states the *Catechism* "make us forget that the Old Testament retains its own intrinsic value as Revelation reaffirmed by our Lord himself (*CCC* 129)."[21]

---

[17] "Catechism of the Catholic Church," no. 156.

[18] "Catechism of the Catholic Church," no. 156.

[19] Pitre, 23 mp3 files.

[20] "Catechism of the Catholic Church," no. 129, vatican.va, http://www.vatican.va/archive/ccc_css/archive/catechism/p1s1c2a3.htm.

[21] "Catechism of the Catholic Church," no. 129.

Section Questions

1. List at least five of the six motives of credibility, or external proofs of the *Catechism of the Catholic Church* that indicate Revelation is reasonable.

2. True or False - Are the motives of credibility what primarily motivate faith in Revelation? Why or why not?

---

[22]   Ivan   Aivazovsky,   "Christ   Walks   on   Water,"   1888, https://commons.wikimedia.org/wiki/File:Po_vodam.jpg, Ivan Aivazovsky [Public domain], via Wikimedia Commons.

Interpreting Scripture

Interpreting the Old Testament in light of Christ's Resurrection and interpreting the Old Testament by bringing out its "own intrinsic value" is part of the interpretative tradition of Scripture that the *Catechism* identifies. According to the *Catechism* there are two main "senses" for interpreting Scripture: literal and spiritual.[23] The literal is the meaning the author intended to communicate through the words of Scripture. Since God is the ultimate author, the author of Scripture includes both the human author of Scripture who participates with the ultimate author of Scripture, God. The spiritual interpretation of Scripture is to be, writes the Catechism, "based on the literal (*CCC* 116)."[24] This spiritual interpretation is subdivided by the Catechism in three sub-senses: the allegorical sense, the moral sense and the anagogical sense.

The word allegory comes from two Greek words: *allos*, meaning "another, different" and *agoreuein* meaning "speak in the assembly".[25] It means that when people and things are being described they are symbolic of a related but different reality. Philip Cary traces the use of the term to ancient Greek philosophers prior to being taken up first by both Judaism and Christianity. Cary explains that according to an allegorical interpretation of Greek Gods, Apollo signifies the sun, Poseidon signifies the sea etc. People and things that are being

---

[23] "Catechism of the Catholic Church," no. 115, vatican.va, http://www.vatican.va/archive/ccc_css/archive/catechism/p1s1c2a3.htm.

[24] "Catechism of the Catholic Church," no. 116, vatican.va, http://www.vatican.va/archive/ccc_css/archive/catechism/p1s1c2a3.htm.

[25] "allegory (n.)," etymonline.com, https://www.etymonline.com/word/Allegory.

described also can represent higher spiritual realities.[26]

[27]

A related term to allegory is typology, which comes from the Greek word *typos*, meaning "a blow, dent, impression"[28] like the symbol that is formed on a page after being struck by a stamp. The stamp is the type and the symbol left behind on the page is the anti-type or fulfillment of the type. When applied to the Old Testament itself, an earlier historical figure, such as Adam prefigures Noah as a new Adam.

---

[26] Phillip Cary, *The History of Christian Theology* Lectures 1-18 (Chantilly: The Great Courses, 2008), 119.

[27] Matthias Stom, "Saint Jerome," first half of 17th century, https://commons.wikimedia.org/wiki/File:MatthiasStom-SaintJerome-Nantes.jpg, Matthias Stom [Public domain], via Wikimedia Commons.

[28] "Type," Online Etymology Dictionary, http://www.etymonline.com/index.php?term=type.

When applied to the Old Testament in light of the New Testament, all types in the Old Testament, whether Adam, Noah, Moses…, are fulfilled in the antitype, that is fulfillment, who is Christ. The types that anticipate Christ will always be similar to Christ in some way while, due to their imperfection, different. As pointed out by Pitre, if there was a one to one correspondence than there wouldn't be genuine typology, from the standpoint of promise and fulfillment, but only identity.[29]

By becoming born in time while fully retaining His divinity, Christ perfectly fulfills the imperfect types of the Old Testament both horizontally in history and vertically, because as divine, He transcends time and space, which constitute history. In Christianity, therefore, the typological, explains Cary, with its focus on horizontal historical relationships and allegorical interpretations, with its focus on vertical, figurative relationships (Apollo: Moon; Aphrodite: Love) are brought together.[30] For example, Christ is both the historical antitype, the fulfillment of Adam, and is the higher reality that transcends history which Adam is an imperfect figure of.

Besides the allegorical and typological interpretation of Scripture the other two kinds of spiritual interpretation are moral and anagogical. The moral interpretation is self-explanatory. The anagogical sense, though, needs to be clarified. The term comes from the Greek word *anagoge* meaning, defines the *Catechism*, "leading (*CCC* 117)".[31] According to this interpretation, Scripture is interpreted

---

[29] Pitre, MP3, 15.

[30] Phillip Cary, *The History of Christian Theology* Lectures 1-18 (Chantilly: The Great Courses, 2008), 122.

[31] "Catechism of the Catholic Church," no. 117, vatican.va, http://www.vatican.va/archive/ccc_css/archive/catechism/p1s1c2a3.htm.

spiritually in reference to heaven. For example, the Exodus of the Old Testament can be interpreted as representing a journey to, writes the *Catechism*, "the heavenly Jerusalem (*CCC* 117)."[32]

The criteria to discern the acceptability of spiritual interpretations of Scripture, including attempts at the intended literal interpretation, is three-fold: Scripture itself, the Magisterium, and Tradition.[191] The *Catechism* refers to these three criteria as "the content and unity of the whole Scripture (*CCC* 112)," "the analogy of faith (*CCC* 114)," and "the living Tradition of the whole Church (*CCC* 113)".[33] We are to interpret passages of Scripture in light of other scriptural passages since earlier scriptural Revelation are in harmony with older scriptural Revelation and the earlier (the Old Testament) is fulfilled in the newer (the New Testament.)

Interpreting a part of Scripture in its narrative biblical context, in its relationship to the logic of Scripture taken as a whole, is referred to by Scott Hahn as a canonical interpretation. In such an interpretation biblical passages are not interpreted "in isolation" but rather, explains Hahn, "in the context of the biblical canon. Its interpretive frame of reference is thus the entire collection of books grouped together into the Bible and deemed authoritative by the believing Church. Its rationale is that Scripture, despite the diversity of its works, has an underlying unity that coalesces around a common perspective of faith."[34] In further clarifying a canonical interpretation Pitre states:

---

[32] "Catechism of the Catholic Church," no, 117.

[33] "Catechism of the Catholic Church," no. 112-114, vatican.va, http://www.vatican.va/archive/ccc_css/archive/catechism/p1s1c2a3.htm.

[34] Scott Hahn, and Curtis Mitch, *Ignatius Catholic Study Bible: The Book of Genesis* (San Francisco: Ignatius Press, 2010), 115.

When he [Scott Hahn] refers to canonical interpretation what it means is that you are interpreting the text in its final form as we have it in the canon. So, in other words you are not speculating a sort of pre-history of the text that may be a scholarly, theoretical construct but the narrative that is there. So, in other words, we are reading the narrative in its narrative flow according to the narrative logic according to its final form in the text. … The reason he has to make this distinction is that in modern Old Testament scholarship, because of the rise of source criticism, there is a tendency to develop theories about hypothetical sources and then give dates to them, like JEDP, for example, and then scholars will say, well this passage is from J which is from the tenth century, and this passage is from P which is from the fifth century, so we can't read them as a unity, we have to read them as two separate passages. What [Hahn] is saying is if you want to speculate about that, that is fine, but in terms of theological exegesis all we have is the final form, so let's look at the canonical form and see if the narrative as we have it makes sense.[35]

Besides Scripture itself the other two reference points identified by the *Catechism* for properly interpreting a passage of Scripture are the Magisterium and Tradition. These two realities inform one another and are related to Scripture by being another mode of Revelation in the sense that they clarify what is at least implicitly taught in Sacred Scripture. The Magisterium refers to how bishops in union with the

---

[35] Pitre, MP 14.

Pope act as, writes Ratzinger, the "external form"[36] of Tradition in ecumenical councils by making explicit with specific "content"[37] what is implicitly revealed in Sacred Scripture, for example the teaching of the Trinity, the Virgin Birth, and the Immaculate Conception.[192]

Section Questions

1. What are the two main "senses" for interpreting Scripture? In responding, specifically sub-divide the second sense into three sub-senses while defining each sense.

2. What are three essential criteria, identified by the *Catechism of the Catholic Church*, for properly interpreting Sacred Scripture?

3. One of the essential three criteria for properly interpreting Sacred Scripture is sometimes termed the canonical interpretation. Define what a canonical interpretation means while including the following terms, final form, isolation, context, primary author, and underlying unity.

---

[36] Joseph Ratzinger, *The Episcopate and the Primacy*, trans. Kenneth Barker (New York: Herder and Herder, 1962), 51.

[37] Ratzinger, *The Episcopate and the Primacy*, 51.

Genesis

Historical Character of Genesis

According to the *Catechism*, Genesis uses symbolic, and figurative language in describing the beginning of the world. For example, the six days of creation in Genesis 1 are identified as how "Scripture presents the work of the Creator symbolically (*CCC* 337)."[2] Similarly,

---

[1] Philip Medhurst, "Creation. Genesis cap 1 v 10. De Vos," 1 January 2000, https://commons.wikimedia.org/wiki/File:The_Phillip_Medhurst_Picture_Torah_3._Creation._Genesis_cap_1_v_10._De_Vos.jpg, By Phillip Medhurst [CC BY-SA 3.0 (https://creativecommons.org/licenses/by-sa/3.0)], from Wikimedia Commons.

[2] "Catechism of the Catholic Church," vatican.va, http://www.vatican.va/archive/ENG0015/__P1A.HTM.

the Fall of Man in Genesis 3, states the *Catechism*, "uses figurative language (*CCC* 390)." However, clarifies the *Catechism*, this figurative language is used to narrate an event, in this case the sin of our first parents, which was an actual historical event "that took place at the beginning of the history of man (*CCC* 390)."[3]

In reference to Pius XII's encyclical *Humani Generis*, Scott Hahn writes, "Gen 1-11 may be regarded as historical in substance but mythopoeic in expression."[4] In this encyclical Pius XII writes, "the first eleven chapters of Genesis, although properly speaking not conforming to the historical method used by the best Greek and Latin writers or by competent authors of our time, do nevertheless pertain to history in a true sense."[5]

The historical core of these chapters from Genesis include, taught the Pontifical Biblical Commission, "creation of all things wrought by God in the beginning of time; the special creation of man; the formation of the first woman from the first man; the oneness of the human race; the original happiness of our first parents in the state of justice, integrity, and immortality; the command given to man by God to prove his obedience; the transgression of the divine command through the devil's persuasion under the guise of a serpent; the casting of our first parents out of that first state of innocence; and also the

---

[3]   "Catechism   of   the   Catholic   Church,"   vatican.va, http://www.vatican.va/archive/ENG0015/__P1C.HTM.

[4] Scott Hahn, and Curtis Mitch, *Ignatius Catholic Study Bible: The Book of Genesis* (San Francisco: Ignatius Press, 2010), 316-320.

[5]   Pius   XII,   "Humani   Generis,"   38,   w2.vatican.va,   http:// w2.vatican.va/content/pius-xii/en/encyclicals/documents/hf_p-xii_enc_12081950_humani-generis.html.

promise of a future restorer."[6] In the next section we will focus our attention on the first event affirmed by the commission as having actually taken place, God's creation of the world.

Section Questions

1. Representing the teaching of the *Catechism of the Catholic Church*, distinguish the historical event in in the Genesis Creation account from its symbolic and figurative aspects.

2. As identified by the Pontifical Biblical Commission, list four of the nine historical aspects that make up the historical core of the Genesis creation account.

Creation and the Trinity

Verse one of Genesis chapter one states, "In the beginning God created the heavens and the earth (Genesis 1:1 *RSVCE*)." The word create is a translation of the Hebrew verb בָּרָא (bārā'). According to the *Lexham Theological Wordbook*, this Hebrew verb is used in the Old Testament "only of God creating, never of humans making things."[7]

---

[6] "Catholic Dogma and the Teaching on Creation and the 1909 Pontifical Biblical Commission on Genesis," philvaz.com, http://www.philvaz.com/apologetics/p100.htm#Question3 .

[7] D. Mangum, D. R. Brown, R. Klippenstein, & R. Hurst (Eds.) *Lexham Theological Wordbook* (Bellingham, WA: Lexham Press, 2014), "Creation". "This verb is used only of creative acts performed by God. It appears five times in the creation narrative of Gen 1–2: God created (*bārā'*) the heavens and the earth (Gen 1:1; 2:4), the creatures of the sea (Gen 1:21), humankind

In contrast, the Hebrew verb עָשָׂה (ʿāśâ), which means to make, is used in reference to both to what God makes and things humans make.[8]

What distinguishes that which God creates from what man makes? When God creates, He does not need to rely on anything that is pre-existing. Instead, He can simply, without doing any violence, teaches Bishop Barron, to preexisting form, create out of nothing.

---

in his image (Gen 1:27), and creation as a whole (Gen 2:3). It also appears in other books, especially Isaiah. Isaiah says that after the exile God will create (*bārāʾ*) a cloud of smoke during the day and a flame of fire by night over Mount Zion (Isa 4:5). God created (*bārāʾ*) the ends of the earth (Isa 40:28); the heavens and earth (Isa 42:5; 45:18); human beings in general (Isa 45:12) and Israel in particular (Isa 43:1); light and darkness (Isa 45:7); and righteousness and salvation (Isa 45:8). He promises to create (*bārāʾ*) the new heaven and new earth (Isa 65:17). Psalms also speaks of God creating (*bārāʾ*) human beings (Psa 89:47); the heavens, angels, and lights of the sky (Psa 148:5); and north and south (Psa 89:12). David asks God to create (*bārāʾ*) a clean heart in him (Psa 51:10)."

[8] D. Mangum, D. R. Brown, R. Klippenstein, & R. Hurst (Eds.) *Lexham Theological Wordbook*, "Creation." "What is of interest is the use of the Hebrew word bārāʾ, occurring in 1: 1, 21 and three times in 1: 27 in connection with the creation of humans to describe their origin. God "created" them. Whenever this verb is used in the Old Testament, God is always the subject. And the verb is never followed by the accusative of material, unlike, for example, the verbs in "[he] formed man of dust" (2: 7 RSVCE) and "the rib . . . he made into a woman" (2: 22 NRSVCE). Although it probably goes too far to say that this use of bārāʾ explicitly teaches *creatio ex nihilo*, it does indeed lean in that direction. We should also note that Genesis 1 uses another verb for God's creating, the verb "make" (1: 7, 16 [2x], 25, 26). The verb ʿāśâ, unlike bārāʾ, often has a human subject." Victor P. Hamilton, *Handbook on the Pentateuch: Genesis, Exodus, Leviticus, Numbers, Deuteronomy* (Grand Rapids: Baker Academics, 2005), 381.

However, when we make something we cannot create as God creates, since we need to rely on pre-existing material out of which we form other objects. This often involves cutting and breaking apart the material we are using.[9]

[10]

This distinction between creating of nothing, *creatio ex nihilo*, and making from something is implied by the two Hebrew verbs: *bara*, which only is used for divine creation, and the Hebrew verb *asa* which includes human making. Not until 2 Maccabees will this implicit difference be made explicit when the mother of the seven brothers who are martyred explains to her youngest son, "I beg you, my child, to look at the heaven and the earth and see everything that is in them, and recognize that God did not make them out of things that existed (2 Maccabees 7:28 *RSVCE*)."

---

[9] Robert Barron, *Catholicism* (New York: Image Books, 2011), location 1068-1078.

[10] James Tissot, "The Creation," 1896 and 1902, https://commons.wikimedia.org/wiki/File:Tissot_The_Creation.jpg, [Public domain or Public domain], via Wikimedia Commons.

In interpreting the first verses of Genesis, the Church Fathers not only brought out the implicit acknowledgement of God creating out of nothing but also saw hidden references to the Trinity, which had not been explicitly revealed to the sacred writers.[11] The Church Fathers, though, were aware of the ultimate author of the text who is the Triune God and who gradually in the Old Testament prepared the way for the Revelation of the Trinity. Irenaeus of Lyons in *Against Heresies* writes that "Scripture tells us in the book of Genesis that He made all things connected with our world by His Word"[12] and, "one god formed all things in the world by means of the Word and the Holy Spirit."[13] Genesis, according to Irenaeus, implies that God the Father created the world through his Word and Holy Spirit. A reference to the Word, that is the Son, is in Genesis chapter one, "And God said…(1:6 *RSVCE*)." Genesis chapter one's reference to the Holy Spirit is "the Spirit of God was moving over the face of the waters (1:2 *RSVCE*)." The Christological meaning of these verses is further illuminated when, points out Pitre, they are seen in light of John Chapter 1, "In the beginning was the Word, and the Word was with God, and the Word was God (John 1:1)." With this first verse of his gospel, John makes explicit what is implicit in the first verse of Genesis. Jesus Christ is the Word of God, is God, and through him the Father

---

[11]   See   Augustine,   "Confessions,"   11.5.7,   newadvent.org, http://www.newadvent.org/fathers/110111.htm.

[12] Irenaeus of Lyons, Irenaeus Against Heresies, in A. Roberts, J. Donaldson, & A. C. Coxe, *The Apostolic Fathers with Justin Martyr and Irenaeus* (Buffalo, NY: Christian Literature Company, 1885), Vol. 1, Book IV, chapter 20, 1.

[13] Irenaeus of Lyons, Irenaeus Against Heresies, Vol. 1, Book IV, chapter 20.

created.[14]

Section Questions

1. With respect to God's creation and human making, how does
    the Hebrew verb בָּרָא (bārā'), used in Genesis 1:1, differ from
    the Hebrew verb עָשָׂה ('āśâ)?

2. How did Church Fathers interpret the first verses of Genesis in
    a Trinitarian manner? In your answer identity how each
    person of the Trinity specifically acts in the Creation of the
    world.

Six Days of Creation

────────────────

[14] Brant Pitre, *Genesis and the Books of Moses: Unlocking the Mysteries of the Pentateuch*, MP3 5.

[15] Julius Schnorr von Carolsfeld, "*Sixth Day of Creation*, (woodcut by Julius Schnorr von Carolsfeld from 1860 *Die Bibel in Bildern*), 1860, https://commons.wikimedia.org/wiki/File:Schnorr_von_Carolsfeld_Bibel_i

Catholic commentators on Scripture, outlines Pitre, have interpreted the six days of creation in a variety of ways.[16] Some, like St. Basil the Great (330-379) interpret the days as referring to six chronological days in which God created the universe.[17] Others hold that the six days represent six stages of creation. Still others interpret the days symbolically and unrelated to how God created the world in time.[18] According to St. Augustine, "What kind of days these were it is extremely difficult, or perhaps impossible for us to conceive, and how much more to say!"[19]

The essential Catholic understanding of Genesis' creation account,

---

n_Bildern_1860_006.png, Julius Schnorr von Carolsfeld [Public domain], via Wikimedia Commons.

[16] Pitre, *Genesis and the Books of Moses,* MP3.

[17] St. Basil the Great, "Haxaemeron (Homily 2)," newadvent.org, http://www.newadvent.org/fathers/32012.htm. "Why does Scripture say one day the first day? Before speaking to us of the second, the third, and the fourth days, would it not have been more natural to call that one the first which began the series? If it therefore says one day, it is from a wish to determine the measure of day and night, and to combine the time that they contain. Now twenty-four hours fill up the space of one day — we mean of a day and of a night; and if, at the time of the solstices, they have not both an equal length, the time marked by Scripture does not the less circumscribe their duration. It is as though it said: twenty-four hours measure the space of a day, or that, in reality a day is the time that the heavens starting from one point take to return there. Thus, every time that, in the revolution of the sun, evening and morning occupy the world, their periodical succession never exceeds the space of one day."

[18] Pitre, *Genesis and the Books of Moses,* MP3.

[19] Augustine of Hippo, *The City of God*, in P. Schaff (Ed.), M. Dods (Trans.), *St. Augustin's City of God and Christian Doctrine* (Buffalo, NY: Christian Literature Company, 1887) Vol. 2, p. 208, book 11, chap. 6.

as represented by the *Catechism,* is that the Triune God who transcends and is not, therefore, dependent on matter, freely and lovingly created a good world out of nothing for His glory. In addition, God providentially sustains and guides what he created. Finally, God blessed the angels and human beings with free will so that we can participate in His providential design in which one day the world will be free from sin and imperfection.[20]

After Genesis chapter one and chapter two describe six days of creation, God "finished his work which he had done, and he rested on the seventh day (Genesis 2:1 *RSVCECE*)." Robert D. Miller asks, "if God finished on the day 7, what was the work did on the seventh day, as He finished?"[21] The answer, comments Miller, is in the verse that follows. According to verse three the work God did before he rested was blessing day seven and hallowing it. This work entailed creating, writes Miller, a "temple in time" that is entered when the sun sets on Friday and is left when the sun sets on Saturday.[22] By rising on Sunday, Jesus created a new "temple in time" that begins the first day of the week, after the seventh day, the day of the Jewish Sabbath. The Christian temple in time is Sunday since Jesus restored creation on the first day of the week, signifying a new beginning.

That God rested on the seventh day is also an important detail since the Hebrew word for seven (שֶׁבַע *sheva*) is the root word for

---

[20]   "Catechism   of   the   Catholic   Church,"   vatican.va, http://www.vatican.va/archive/ccc_css/archive/catechism/p1s1c2a3.htm, 290-314.

[21] Robert D. Miller II, *Understanding the Old Testament* (Chantilly: The Teaching Company, 2019), 28.

[22] Miller, 28.

swearing an oath to create a covenant (שָׁבַע *shava*).[23] By resting on the seventh, the use of the Hebrew word *sheva* implies, comments Brant Pitre, that God entered into a sacred covenant with all of creation.[24]

Section Questions

1. True or False. Augustine taught that the six days of creation took place in six consecutive, chronological days, while St. Basil interpreted the six days of creation as referring to six stages of creation.

2. List at least four Catholic teachings on Creation, as taught by the *Catechism of the Catholic Church* (290-314).

Seventh Day and Covenant

The biblical understanding of a covenantal relationship is distinctly different from the modern understanding of a contract. In distinguishing the two, Hahn and Pitre explain that whereas a covenant is an exchange of persons, in which the people commit themselves to one another, a contract entails an exchange of property.[25] The exchanges between people that take place in covenants

---

[23] "7650. shaba," biblehub.com, https://biblehub.com/hebrew/7650.htm; Scott Hahn, *Catholic Bible Dictionary* (New York: Doubleday, 2009), 24, 658; James Strong, Strong's Hebrew Dictionary of the Bible (Miklal Software Solutions, Inc.. Kindle Edition), Kindle Locations 28983-28985.

[24] Pitre, *Genesis and the Books of Moses*, MP3 5.

[25] Scott Hahn, *A Father Who Keeps His Promises: God's Covenant Love in Scripture* (Cincinnati: Servant Books, 1998), 24; Brant Pitre, *The Old*

and contracts entail laws. However, due to the relational dimension of both contracts and covenants, neither is reducible to laws. Covenants and contracts establish relationship between people which laws then, writes Hamilton, "regulate or perpetuate...by orderly means."[26] Contracts establish a new business relationship, whereas covenants establish new personal/familial relationships. According to the bible, marriage is to be understood as a covenant and not a contract, and the biblical laws associated with marriage are intended to foster and protect this family relationship.

Testament-A Historical and Theological Journey through Jewish Scripture Outline, 26. Pitre draws on the following work. Scott W. Hahn, Kinship by Covenant: A Canonical Approach to the Fulfillment of God's Saving Promises (Anchor Yale Bible Reference Library; New York: Doubleday, 2009).

[26] Victor P. Hamilton, *Handbook on the Pentateuch, Second Edition* (Grand Rapids: Baker Academic, 2005), 189.

[27] Julius Schnorr von Carolsfeld, "The Sabbath (woodcut by Julius Schnorr von Carolsfeld from the 1860 Die Bibel in Bildern)," 1860, https://commons.wikimedia.org/wiki/File:Schnorr_von_Carolsfeld_Bibel_i n_Bildern_1860_007.png, Julius Schnorr von Carolsfeld [Public domain], via Wikimedia Commons.

When a man and woman marry, they exchange themselves and seal their marriage with an oath to God the father of all. In so doing, a sacred family relationship, and not merely a business relationship, is established between the man and woman. In contrast, a contract, such as between a cell phone provider and the customer, entails only a legally binding business commitment between a company and the individual with the understanding that if the individual or company breaks the contract legal action may be taken in which the laws of the contract and the state are invoked, not the laws of God.

The implied Genesis covenantal relationship between God and all creation means that God on the seventh day God entered into a sacred family relationship with everything he created as a loving, immanent, close Father and not simply as a distant, transcendent God.

Section Questions

1. As interpreted by Robert D. Miller, what did God create on the seventh day before resting?

2. According to Brant Pitre, creation imply about the relationship between creation and God?

3. As explained by Scott Hahn, how does a modern contract differ from a biblical covenant?

Adam and Eve

Before the creating the first Sabbath on the seventh day, God created man and woman. According to Genesis, chapter one, "…God said, 'Let us make man in our image, after our likeness'. … So, God created man in his own image, in the image of God he created him; male and female he created them (Genesis 1:26-27 *RSVCE*)." Genesis 5:3, explains Hahn, helps to interpret the meaning that man is created in the "image" and "likeness" of God. This verse states, "When Adam had lived a hundred and thirty years, he became the father of a son in his own likeness, after his image, and named his Seth (*RSVCE*)." The expression image and likeness in Genesis 1 indicates that Adam and Eve are related to God as children in an analogous way (similarity with a difference) as Seth is related to his Father, Adam as a son. [28]

That both the first man and first woman were created in the image and likeness of God means, comments Miller, "that to have a full image of God, you need males and females both. … [A] roomful of men does not give you an image of God. A roomful of women does not give you an image of God. If you want to know the image of God, you're going to need men and women both." [29]

Pitre explains that it is not clear why the plural pronoun "us" is used. One common explanation is that God is speaking in the royal we, that even popes once used in formal settings. Pitre dismisses this explanation since apart from this text God is referred to only with a singular pronoun. Another explanation is that God is speaking to the angelic court or, as some Jewish commentaries pose, perhaps to

---

[28] Hahn, *Catholic Bible Dictionary*, 23.
[29] Miller, 26.

creation itself. The difficulty with this explanation, points out Pitre, is that man is created in the image of God and not in the image of angels or creation.

A Patristic explanation is that the "us" is a veiled reference to the

---

[30] Hieronymus Bosch, "The Garden of Earthly Delights," c. 1450-1516, https://commons.wikimedia.org/wiki/File:Hieronymus_Bosch_-_The_ Garden_of_Earthly_Delights_-_The_Earthly_Paradise_(Garden_of_ Eden).jpg, [Public domain], via Wikimedia Commons.

Trinity that is revealed in the New Testament. For example, according to the *Epistle of Barnabas* (c. 130 A.D.) with the pronoun us God, "refer[s] to the Son."[31] Similarly, the *Apostolic Constitutions* (300s A.D.) states, "the divine Scripture testifies that God said to Christ, His only-begotten, "Let us make man after our image."[32]

Genesis names the first two humans created Adam, from the Hebrew word *Adama* (אֲדָמָה) meaning dirt or ground[33], and Eve, from the Hebrew word *Chavvah* (חַוָּה) meaning life,[34] "because she was the mother of all living (Genesis 3:20 *RSVCE*)." As "dirt" Adam is to be the protective ground that supports his wife, Eve "life" is to walk on. After being created as a supportive ground, Adam is commanded to "keep" the garden. The English translation "keep" comes from the

---

[31] "The Epistle of Barnabas," 6.12, earlychristianwritings.org, http://www.earlychristianwritings.com/text/barnabas-lightfoot.html.

[32] "Apostolic Constitutions," section 1, book V, chapter VII, newadvent.org, http://www.newadvent.org/fathers/07155.htm. Another example from St. Augustine is, "For God said, Let us make man in our image, after our likeness; and a little after it is said, So God created man in the image of God. Certainly, in that it is of the plural number, the word our would not be rightly used if man were made in the image of one person, whether of the Father, or of the Son, or of the Holy Spirit; but because he was made in the image of the Trinity, on that account it is said, After our image. But again, lest we should think that three Gods were to be believed in the Trinity, whereas the same Trinity is one God, it is said, So God created man in the image of God, instead of saying, In His own image." Augustine, "On the Trinity," Book XII, Chapter 6, 6, newadvent.org, http://www.newadvent.org/fathers/130112.htm.

[33] Strong's Concordance, "127. Adamah," biblehub.com, http://www.biblehub.com/hebrew/127.htm.

[34] Strong's Concordance, "2332. Chavvah," biblehub.com, http://biblehub.com/hebrew/2332.htm.

Hebrew verb *shamar* (שָׁמַר) meaning to guard and to watch (Genesis 2:15).[35] The mutually subordinate friendship between Adam and Eve is also intended by God to be friendship that is a life-long commitment to only one other spouse as the verse 24 indicates, "Therefore a man leaves his father and his mother and clings to his wife, and they become one flesh (Genesis 2:24 *RSVCE*)." After the Fall, the original intention of marriage to be between one man and one woman who become united in a life-long friendship as "one flesh" is soon forgotten and polygamy, beginning with Lamech, a fourth-generation descendant of Cain, becomes common.[36]

How the first woman is named indicates the mutual subordinate relationship of life-long equal friends that Adam and Eve are to live in accordance with. Adam is to be subordinate to Eve as the ground she walks on and Eve is to be subordinate to Adam who is to protect her by guarding the garden. In chapter two, after Adam names the animals he refrains from naming Eve in the same way and instead says "she shall be called Woman (*ishshah* אִשָּׁה) (Genesis 2:23 *RSVCE*)." In commenting on Adam's avoidance of naming the first woman, Miller writes, "If the man names the woman, then he decrees her destiny and he owns her. The man does not name the woman. … 'This one shall be called,' passive voice … It's a grammatical attempt to avoid saying he names her."[37]

After the Fall, Adam is not as delicate in relating to his wife, the first woman, and instead of saying "This woman shall be Eve since she

---

[35] Strong's Concordance, "8104. Shamar," biblehub.com, http://biblehub.com/hebrew/8104.htm.

[36] Miller, 46.

[37] Miller, 46.

is the mother of the living," he abrogates the responsibility of naming the first woman upon himself, "The man called his wife's name Eve (Genesis 3:20 RSVCE)." By so doing, Miller explains, Adam names the first woman "the same way he named the coyote and the raccoon. In other words, Israel acknowledges that women are oppressed. If you look at the laws, a woman is the property of her father until she is married and becomes the property of her husband, just like his plow. But Genesis 2 says, startlingly, that's the way it is but it's not what God intended."[38]

Prior to taking upon himself the role of naming the first woman, Adam repeatedly failed to fulfill his vocation to protect the garden, and, consequently, failed to heroically love his wife who was formed out of Adam's rib as he slept. Instead, Adam remained silent while the serpent, representing the devil, explains Pitre, subverted the family order by engaging first with Eve and not with the guardian of the garden who is Adam. When Adam speaks it is blame Eve, observes Miller, "The woman whom you gave to be with me, she gave me the fruit of the tree, and I ate (Genesis 3:12 *RSVCE*)."[39] A noble response would have been to acknowledge his cowardice before God, to acknowledge his choice of fearfully in silence not protecting Eve from evil. Adam's silence is evident since the devil, although directing his temptation to Eve, uses the second person plural of die (תְּמֻתוּן) and eat (אֲכָלְכֶם) when tempting Eve (Genesis 3:4-5).[40] This means that the devil was speaking to both Adam and Eve in the you plural while directing his temptation to Eve. Throughout this attack Adam says not a word.

---

[38] Miller, 48.

[39] Miller, 59.

[40] Hahn, *Catholic Bible Dictionary*, 280.

Not only was Adam to guard the garden as future priests guarded the holiness of the Tabernacle, and later the Jerusalem Temple but he was also to fulfill a kingly role.[41] Adam's priestly guardian role in relationship to Eden and Eve is evident, explains Hahn, in that the two Hebrew verbs in Genesis 2:15 "to till" and "to keep" "only occur together elsewhere in the Pentateuch where priestly duties are assigned to the Levites in the tabernacle (see Nm 3:7-8; 8:26; 18:5-6)."[42] In addition, Hahn points out the Garden of Eden, the tabernacle, and temple are all described in similar ways.[43]

One early example of identifying Adam as not only a priest who was to guard Eden but also a king who was to rule over Eden and extend his rule over all of creation is from the eastern monk Symeon the New Theologian (949-1022). In his discourses Symeon writes:

> In the beginning God made man king of all the things that are on the earth (Gen. 1:26, 28); indeed of all things that are under the vault of the sky. In fact sun, moon, and stars were brought into being for man. What then? When he was king of all these visible objects, did they harm him with regard to virtue? In no way whatever. On the contrary, had he continued to give thanks to God who had made him and given him all things, he would have fared well. He he not transgressed the commandment of his Master he would not have lost this kingship, he would not have deprived himself of the glory of

---

[41] Leviticus 8:35; Numbers 1:53, 3:8, 38, 31:47.

[42] Scott W. Hahn, *A Father Who Keeps His Promises* (Ann Arbor, Mich: Charis, 1998), 54.

[43] Hahn, *A Father Who Keeps His Promises*, 54-56.

God.[44]

Echoing St. Symeon and other early Christians' understanding of Adam as a king Bishop Barron writes that:

> Adam prior to the Fall was interpreted not only as a priest but also as a king, specifically a king on the march, for his purpose was not only to cultivate the Garden but also to expand its borders outward, making the whole world a place where God is correctly praised. Under this rubric, we can understand the Fall as a failure in kingship. Compromised in his basic identity, Adam was no longer able to defend the Garden, much less increase its empire. Consequently, he and Eve were expelled from paradise. We should read this not as an arbitrary punishment, but rather as spiritual physics. From the loss of priestly and kingly identity follows, as night follows day, the loss of the Garden. The Fall, of course, is described in the third chapter of Genesis, and it is most instructive to read the ensuing chapters, which proffer a concentrated account of the permutations and combinations of dysfunction that follow from the original disintegration. We find stories of corruption, violence, envy, murder, imperialistic machination, and cruelty. St. Augustine did not miss the Bible's identification of the fratricide Cain as the founder of cities, seeing in this the skewing of the political order that ought to have followed from right kingship. He practically delighted in the echo of this

---

[44] Symeon the New Theologian, *Symeon the New Theologian: The Discourses,* trans. C.J. De Cantanzaro (New York: Paulist Press, 1980), 94.

identification in the story of Rome's founding by another fratricide.[45]

As explained by Pitre, unlike the Old Adam who was tempted by the devil with disordered pleasure (eating the forbidden fruit), with possessions (possessing the forbidden fruit), and with power (being like God but on one's own terms) and fell, Jesus as the New Adam when faced by a variation on these three-fold temptations did not sin.[46] After being led "by the Spirit into the wilderness" (Matthew 4:1 *RSVCE*), Satan similarly tempted Jesus as the new Adam in a three-fold manner consisting of "lust of the flesh, lust of the eyes and pride" (1 John 2:7 *RSVCE*). Satan does so by tempting Jesus to turn stones into bread (lust of the flesh), by offering him all the kingdoms of the world (lust of the eyes), and by tempting Jesus to jump from a high point on the temple and land miraculously unharmed (pride). Jesus successfully counters each temptation with temperance, meekness and humility.

Hahn and Pitre additionally explain that Jesus' ultimate visible expression as a perfect, new Adam was his willingness to die on the cross for his bride, the Church. Like Adam Jesus experienced fear of death as is evident in Jesus' words, "Father, if you are willing, remove this chalice from me." Unlike Adam, though, Jesus immediately followed this fearful reaction with perfect submission to His Heavenly Father's will, "nevertheless not my will, but yours, be done (Luke 22:42

---

[45] Robert Barron, "Evangelizing the Nones," January 2018, First Things, https://www.firstthings.com/article/2018/01/evangelizing-the-nones.

[46] Brant Pitre, *The Old Testament-A Historical and Theological Journey through Jewish Scripture Outline*, 29.

RSVCE)." With these words Jesus indicated that although he is afraid of dying on the cross, a natural reaction of human nature, he will do so if the Father wants him to. Jesus then does so and fulfills his role of guardian, as keeper of his bride the Church even if this means sacrificing his life for her.[47] Then, through His death and resurrection, Jesus restores the life of grace that Adam had been called to and had lost.

Adam's main sin was failing as a protector, as a defender of life, as a defender of truth against falsehood, especially against the lies that Eve was tempted with. A principle lie, identified by Benedict XVI, that Eve encountered and fell for is similar to what King David experienced when lustfully gazing upon the naked beauty of the married woman, Bathsheba. Both David and Eve desired to possess and dominate the beautiful object of their desire. Bathsheba, in case of David, and the forbidden fruit that was a delight to Eve's eyes. In describing this temptation in the form of "deceptive and false" beauty, beauty not formed by truth, principally by the truth of sacrificial love that both Adam and Eve were called to and not selfish, overly possessive love, Benedict XVI comments:

> Falsehood, however, has another stratagem: a beauty that is deceptive and false, a dazzling beauty that does not bring human beings out of themselves into the ecstasy of starting off toward the heights but instead immures them completely within themselves. Such beauty does not awaken a longing for the ineffable, a willingness to sacrifice and to lose oneself, but instead stirs up the desire, the will for power, possession, and

---

[47] Pitre, *The Old Testament*, 23 mp3 files.

pleasure. It is that sort of experience of beauty that Genesis tells about in the account of the Fall. Eve sees that the fruit of the tree is "beautiful" to eat and is "delightful to the eyes". "Beauty," as she experiences it, arouses in her a desire for possession, making her, so to speak, turn in upon herself.[48]

Like the old Adam, Eve lost her role. Eve lost her role as "mother of all living (Genesis 3:20 *RSVCE*)," but not completely. In affirming that Eve kept her status as mother of all in some manner, Benedict XVI asserts that Genesis 3:20 indicates Eve did not completely lose her role as mother of the living since she called Eve (*Chavvah*), meaning life, after the account of the Fall. According to Benedict XVI, this placement implies that even after the Fall Eve retained her status of being "very good" (Genesis 1:31) and a mother of the living, but in a wounded manner that was waiting to be healed.[49]

God promises, in what is called the first gospel (protoevangelium Genesis 3:15), that one day this healing will take place with the aid of a New Eve, a new woman who would fulfill her role as a perfect mother of all. She, through her "seed," prophecies Genesis, will crush the head of Satan. Hamilton points out that in the Septuagint the seed of the woman is translated into Greek as σπέρματός (*spermatos*), from which

---

[48] Joseph Ratzinger, *On the Way to Jesus Christ*, trans. M.J. Miller (San Francisco: Ignatius Press, 2005), 38-40. Ratzinger applies this temptation to today with, "Could anyone possibly be unacquainted with the images, for example, in advertising that are made with the utmost shrewdness so as to tempt a man irresistibly to grab what he wants, to seek momentary satisfaction rather than to set out on a path toward the other?"

[49] Joseph Ratzinger, *Daughter Zion: Meditations on the Church's Marian Belief*, trans. J.M. McDermott (San Francisco: Ignatius Press, 1983), 16.

the English word semen originates. This word is typically used in reference to a man, not to a woman, and yet here it is used in reference to a woman. Could this be interpreted as a subtle indication from God who is the primary author of Scripture of the Virgin Birth?[50]

By being perfectly obedient to God, Mary became the new mother of the living who restores supernatural life to humans by her son Jesus, by her "seed" Jesus. Pitre explains that God out of mercy banished Adam and Eve from Eden since if they had continued to eat from the central tree in the garden, the tree of life, they would have lived forever but only physically since they had lost sanctifying grace, they had lost their spiritual communion, their spiritual life that God has invited them to participate in. Jesus, according to patristic commentary, as the new tree of life by his death on the cross, restores us to sanctifying grace by Baptism, represented by water flowing from his pierced side, and Jesus deepens this restoration through the Eucharist, represented by the blood flowing from his side.[51]

Banished from Eden and from eating from the old tree of life, Adam, Eve, and their descendants were "at enmity" (Genesis 3:15 *RSVCE*) with Satan who lusted after them to consume them in

---

[50] Victor P. Hamilton, *Handbook on the Pentateuch, Second Edition* (Grand Rapids: Baker Academic, 2005), 45. "Victor P. Hamilton, *Handbook on the Pentateuch, Second Edition* (Grand Rapids: Baker Academic, 2005), Victor P. Hamilton, *Handbook on the Pentateuch, Second Edition* (Grand Rapids: Baker Academic, 2005), 45-46. "In the Old Testament descent is virtually always through the male. The son is the seed of his father rather than of his mother. Exceptions are rare, as in the cases of Hagar's seed (Gen. 16:10) and Rebekah's seed (Gen. 24:60), but both references, by context, clearly point to individuals, not an individual. (Eve later will refer to Seth as her "other seed" [Gen. 4:25].)."

[51] Hahn, *The Catholic Bible Dictionary*, 923.

accordance with Satan's curse of to eat "dust...all the days of your life (Genesis 3:14 *RSVCE*)." Pitre points out that the dust represents man whose very name means dirt or ground and represents that which can never satisfy Satan's lust to be like God, whose image man is created in. Eating dust well represents this insatiable desire of Satan since dust is completely unnourishing (Genesis 3:14 *RSVCE*).[52] When Jesus takes on the flesh of man, he restores what Adam and Eve lost. Through Jesus, we once again become capable of being "partakers in divine nature (2 Peter 1:4 *RSVCE*)" as assisted by the aid of Mary who is given through Jesus fulness of grace (Luke 1:28 *RSVCE*).[53]

[54]

The dust that Satan is condemned to lust after corresponds with

---

[52] Brant Pitre, *Genesis and the Books of Moses: Unlocking the Mysteries of the Pentateuch,* MP3, 7.

[53] Pitre, *Genesis and the Books of Moses,* MP3, 7.

[54] James Tissot, "Adam is Tempted by Eve," c. 1896-1902, https://commons.wikimedia.org/wiki/File:Tissot_Adam_Is_Tempted_by_E ve.jpg, James Tissot [Public domain], via Wikimedia Commons.

his sin of enticing Eve to eat forbidden fruit. Hamilton comments that God's fitting a punishment to match a sin is repeated in other passages of Genesis. For example, Cain who once lived the life of a stable farmer was punished with exile and condemned to a nomadic lifestyle.[55]

St. Irenaeus (130-202) teaches that Jesus and Mary fulfill Genesis 3:15, which describes a woman who together with her "seed" crush the head of a serpent, representing Satan, who bites at the heel. Jesus, born of the New Eve, Mary, is the seed who crushes Satan. "[I]n his work of recapitulation" writes Irenaeus, it was fitting that Jesus, as the New Adam, be born of a sinless woman, since by being sinless Mary does not fall under Satan's power, and, hence, is truly the mother of the living.[56] The sinless woman Mary is invited by Jesus to participate in the work of redemption of crushing Satan's head and we, as adopted sons of God in Jesus, are also invited to participate in this work of redemption, ending Satan's kingdom while extending God's kingdom.

---

[55] Victor P. Hamilton, *Handbook on the Pentateuch, Second Edition* (Grand Rapids: Baker Academic, 2005), 76.

[56] Irenaeus of Lyons, Irenaeus Against Heresies, Irenæus against Heresies, in A. Roberts, J. Donaldson, & A. C. Coxe, eds., *The Apostolic Fathers with Justin Martyr and Irenaeus* (Buffalo, NY: Christian Literature Company, 1885), vol. 1, book v, chap. xx, 548. "For indeed the enemy would not have been fairly vanquished, unless it had been a man [born] of a woman who conquered him. For it was by means of a woman that he got the advantage over man at first, setting himself up as man's opponent. And therefore does the Lord profess Himself to be the Son of man, comprising in Himself that original man out of whom the woman was fashioned (*ex quo ea quæ secundum mulierem est plasmatio facta est*), in order that, as our species went down to death through a vanquished man, so we may ascend to life again through a victorious one; and as through a man death received the palm [of victory] against us, so again by a man we may receive the palm against death."

Participating in redemption entails suffering in union with Jesus, and because of this union, because of participating in Jesus' love, is a suffering which has become light by love in contrast with suffering that is heavy, absent of love, and accompanied by resentment or least hopeless resignation.

Expanding on Irenaeus' interpretation, Pitre points out that Jesus, as the redeemer, with Mary, who participates in His work of redemption, dies since He is bitten by the serpent/Satan prior to Jesus crushing the serpent's head. As a divine person whose human nature, which truly experiences death, Jesus rises from the dead and through this death conquers death's agent, the devil.[57] By rising from the dead, Jesus, the New Adam, together with Mary, the New Eve, undo the sin that the Old Adam and Old Eve had committed. Jesus fulfills his role as New Adam by being the perfect redeemer and Mary, as the true mother of the living, does so by participating in Jesus' one redemption.

Jesus also fulfills his role as New Adam by giving life to the New Eve. As Eve was formed out of Adam's side as he slept so the New Eve, the Church, was born out the side of Jesus as he hung upon the cross. As the Gospel of John describes, after Jesus had died, "one of the soldiers pierced His side with a spear, and at once there came out blood and water (John 19:34 *RSVCE*)." The blood and water, according to Church Fathers, represents the Sacraments of the Church, especially the Eucharist, associated with the blood, and Baptism, associated with the flowing water, that like Ezekiel's image of water flowing out of the Temple gives life (Ezekiel 47). St. Augustine in making this connection writes:

---

[57] Pitre, *The Old Testament*, 23 mp3 files.

2. Then came the soldiers, and broke the legs of the first, and of the other who was crucified with Him. But when they came to Jesus, and saw that He was dead already, they broke not His legs: but one of the soldiers with a spear laid open His side, and immediately came there out blood and water. A suggestive word was made use of by the evangelist, in not saying pierced, or wounded His side, or anything else, but opened; that thereby, in a sense, the gate of life might be thrown open, from whence have flowed forth the sacraments of the Church, without which there is no entrance to the life which is the true life. That blood was shed for the remission of sins; that water it is that makes up the health-giving cup and supplies at once the laver of baptism and water for drinking. This was announced beforehand, when Noah was commanded to make a door in the side of the ark, Genesis 6:16 whereby the animals might enter which were not destined to perish in the flood, and by which the Church was prefigured. Because of this, the first woman was formed from the side of the man when asleep, Genesis 2:22 and was called Life, and the mother of all living. Genesis 3:20 Truly it pointed to a great good, prior to the great evil of the transgression (in the guise of one thus lying asleep). This second Adam bowed His head and fell asleep on the cross, that a spouse might be formed for Him from that which flowed from the sleeper's side. O death, whereby the dead are raised anew to life! What can be purer than such blood? What more health-giving than such a wound?[58]

---

[58] Augustine, "Tractates on the Gospel of John: Tractate 120 (John 19:31-20:9)," 2, newadvent.org, http://www.newadvent.org/fathers/1701120.htm.

Section Questions

1. How is Genesis 5:3 similar to Genesis 1:26 which describes God creating human beings in His image and likeness? Why is this similarity important in understanding how we are related to God?

2. Genesis 1:26 "God created man in his own image, in the image of God he created him: male and female he created him (Genesis 1:27 *RSVCE*)." With respect to complementarity of the sexes, what does this verse from Genesis reveal who God is?

3. Genesis 1:26 "Let us make man in our image, after our likeness" Provide three possible explanations for the use of the first-person plural pronoun. Include in your answer the Patristic explanation.

4. State what Adam's and Eve's names mean in Hebrew. Dirt/Ground and Life.

5. According to the Hebrew, Adam is called by God to the priestly role of *shamar* (שָׁמַר) to guard, to watch (Genesis 2:15) the Garden, above all Eve. How does Adam specifically fail in his role as guardian?

6. As explained by Symeon the New Theologian and Bishop Barron, how was Adam called by God to be a king?

7. Compare Jesus and Adam with respect to the three temptations "lust of the flesh, lust of the eyes and pride (1 John 2:7)." Do so by specifying how Adam fell for each temptation while Jesus emerged victorious after each temptation.

8. According to Benedict XVI, Genesis 3:20 indicates that Eve did not completely lose her role as "mother of all living." In reference to the placement of Genesis 3:20, how does Benedict XVI argue for this interpretation?

9. Genesis 3:15 refers to the woman's seed. How can this be interpreted spiritually as fulfilled in Mary and Jesus?

10. With respect to the Tree of Life, how was God's act of banishing Adam and Eve from the Garden of Eden a merciful action? In addition, hoe does Jesus restore an ordered relationship to the Tree of Life? In your answer refer to sanctifying grace.

11. With respect to disordered love, why is Satan's punishment of eating dust a fitting punishment for Satan?

12. How are the woman and her seed in Genesis 3:15 fulfilled in Jesus and Mary. In your answer include the following: Mystical Body, Jesus, Mary, Heel, Recapitulation.

Eden

The "great good" that Augustine refers to was formed out of Adam's side in Eden and was Eve, a woman. In Eden, Adam along with Eve enjoyed harmony with God, with themselves, and with all of creation. This garden (Gan Eden עֵדֶן גַּן,) included various trees and rivers. Among the various trees were the Tree of Life that Adam and Eve were allowed to eat from, and the Tree of Knowledge of Good and Evil, the one tree they were forbidden to eat from. (Genesis 2:9)

The following verses (Genesis 2:10-11 *RSVCE*) read, "A river flowed out of Eden to water the garden, and there it divided and became four rivers… Pishon … Gihon … Tigris … Euphrates." Since water flows downward this means that the Garden of Eden was situated in an elevated place. For this reason, explains Pitre with

---

[59] James Tissot, "Adam and Eve Driven from Paradise," 1896-1902, https://commons.wikimedia.org/wiki/File:James_Jacques_Joseph_Tissot_-_Adam_and_Eve_Driven_From_Paradise_-_Google_Art_Project.jpg, [Public domain], via Wikimedia Commons.

reference to Jewish tradition,[60] Ezekiel calls Eden "the holy mountain of God (Ezekiel 28:14 *RSVCE*)."

Pitre further explains that the ancient Jewish people identified Jerusalem, built upon Mount Moriah, with the site of Eden. One justification for this view is that the spring of the Gihon River is in Jerusalem (Genesis 1:38) and is still active today.[61] It was fitting, therefore, that Jesus was crucified relatively near this site since He is the source of living waters of eternal life (John 4:14). He restores life from the very site that life was lost at.

If, though, Eden is located in reference to rivers whose location is known then Eden's location becomes problematic. This is because, explains Miller:

> The Gihon is a little stream in Jerusalem. There's no way to describe it as winding through the whole of the land of Ethiopia, which is Cush. The Tigris and Euphrates are the rivers of Mesopotamia. There's no way to make them branches of a river in Jerusalem, yet alone in Ethiopia. And even the little details are wrong. The Tigris doesn't flow east of Assyria. It flows west of Assyria.[62]

Miller proposes that these discrepancies are deliberate which means that:

> most Israelites reading this would realize how bizarre these

---

[60] Pitre, *Genesis and the Books of Moses*, MP3, 6.

[61] Pitre, *Genesis and the Books of Moses*, MP3, 6.

[62] Miller, 43.

directions are. I think the point of this bizarre travelogue is precisely to keep people from trying to find Eden, because there's no way to match these rivers up. And at the same time, because of what will happen in Genesis 3, they want you to understand these events as taking place in real places, on this earth. This isn't something that happened in a completely alternate reality. Which means the decisions that Adam and Eve make are intimately related to decisions you may or may not make.[63]

Sadly, due to the decisions they made, Adam and Eve were banished from the garden, and out of divine love prevented from eating from the central tree of life, for if they had continued to eat from this tree they would have been condemned to an eternal state of misery on earth due to their acquired sinful state. The Hebrew word used for God driving out Adam and Eve from the Eden is *garash* (גָּרַשׁ), a verb that is often used in reference to a woman who is cast out of a marital relationship by divorce, observes Miller. "To be exiled from Eden," concludes Miller, means "a loss of fellowship with God,"[64] a loss of a marital relationship between God and Human Beings.

In the subsequent chapters after the Fall, Genesis depicts man's life span as decreasing from life spans of hundreds of years before the Flood to lifespans of under two hundred years, such as Noah who, either symbolically or literally, lived over 600 years (Genesis 7:6) to Jacob who, in comparison, only lived 147 years (Genesis 47:28). Eventually, as testified by Psalm 90, men are listed as living a life span

---

[63] Miller, 43-44.
[64] Miller, 63.

similar to ours "seventy years, or if due to strength, eighty years (Psalm 90: 10 *NASB*)."

As Pitre astutely observes, the Genesis account of a progressive degeneration from original perfection to our current state is contrary to a common modern belief that human beings are progressing as time moves on.[65] A Catholic response in accordance with Jesus's own words is that it is not an either/or question of whether the older is better than the newer or the newer better than the older, a trend particularly evident in our technologically advanced times, but rather is a question of what to revere from the past and what to appreciate in the present and what to preserve and possibly improve in the future. "[E]very scribe trained for the kingdom of heaven is like a householder who brings out of his treasure what is new and what is old (Matthew 13:51 *RSVCE*)."

Section Questions

1. According to Miller, how does the Genesis description of the four rivers that flow down from and out of Eden indicate its location, and why is this significant?

Two Cities

Immediately after the Fall, Genesis chapter four focuses on the first two children, Cain, the first-born son, and Abel. Even though Cain was the older son, Abel was favored by God. Cain responds to this favoritism not with happiness and gratitude that his brothers is so

---

[65] Pitre, *Genesis and the Books of Moses,* MP3 10.

loved by God but rather with spiritual envy, with sadness that his brother is favored and not him. Out of envy Cain then murders Abel.

God's favoritism of Abel over Cain was not without rational basis. As indicated by Pitre, it is important to note that Abel is described as offering "the firstlings of his flock and of their fat portions" while Cain only offers "an offering of the fruit of the ground (Genesis 4:3-4 *RSVCE*)." If this detail is overlooked, then it might seem that God is favoring Abel for no reason. However, when this detailed in reflected upon it becomes evident that the passage implies Abel was sacrificed, offered to God, that which was most precious from his flock, the first-born, and that which was most precious of their meat, the fat. In contrast, Cain merely offers some fruit of the ground without taking the extra care to offer the first, the best of what he has cultivated.[67]

After Cain murders his brother God asks Cain where Abel is. Cain

---

[66] James Tissot, "Cain Leadeth Abel to Death," c. 1896-1902, https://commons.wikimedia.org/wiki/File:Cain_leadeth_abel_to_death_tissot.jpg, [Public domain], via Wikimedia Commons.

[67] Pitre, *Genesis and the Books of Moses*, MP3 9.

responds with, "I do not know; am I my brother's keeper (Genesis 4:9 *RSVCE*)?" Hamilton comments that the Hebrew word for keeper comes from the word, to guard, watch, preserve (*shamar*, שָׁמַר), the same word that is used for Adam's vocation to guard the garden, especially since Eve the woman Adam is to love is present in the garden. The verb *shamar* and its associated noun indicate the keeper is a master in relationship to what he is guarding and watching over, and yet this type of relationship is not the fraternal relationship Cain was to have with his brother. As Hamilton points out this relationship is appropriate for, "[z]oos, bees, and prisoners" but not between brothers.[68]

The fratricide is immediately followed by Cain establishing a city called Enoch, named after Cain's son. Cain's fourth generation descendant Lamech is the first man identified by the bible who is married to more than one wife: A'dah and Zillah. A'dah's son Ju'bal is called "the father of all those who play the lyre and pipe (Genesis 4:21 *RSVCE*)." Zillah's son, Tu'bal-cain, "was the forger of all instruments of bronze and iron (Genesis 4:21 *RSVCE*)," in other words, according to Pitre, instruments of war. This verse is followed by Lamech boasting to his wives of his "seventy-seven-fold," vengeful anger represented by killing a man who only wounded him. As St. Augustine teaches, Cain's city is founded by a man who murdered his brother, and, furthers Pitre, known for beginning polygamy, for its vengeful, warlike spirit, and its development of entertainment.[69]

---

[68] Hamilton, 59.

[69] For Augustine this fratricidal act of the first earthly city corresponds to the founding of Rome by Romulus who murdered his brother Remus. Augustine of Hippo, *The City of God*, trans. M. Dods (Buffalo: Christian

For Augustine, the city of Cain represents the fallen city of man, while Abel represents the city of God. These two cities undergo in this world "a series of deaths and births."[70] Biblical founders of the violent, this world centered, death and pleasure driven city of man are Cain, Enoch (Cain's son not Enoch son of Jared), Ham (Noah's son), and Ishmael (Abraham's son). The founders of the peaceful, other world directed, life affirmative, prayerful, moral, God centered city of God are Abel and Seth (Adam's sons), Shem (Noah's son), Isaac (Abraham's son), and definitively in its fullest sense, Jesus Christ.

The two cities are depicted in the Old Testament as dying and being reborn since, writes Augustine, in the "wicked war with the wicked" some of the citizens of the city of God in its imperfect state on earth are seduced by the wicked, corrupted, and destroyed.[71] A seduction of members in the city of god by the idolatrous, violent, lustful city of man is described in Genesis chapter six with "the sons of God [the descendants of Seth] came into the daughters of men [the descendants of Cain], and they bore children to them (Genesis 6:4 *RSVCE*)." In Hebrews, the expression "came into" is a typical expression for sexual intercourse. Upon seeing the citizens of the city of God becoming more and more like the city of man, God then decides to "blot out man…from the face of the ground (Genesis 6:7 *RSVCE*)" except for Noah who was just and favored by God.[72]

A verse that follows God's decision to "blot out man" describe the extent of man's corruption: "Now the earth was corrupt in God's sight,

---

Literature Company, 1887), 15.5, 286; Pitre, *Genesis and the Books of Moses*, MP3.

[70] Augustine of Hippo, *The City of God*, 15.1.2, 286.

[71] Augustine of Hippo, *The City of God*, 15.5.1, 287.

[72] Augustine of Hippo, *The City of God*, 15.22, 302.

and the earth was filled with violence. And God saw the earth, and behold, it was corrupt; for all flesh had corrupted their way upon the earth (Genesis 6:11-12 *RSVCE*)." In focusing on the word "corrupt" in this verse, Hamilton observes that it comes from the Hebrew root destroy (שָׁחַת *shachath*).[73] Hamilton comments, "Is this one way by which God destroys? Rather than interrupt and impede, he allows the evil started by humankind to run to its inevitable conclusion. … Similarly, the apostle Paul, in speaking of the expression of God's wrath against sin, uses the expression 'God gave them up' (Rom. 2: 24, 26, 28), surely more passive than active, more gentle than raging."[74]

Another interesting detail that Hamilton comments on is that God's first reaction to the corruption and wickedness of man is not to angrily "blot out man (Genesis 6:7 *RSVCE*)." Rather, His initial reaction is grief: "[I]t grieved him to his heart (Genesis 6:6 *RSVCE*)."[75] We can interpret this as meaning God suffering with man, and this suffering will find its perfect, visible expression in Jesus who is *Immanuel*, meaning in Hebrew God with us (עִמָּנוּאֵל Imanu'el).

The power that enables the citizens of the corrupt city of man to be terrifying and giant like (Genesis 6:4) is, indicates Pitre, from the fallen angels, principally Satan, represented in Genesis 3 by a serpent. For this reason, interprets Pitre, Ezekiel in chapter twenty-eight identifies the power behind the corrupt King of Tyre with the one who was "in Eden the garden of God … [who was] blameless … till iniquity was found in you…[who] was filled with violence, and…sinned."

---

[73] "7843. shachath, Strong's Concordance," biblehub.com, http://biblehub.com/hebrew/7843.htm.

[74] Hamilton, 67.

[75] Hamilton, 68.

(Ezekiel 28:13-16 *RSVCE*) Reflecting the belief in an angelic world that interfaces with worldly politics, Paul cautions Christians from becoming overly engaged in battling with political forces of this world, "For we are not contending against flesh and blood, but against the principalities, against the powers, against the world rulers of this present darkness, against the spiritual hosts of wickedness in the heavenly places (Ephesians 6:12 *RSVCE*)."[76]

[77]

---

[76] Pitre, *Genesis and the Books of Moses,* MP3, 7.

[77] Arthur Rackham / Publicdomain, "The giants Fafner and Fasolt seize Freyja in Arthur Rackham's illustration of Richard Wagner's *Der Ring des Nibelungen*," https://commons.wikimedia.org/wiki/File:Rhinegold_ and_the_Valkyries_p_032.jpg.

Section Questions

1. Why does Augustine and Pitre, identify the City of Cain, Enoch, with the City of Man, a city of death that promotes a culture of death? With specific reference to Scripture, include the following in your response: Musical Instruments, Weapons of Warfare, Polygamy, and Vengeance.

First Born Sons

As is evident with Cain and Abel, in the Old Testament the younger son is often favored by God over the first-born son. However, this is not always the case. For example, the first-born son of Noah, Shem, is blessed by God with a long life (Genesis 11:11) and does not as a result become sinfully proud of his status. For this reason, Shem is considered as one of the founders of the city of God. Abraham, points out Hahn, is yet another example of a first-born son who is favored by God and remains a just, upright man.[78] Although Israel, as a nation, is identified as the first-born son of God, in an adoptive sense, "Thus says the Lord, Israel is my first-born son (Exodus 4:22 *RSVCE*)"[79], unlike Shem and Abraham, Israel repeatedly becomes sinfully proud of its status and forgot that it is a first-born son for the sake of the other nations, to lead them also to worship of the one true

---

[78] Scott Hahn, *A Father Who Keeps His Promises: God's Covenant Love in Scripture* (Cincinnati: Servant Books, 1998), 90.

[79] Hahn references: Hos 11:1, Wis 18:3, Deut 14:1, Is 63:8, Wis 9:7, Jer 31:9, Sir 36:11, Jer 31:3, Deut 7:6-8, Wis 14:3, Sir 23:1. Scott Hahn, and Curtis Mitch, *Ignatius Catholic Study Bible: The Book of Exodus* (San Francisco: Ignatius Press, 2012), loc. 2891.

God.[80]

This was one of reasons why Jesus became angry in the Jerusalem Temple by overturning tables and chasing people out with the words, "My house shall be called a house of prayer for all nations? But you have made it a den of robbers (Mark 11:17 *RSVCE*)." As explained by James Mallon, in this verse Jesus is quoting from Isaiah 56:6 in which Israel is portrayed as "a house of prayer for all people" and not just for the Israelites.

In other words, Israel was given the first-born status not for self-

<hr />

[80] Pitre cautions against interpreting the term Son of God in a univocal sense, in the sense that it has one meaning regardless of context. Rather, the context will determine different meanings. The Sethites (Genesis 6:2), according to Augustine's interpretation, Israel (Exodus 4:23) and King David (Psalm 2:7) are all referred to as sons of God but in different senses. Pitre, *Genesis and the Books of Moses,* MP3 10.

[81] Francesco Hayez (1791-1881), "Meeting of Esau and Jacob," https://commons.wikimedia.org/wiki/File:Francesco_Hayez_061.jpg, [Public domain or Public domain], via Wikimedia Commons.

glorification but rather so that they could lead their younger brothers and sisters, represented by non-Israelite nations, to God for God's glory. Reflecting the ancient understanding of first-born sons as leaders of their families after their father, Israel was to fulfill this adoptive role as first-born among the nations by serving the other nations as priests who, asserts Hahn, mediate God's truthful, love (see Exodus 19:6).[82] Jesus became angry because the excessive money changing in the Court of the Women, close to the Court of the Gentiles, were a great distraction to the Gentiles and to women in a place intended by God for worship. Jesus held that many of His people had forgotten they had been chosen as first-born for the sake of all nations and that, consequently, the Temple was intended by God to be a temple of worship for all people, for all nations and not just for Israelite men.[83]

---

[82] Hahn references: Gen 1:26, Gen 2:15, Ex 19:6, Ps 89:27, 2 Sam 6:17. Scott Hahn, and Curtis Mitch, *Ignatius Catholic Study Bible: The Book of Exodus* (San Francisco: Ignatius Press, 2012), loc. 3360.

[83] James Mallon, *Divine Renovation: From Maintenance to a Missional Parish* (Toronto: Novalis, 2014), Loc. 179-197; Randall Price, *Rose Guide to the Temple* (Torrance: Bristol Works, 2012), 4001-4014. "The expansive Court of the Gentile sported at its entrance a popular bazaar underneath the protective roof of the Stoa. Here moneychangers exchanged local coinage for the pure silver Tyrian shekel (acceptable because Roman currency was defiling, and the Jews were forbidden by the Romans to coin their own money) so that a proper offering could be made to the Temple. Here, too, vendors sold animals for use as burnt offerings. Although Mishnah Berakot 9:5 states that the selling of animals for sacrificial purposes was not permitted within the Temple walls, the Gospels clearly state that this selling took place within the Temple (John 2:15). This has been confirmed from the archaeological excavations at the southwest and southern corners of the Temple Mount under the direction of Benjamin Mazar and Meir Ben-Dov.

Except for Adam, Israel (as a nation), Noah, Shem, and Abraham, all other first-born sons that are identified in the Old Testament, explains Hahn, are not specially favored by God. Instead, God favors and blesses the younger son over the elder son: Abel instead of Cain, Isaac instead of Ishmael, Jacob instead of Esau, Perez instead of Zerah, Joseph instead of Reuben, Ephraim instead of Manasseh, David instead of Eliab.[84]

Just because God favors a younger son over the first-born son, does not mean God allows the younger son to abuse his privileged status without punishment. An example, indicates Hahn, is the account of Jacob's life. Jacob deceitfully stole his older brother's birthright (Genesis 27:29) by tricking his old, nearly blind father to think that he

---

However, these excavations helped resolve the difficulty, revealing that a smaller Temple market was isolated inside the Royal Stoa, but did not spread out into the Court of the Gentiles proper. This market was still considered *inside* the Temple complex, even though removed from the actual Temple precincts. For example, John 7:28 says that Jesus "cried out in the Temple," although the text locates Him in the area of the Temple treasury within the Court of the Women (John 8:20). Although the next court after the Court of the Gentiles, this court was still outside the area of greater sanctity (since lepers could enter here). Despite this, the Gospel writers considered this to be 'in the Temple.' This helps us understand Jesus' concern over the sanctity of the Temple at His entrance to the Royal Stoa situated on the threshold of the Temple court (Matthew 21:13; Mark 11:17; Luke 19:46), and also why His clash with the Temple vendors was a fairly modest incident, permitting His daily return to the Temple precincts to address the Temple crowds (Luke 19:47; see also Matthew 21:14). If it had occurred in the more public open area of the Court of the Gentiles it would have been considered not just a religious demonstration, but also a political threat, and would have brought an immediate arrest by either the Temple guards or the Roman authorities."

[84] Hahn, *The Ignatius Catholic Study* Bible, Kindle Locations 4812-4819.

was blessing the first-born, Esau. Years later, God justly allows Jacob to experience what it feels to be similarly deceived when his uncle Laban tricks him to marry Leah instead of Rachel, whom Jacob loves and willingly works seven more years to marry (Genesis 29). Similarly, at the end of his life Jacob is once again deceived in a similar way that he fooled his father. In chapter thirty-seven of Genesis, Joseph's brothers trick their father Jacob to think that his favorite son Joseph was killed by a wild animal. They do so by presenting to Jacob Joseph's robe in goat blood while claiming they do not know what happened to their brother Joseph.[85]

Section Questions

1. Explain the role of the following first-born sons to other sons: Adam, Israel, Noah, and Abraham. Include in your answer how Israel often failed to live up to its first-born status.

Noah

Adam was the first, adopted son of God. Due to Adam's sin, and the increasing intensity of sin both by those of the line of Seth and those of the line of Cain, God sent a great flood to destroy mankind except for Noah, his family, and the animals protected by the ark. After the flood, Noah became a new Adam, and, in a sense the new first adopted son of God as a just man and just father. As an imperfect fulfillment of the first Adam, Noah prefigures Jesus Christ the first and only Son of God, eternally begotten by the Father. Jesus is also the

---

[85] Hahn, *The Ignatius Catholic Study Bible*, Kindle Locations 4579-4582.

perfect savior of the world as the New Adam and the new Noah who is the originator of the new creation of grace under the New Covenant.

When Noah is seen as prefiguring Christ, as a type of Christ then the various aspects of his life can be spiritually interpreted as fulfilled in Christ. This is precisely what St. Peter does with, "…when God's patience waited in the days of Noah, during the building of the ark, in which a few, that is, eight persons, were saved through water. Baptism, which corresponds to this, now saves you, not as a removal of dirt from your body but as an appeal to God for a clear conscience, through the resurrection of Jesus Christ (1 Peter 3:20-21 *RSVCE*)." Echoing St. Peter's spiritual interpretation, St. Augustine describes the flood which wiped out the sinful descendants of Adam, as fulfilled in baptism that similarly washes away sin, but, differently from the flood, offers us salvation in way that the flood of old did not.[86]

The forty days (Genesis 7:4) the flood lasted and 150 days (Genesis 8:3) that the water reached its maximum height[87] in which Noah's and his family's trust in God was tested anticipates Jesus forty days in the desert where he was tempted by the devil's suggestions. These forty days of Noah are echoed by Moses' fasting for forty days on Mount Sinai, and the Israelites' forty years in the desert. They also are related

---

[86] Augustine of Hippo, *Reply to Faustus the Manichaean*, in *St. Augustin: The Writings against the Manichaeans and against the Donatists*, ed. P. Schaff, trans. R. Stothert (Buffalo: Christian Literature Company, 1887), vol. 4, p. 189).

[87] Hamilton, 71.

"[D]oes the text indicate an inconsistency in the duration of the flood, forty versus 150 days? Was not the actual downpour forty days and nights, followed by five months (150 days) of rising water until the water level peaked?"

to the prophet Elijah's forty days of fasting on Mount Sinai, to name just a few Old Testament biblical references.[88]

[89]

The dove that returns to Noah, signaling that the flood has

---

[88] See: Ex.24:18; Deut. 9:9, Ex. 16:35; Ps 95:10, 1 Kings 19:8; Mt. 4:1-2. Steve Ray also provides others including, "...Israel is in the hand of the Philistines for 40 years (Judg 13:1) .... 40 days Ezekiel lies on his side to symbolize the punishment of Judah (Ezek 4:6); Jonah prophesies that Nineveh will be destroyed in 40 days—unless they fast and repent (Jonah 3:4); Punishment limited to 40 stripes — lashes (Deut 25:3; cf. 2 Cor 11:24)…. There were 40 days before purification in the Temple—40 days for Mary's purification (Lk 2:22-24; Lev. 12:1-8, CCC 583)." Steve Ray, "Here We Are-Stuck in 40 Days of Lent!" catholicconvert.com, http://www.catholicconvert.com/blog/2008/02/16/here-we-are-stuck-in-40-days-of-lent/.

[89] "An Islamic Depiction of Noah in a 16th-century Mughal Miniature," c. 1590, https://commons.wikimedia.org/wiki/File:Noah%27s_Ark_by_Miskin.jpg, By Miskin [Public domain], via Wikimedia Commons.

sufficiently receded, anticipates the Holy Spirit, interprets St. Jerome among other Church Fathers.[90] The Holy Spirit is not only associated with the cleansing waters of baptism, but also with fire as indicated in Acts Chapter two when describing Pentecost (Acts 2:3). St. John Chrysostom compares this fiery presence of the Holy Spirit to the burning bush that Moses saw that rather being consumed by the fire became transformed by the fire while keeping its form.[91]

God keeps his promise to Noah never again to flood the world with the destructive force of water. This is evident, as explained by Pitre and Hahn, by the Hebrew word for rainbow (קֶשֶׁת, *qesheth*). *Qesheth* means both a rainbow, and a bow used to kill men in war or animals in hunting.[92] Due to this double meaning, the rainbow has been interpreted, explains Hahn, as "a sign that God will no longer make war against humanity: God hangs us his war bow and retires it from service [or]… as a bow drawn and aimed at heaven, a symbolic threat the represents God's covenant oath."[93]

---

[90] Jerome, *The Dialogue Against the Luciferians*, in *St. Jerome: Letters and Select Works*, ed. P. Schaff & H. Wace, trans. W. H. Fremantle, G. Lewis, & W. G. Martley, (New York: Christian Literature Company, 1893), vol. 6, p. 331. New York: Christian Literature Company.

[91] John Chrysostom, *Homilies of St. John Chrysostom, Archbishop of Constantinople, on the Acts of the Apostles*, in *Saint Chrysostom: Homilies on the Acts of the Apostles and the Epistle to the Romans*, ed P. Schaff, trans, J. Walker, J. Sheppard, H. Browne, & G. B. Stevens, (New York: Christian Literature Company, 1889), vol. 11, p. 25.

[92] Strong's Concordance, "7198. Qesheth," biblehub.com, http://biblehub.com/hebrew/7198.htm.

[93] Scott Hahn, *Catholic Bible Dictionary* (New York: Doubleday, 2009), 126.

God has kept his oath not to destroy mankind with a flood of water. Pitre points out this does not mean that God will not purify mankind by other means.[94] According to Scripture, God will send out his Holy Spirit in full force at the end of time to bring forth a New Heavens and a New Earth (Is. 65:17; 2 Peter 3:13; Rev. 21:1). Those who are not living on earth during the Second Coming of Christ, will be transformed by fire in purgatory[95] as St. Paul states, "for the Day will disclose it, because it will be revealed with fire, and the fire will test what sort of work each one has done…. If any man's work is burned up, he will suffer loss, though he himself will be saved, but only as through fire (1 Cor. 3:13-15 *RSVCE*)." St. Peter even explicitly compares the flood of Noah to Jesus's Second Coming at the end of time:

> …the world that then existed was deluged with water and perished. But by the same word the heavens and earth that now exist have been stored up for fire, being kept until the day of judgment and destruction…the day of the Lord will come like a thief, and then the heavens will pass away with a loud noise, and the elements will be dissolved with fire, and the earth and the works that are upon it will be burned up… … heavens will be kindled and dissolved, and the elements will melt with fire! But according to his promise we wait for new heavens and a new earth in which righteousness dwells. (2 Peter 3: 6-13 *RSVCE*)

---

[94] Pitre, *Genesis and the Books of Moses,* MP3 10.
[95] Pitre, *Genesis and the Books of Moses,* MP3 10.

The ark that protected Noah, his family, and the animals from the flood has commonly been interpreted as representing the Church. The early bishop of Carthage, St. Cyprian (200-258) writes "the one ark of Noah was a type of the one Church."[96] St. Augustine furthers this typology by spiritually interpreting various aspects of the ark. For example, the door of the ark is compared to the side of Christ that "was pierced with the spear" and out of which blood and water flowed, representing the sacramental Church.[97]

In accordance with this typology, Bishop Barron reminds Catholics that we are not to stay in a protective ecclesial environment, but rather as Noah and his family exited the ark and then set about restoring order to the world, we are called to go out into the world, proclaim the Good News of Jesus Christ so that people will order their many loves to the source of all love, God.[98] In addition, the central way by which we are to bring order to a fallen world is represented by what Noah did shortly after disembarking from the ark. He worshiped God and offered sacrifice on the Mountain of Ararat from the seven pairs of animals, distinguished from the non-numbered pair of animals, that

---

[96] Cyprian of Carthage, *The Epistles of Cyprian,* in *Fathers of the Third Century: Hippolytus, Cyprian, Novatian, Appendix*, eds. A. Roberts, J. Donaldson, & A.C. Coxe, trans. R.E. Wallis (Buffalo, NY: Christian Literature Company, 1886), vol. 5, p. 398.

[97] Augustine of Hippo, *The City of God*, in *St. Augustine's City of God and Christian Doctrine*, ed. P. Schaff, trans. M. Dods, (Buffalo, NY: Christian Literature Company, 1887), vol. 2, p. 306.

[98] Robert Barron, *Catholicism: A Journey to the Heart of the Faith* (New York: Crown Publishing Group, 2011), Kindle Location, 2079.

he had provided shelter from the flood.[99] We are to worship God by participating in the one sacrifice of Jesus Christ through the celebration of the Eucharist, "the font [source] and apex [summit] of the whole Christian life."[100] The Eucharist, in the fulfillment of the Garden of Eden, Tabernacle, and Jerusalem Temple, is to be the focal point around which we are to re-order a fallen world to God.

God responds to Noah by establishing a covenant with him (Genesis 6:18; Genesis 9:9). As Pitre indicates, the first time God makes a covenant with Noah, before the flood in Genesis 6:18, and with all of creation (Genesis 9:10), is the first time that the Hebrew word for covenant (בְּרִית, *berith*) is used in the Old Testament explicitly, although the reality the word *berith* points to is implied in the earlier relationships God established with all of creation and with Adam and Eve.[101] Representing Tradition, the *Catechism of the Catholic Church* teaches that, "The Covenant with Noah remains in force during the times of the Gentiles, until the universal proclamation

---

[99] Brant Pitre, *Genesis and the Books of Moses: Unlocking the Mysteries of the Pentateuch,* MP3 10. "[S]ome of the supposedly telltale evidences of confluence in the text may not be all that evident. Are 'two pair' and 'seven' mutually exclusive? Why cannot the 'two' of 6:19– 20 and 7:9,15 be the standard number of animals (a male and female for breeding— even the unclean animals are preserved!) taken into the ark? 'Seven' would apply only to sacrificial animals— that is, animals in a category by themselves." Hamilton, 71.

[100] "Lumen Gentium," no. 11, vatican.va, http://www.vatican.va/archive/hist_councils/ii_vatican_council/documents/vat-ii_const_19641121_lumen-gentium_en.html.

[101] Pitre, *Genesis and the Books of Moses,* MP3 10; Pitre, *Genesis and the Books of Moses,* Outline, 39.

of the Gospel."[102]

[103]

It is important to note that this covenant precedes the covenant God later makes with the Hebrew people, whose first Father (Patriarch) is Abraham, and from these people with Israel, whose Father is Jacob, also called Israel after he wrestled with the angel.[104] God's reaffirmation of the Noahic covenant in Genesis Chapter nine reads, "I establish my covenant with you and your descendants after you, and with every living creature that is with you (Genesis 9:9-10 *RSVCE*)." The covenant God makes with Noah, a gentile, is a covenant that applies to all people, who in some way are descendants of the

---

[102] "Catechism of the Catholic Church," no. 58, vatican.va, http://www.vatican.va/archive/ENG0015/__PG.HTM.

[103] James Tissot, "Noah's Sacrifice," c. 1896-1902, https://commons.wikimedia.org/wiki/File:Tissot_Noah%27s_Sacrifice.jpg, James Tissot [Public domain], via Wikimedia Commons.

[104] Hahn further clarifies that, "According to Scripture, all Israelites are Hebrews (descendants of Eber, Gen 11:16) but most Hebrews are not Israelites (descendants of the Jacob, Ex 1:1-4)." Scott Hahn, and Curtis Mitch, *The First and Second Book of Samuel* (San Francisco: Ignatius Press, 2016), loc. 2246.

nations which descended from Noah identified in Genesis chapter 10. Among these nations are the descendants of Noah's son Shem, who as traced by the Bible, is the father of the Semitic (Shemitic) people, and, consequently, the father of Abraham, Isaac, Jacob and the Israelites.

Due to being after the Fall when all humankind has been touched by sin, the two previously mentioned cities once again emerge and vie with one another. As a reminder, these two cities are the city of man, or the city of death, characterized, explains Augustine, by excessive self-love and a city of God, a city of life, ordered by love of God. Both cities try to persuade the other city's citizens to switch their allegiance. As salvation history unfolds in time, God chooses one nation, the Israelites, so that through this choice all the members from the other nations may be gathered slowly back to God in the city of God, in the city of life whose essential focus is worship and love of God, and its corresponding ordered love of neighbor. In teaching on this principle of Genesis that God chooses in salvation history to call one nation (Israel) for the sake of the other nations, the *Catechism* teaches:

> After the unity of the human race was shattered by sin God at once sought to save humanity part by part. The covenant with Noah after the flood gives expression to the principle of the divine economy toward the "nations," in other words, towards men grouped "in their lands, each with its own language, by their families, in their nations." … In order to gather together scattered humanity God calls Abram from his country. … After the patriarchs [Abraham, Isaac, and Jacob as fathers of Israel] God formed Israel as his people … Israel is the priestly people of God "called by the name of the Lord," and "the first to hear the word of

God." The people of "elder brethren" in the faith of Abraham.[105]

Section Questions

1. How is Jesus a New Noah? With specific reference to Scripture, include in your response the following: First-Born Sons, Baptism, Ark, Creation, Number 40, Dove, Rainbow, Fire.

Meat Eating Concession

Before the sons of Noah (Shem, Ham, and Ja'pheth) and their descendants spread across the face of the earth to fulfill the command "Be fruitful and multiply (Genesis 9:1 *RSVCE*)" God grants them permission to eat animals with, "Every moving thing that lives shall be food for you; and as I gave you the green plants, I give you everything (Genesis 9:3 *RSVCE*)." As the text implies and is confirmed by Genesis chapter one, verse twenty-nine, in the beginning Adam and Eve were given only plants, and fruit from trees to eat as food. Why does the Adamic covenant and the Noahic covenant differ with respect to what food is permissible to eat? Why does Scripture indicate that in the original state of nature, in the time before the Fall, Adam and Eve were vegetarians and were commanded by God to be such, and why after Noah, as a new type of Adam, does God grant permission to eat animals, and explicitly state that the animals shall live in "fear of you (Genesis 9:2 *RSVCE*)"?

---

[105] "Catechism of the Catholic Church," no. 56-63, vatican.va, http://www.vatican.va/archive/ENG0015/__PG.HTM.

One detail in the text that describes the time right after the Fall of Adam and Eve subtly prepares for this change from a vegetarian diet to a carnivorous diet. Hamilton notes that right after Adam and Eve sin but before the serpent is cursed, Adam and Eve "knew that they were naked; and they sewed fig leaves together and made themselves aprons (Genesis 3:7)." This contrast with their attitude towards nakedness before the Fall. Before the Fall, Adam and Even "were both naked, and were not ashamed (Genesis 2:25 *RSVCE*), and consequently, were not motivated to make clothes for themselves. According to the mindset of the Old Testament, being naked and not being ashamed is unusual since, "Every time nakedness is used in the Old Testament, it is symbolic of poverty. POWs [Prisoners of War] are paraded naked away into captivity. So, if we're going to be told that they were naked, the audience will assume they were ashamed unless

[106] Providence Lithograph Company, "*The Garden of Eden* (illustration from Bible card published 1906 by the Providence Lithograph Company)," 1906, https://commons.wikimedia.org/wiki/File:Man_Made_in_the_ Image_of_God_(crop).jpg, By the Providence Lithograph Company (http://thebiblerevival.com/clipart/1907/gen1.jpg) [Public domain], via Wikimedia Commons.

told otherwise."[107]

After God curses the serpent and punishes Adam and Eve, God then makes "for Adam and for his wife garments of skins and clothed them (Genesis 3:21)."[108] Miller argues that since the literal translation of the Genesis 3:21 is God clothing Adam and his wife in garments of skin (singular) the verse may "mean 'skin clothing,' or hides … both rabbinic tradition and early Christian tradition understood this to mean human skin, in the sense of … 'mortal flesh.' In other words, another way of saying "you will eventually die" is to say, "clothed in mortality." It's related to 'to dust you shall return.'"[109]

St. Jerome, as a representative of similar patristic commentary, in commenting on God allowing Noah and his descendants to eat meat, which may be anticipated by Genesis 3:21, writes:

> [J]ust as divorce according to the Savior's word was not permitted from the beginning, but on account of the hardness of our heart was a concession of Moses to the human race, so too the eating of flesh was unknown until the deluge. But after the deluge, like the quails given in the desert to the murmuring people, the poison of flesh-meat was offered to our teeth. The Apostle writing to the Ephesians teaches that God had purposed in the fullness of time to sum up and renew in Christ Jesus all things which are in heaven and in earth. Whence also the Savior himself in the Revelation of John says, "I am Alpha and Omega, the beginning and the ending." At the beginning

---

[107] Miller, 45-48.
[108] Hamilton, 261.
[109] Miller, 62.

of the human race we neither ate flesh, nor gave bills of divorce, nor suffered circumcision for a sign. Thus, we reached the deluge. But after the deluge, together with the giving of the law which no one could fulfil, flesh was given for food, and divorce was allowed to hard-hearted men, and the knife of circumcision was applied, as though the hand of God had fashioned us with something superfluous. But once Christ has come in the end of time, and Omega passed into Alpha and turned the end into the beginning, we are no longer allowed divorce, nor are we circumcised, nor do we eat flesh, for the Apostle says, "It is good not to eat flesh, nor to drink wine." For wine as well as flesh was consecrated after the deluge.[110]

The last two sentences of St. Jerome's above excerpt need to be interpreted carefully. With these words St. Jerome states that Christ has brought us back to the pre-Fall times when divorce did not occur, circumcision not done, and flesh was not eaten. The quotation of the "Apostle" comes from the Letter to the Romans, "it is right not to eat meat or drink wine or do anything that makes your brother stumble (Romans 14:21 *RSVCE*)." Right before this verse we read, "Everything is indeed clean," which reflects Peter's vision from God showing him "all kinds of animals… And there came a voice to him, 'Rise, Peter, kill and eat (Acts 10: 12-13 *RSVCE*).'"

Clearly, St. Jerome is not teaching that it is forbidden to eat meat, just that we need to do so in moderation if we choose to eat meat while

---

[110] Jerome, *Against Jovinianus*, in *St. Jerome: Letters and Select Works*, eds. P. Schaff & H. Wace, trans. W. H. Fremantle, G. Lewis, & W. G. Martley (New York: Christian Literature Company, 1893), vol. 6, p. 360.

remembering that flesh eating as described in the Old Testament was permitted by God because our hardness of heart. As St. Jerome says in another passage, "We do not deny that fish and other kinds of flesh, if we choose, may be taken as food; but as we prefer virginity to marriage, so do we esteem fasting and spirituality above meats and full-bloodedness."[111]

Anthony Pagliarini rightly observes, though, to simply deem meat eating, and the latter concession that Israel may have a king, as a curse is not biblically correct since eating meat and kingship are latter portrayed as a blessing.[112] With respect to meat-eating Pagliarnini writes:

> On the one hand, the new diet is an abiding sign of the violence that brought the flood. On the other, it becomes the means of refiguring that violence in the service of communion. … In addition to the ordinary dietary stipulations that themselves further specify the prescriptions of Genesis 1, animal sacrifices fully elevate that new concession of meat into a form of

---

[111] Jerome, *Against Jovinianus*, in *St. Jerome: Letters and Select Works*, eds. P. Schaff & H. Wace, trans. W. H. Fremantle, G. Lewis, & W. G. Martley (New York: Christian Literature Company, 1893), vol. 6, p. 401.

[112] "It is better, I suggest, to view the concession of meat as an analogy with the grant of kingship in 1 Sam 8. It is in one respect a concession, a decision to 'harken to the voice of the people' who 'have rejected [God] from being king over them" (1 Sam 8:7). All the same, however, the kingship is a blessing and becomes the abiding means for the exercise of God's providence (cf. 2 Sam 7:8-16) Anthony Pagliarini, "Ordering All Things Well," *Communio*, vol. XLIV, no. 3, Fall (2017), 568.

worship and even table fellowship with God. Paradoxically, Fall and flood imbue eating with an ever-greater significance. (*O felix culpa.*)[113]

Section Questions

1. With respect to eating meat, contrast Genesis 1:29 with Genesis 9:3. Then explain how God transforms meat eating. With specific reference to Scripture, include the following in your response: Concession, Kingship.

Tower of Babel

Genesis chapter eleven, describes God checking the pride and resulting violence of the nations that descend from Noah. In the section on the tower of Babel, God halts the growing pride by causing a confusion of languages among "the whole earth" that once had only "one language and few words (Genesis 11:1 *RSVCE*)." The "one language" ought not be interpreted, argues Hamilton, to mean there was only one language since chapter ten states that the nations were divided by languages. Instead, it indicates that before the tower of Babel incident, there was an "international language that makes cooperation and interchange possible among people of different languages."[114] As the *Catechism* teaches, the division of the human race into many nations with many languages without a common language, "is intended to limit the pride of fallen humanity united only in its

---

[113] Anthony Pagliarini, "Ordering All Things Well," 569.
[114] Hamilton, 76.

perverse ambition to forge its own unity at Babel"[115] by building "a tower with its top in the heavens (Genesis 11:4 *RSVCE*)."

The pride exhibited by the inhabitants of Shinar in their attempt to build a tower is, indicates Pitre, even noticeable in the pronoun they use.[117] The pronoun used is the first-person, plural "us". "[L]et us make...let us build... let us make a name for ourselves (Genesis 11:4 *RSVCE*)." In the context of Genesis 11, this pronoun is used in an exclusive, competitive sense of us against other nations, and even against God whom they want to control, represented by the tower piercing heaven itself (Genesis 11:4).

The desire of the inhabitants of Shinar to dominate, rule, control and "make a name for themselves" is contrary to the very purpose of

---

[115] "Catechism of the Catholic Church," no. 57, vatican.va, http://www.vatican.va/archive/ENG0015/__PG.HTM.

[116] Pieter Bruegel the Elder, "The Tower of Babel," c. 1563, https://commons.wikimedia.org/wiki/File:Pieter_Bruegel_the_Elder_-_The _Tower_of_Babel_(Vienna)_-_Google_Art_Project.jpg, Pieter Brueghel the Elder [Public domain], via Wikimedia Commons.

[117] Brant Pitre, "Pentecost and Speaking in Tongues, (Pentecost Sunday, Year A)," catholicproductions.com.

God making man. God created man, as Isaiah asserts, for God's glory and not for self-glorification (Isaiah 43:7). For this reason, St. Paul writes "So, whether you eat or drink, or whatever you do, do all to the glory of God (1 Cor. 10:31 *RSVCE*)." When we truly seek God's glory and not our own glory then, as a consequence, we, at the same time, seek the benefit without excessive favoritism of all since all human beings are God's adopted sons and daughters.

God responds to the prideful assertion of the Shinarites by "scatter[ing] them abroad from there over the face of all the earth and … confus[ing] the language of all the earth (Genesis 11: 8-9 *RSVCE*)." Consequently, the name of the city, Babel, is given in Genesis since it likely originates from the Hebrew word *balal* (בָּלַל) meaning confuse.[118]

Like a mirror image of Genesis 11 and a reversal of Genesis 11, explains Pitre, Acts chapter two describes many people gathered together, this time in Jerusalem (יְרוּשָׁלַם), which, according to a traditional etymological definition, comes from two Hebrew words *yarah* (יָרָה) meaning foundation and *shalem* (שָׁלֵם), meaning peace. For this reason, Jerusalem is often referred to as a city of peace (Hebrews 7:1-2).[119] In this most fitting city God sends His Holy Spirit

---

[118]   Strong's   Concordance,   "1101.balal,"   biblehub.com,   http://biblehub.com/hebrew/894.htm.

[119]   Strong's   Concordance,   "3389.   Yerushalaim,"   biblehub.com, http://biblehub.com/hebrew/3389.htm;   Brant   Pitre,   "Pentecost   and Speaking   in   Tongues,   (Pentecost   Sunday,   Year   A),"   catholicproductions.com. "For this Melchiz'edek, king of Salem, priest of the Most High God, met Abraham returning from the slaughter of the kings and blessed him; and to him Abraham apportioned a tenth part of everything. He is first, by translation of his name, king of righteousness, and then he is also king of Salem, that is, king of peace (Hebrews 7:1-2 RSVCE)."

down upon the Apostles gathered around Mary. The gift of the Holy Spirit and the unifying language of ordered, truthful love the Spirit provides, caused a large crowd of people, who spoke many different languages, to hear the Apostles speaking in their own languages (Acts 2:6).

The Catholic Church that was born on Pentecost is a universal Church with one common language, the language of truthful love, the language of the Holy Spirit which knits us together into one mystical body (1 Corinthians 12:12-31). As one body united by God we are not to dominate others, as the inhabitants of Shinar desired, for, as St. Paul writes, "God has so composed the body, giving the greater honor to the inferior part, that there may be no discord in the body, but that the members may have the same care for one another (1 Corinthians 12:24-25 *RSVCE*)."

Section Questions

1. Describe the similarities and differences between Pentecost (Acts 2) and the Tower of Babel (Genesis 11). With specific reference to Scripture, include the following in your response: Use of pronoun "Us" in Genesis 11:4, international language, and unity.

Sodom and Gomorrah

The cities of Sodom and Gomorrah (Genesis 19-20) were like Babel in that they all were united tenuously by vice and, therefore, always at the edge of descending into chaos. A common that weakly united the people was lust ad evident by the "men of Sodom, both young and old" who surrounded Lot's house and lustfully demanded, "Where are the men who came to you tonight? Bring them out to us, that we may know them (Genesis 19:4-5 *RSVCECE*)." As Bishop Barron comments, with these words, a "gang rape" was being proposed "violent, impersonal, self-interested, and infertile…the precise opposite of what God intends for human sexuality."[120] In response, God tells Abraham that He will destroy this vicious city unless "fifty righteous" people are found in it. Abraham then intercedes for the city by asking God to spare the city for forty-five righteous people (second for 40, third for 30, fourth for 20, fifth for 10). Since not even ten righteous people could be found in the city, God destroyed it with fire and brimstone.

[121]

---

[120] Robert Barron, *Letter to a Suffering Church* (Park Ridge: Word on Fire, 2019), Kindle location 156 of 738.

[121] John Martin, "The Destruction of Sodom and Gomorrah," 1852, https://commons.wikimedia.org/wiki/File:John_Martin_-_Sodom_and_Gomorrah.jpg, [Public domain], via Wikimedia Commons.

In commenting on Abraham's intercessory role, Roy H. Schoeman notes that throughout Scripture, beginning with Noah, a few intercede for many, a few are called for the salvation of all. Both Jewish and Catholic tradition further expand on this basic pattern of salvation history. "Talmudic Judaism" writes Schoeman, "teaches that the continued existence of the entire world is being supported by the prayers of thirty-six righteous men."[122] And in Christianity, continues Schoeman, "This same principle-that for the sake of just a few faithful souls, entire countries or even the entire world are spared divine justice – is frequently reflected in private revelations made to Christian saints [such as to the children of Fatima or to Sister Faustina]."[123]

A related principle that repeats in salvation history is a small group of people, a "remnant," will remain faithful to God while the many abandon God and His ways (Isaiah 11:16; Malachi 3:16). In Catholicism this few faithful are the saints, explains Schoeman. These holy people, writes Paul, are "a remnant, chosen by grace (Romans 11:5)" who help to save the majority. The relationship of God with the minority, and through them, with the majority, "is not" writes Schoeman:

> established and maintained on the basis of 'averages', or on the behavior of the majority. The majority of mankind, throughout all of human history, has always turned away from God, has failed Him, and will continue to do so. God's

---

[122] Roy H. Schoeman, *Salvation is from the Jews* (San Francisco: Ignatius Press, 2003), 29. See Talmud Tract Sanhedrin 97b, The Babylonian Talmud.

[123] Roy H. Schoeman, *Salvation is from the Jews* (San Francisco: Ignatius Press, 2003), 29. See Talmud Tract Sanhedrin 97b, The Babylonian Talmud.

relationship with the entire human race is established and maintained on the basis of His relationship with a 'chosen few', with those few souls who truly give their hearts to Him, in whom He can truly find delight. It is for the sake of these few that He pours out His mercy upon the rest."[124]

Section Questions

1. With respect to the concept of a faithful remnant comment on Sodom and Gomorrah. With specific reference to Scripture, include the following in your response: Salvation History, Abraham, One, Few, Saints.

Abraham and Isaac

Over a thousand years before Pentecost, God began his plan to gather back fallen humanity scattered among many nations with diverse languages by choosing one man, Abraham (c. 2000 BC).[125] For this reason, implies the *Catechism*, Abram is given the name Abraham which means "the father of a multitude of nations (Genesis 17:5 *RSVCE*)."[126] A reason that God chose Abram was because Abram "believed the Lord; and he reckoned it to him as righteousness (Genesis 15:6 *RSVCE*)." The word believe is a translation of the Hebrew root word *aman*, (אָמַן) meaning trusting, believing,

---

[124] Roy H. Schoeman, *Salvation is from the Jews* (San Francisco: Ignatius Press, 2003), 31-32.

[125] "Catechism of the Catholic Church," no. 59, vatican.va, http://www.vatican.va/archive/ENG0015/__PG.HTM.

[126] "Catechism of the Catholic Church," no. 59.

confirming.[127] The English word Amen comes directly from this Hebrew word. In its biblical context, explains Miller, "It has to do not with believing a piece of information but with considering someone reliable. Abraham accepted God as reliable."[128]

Before receiving a new name, Abram is called by God to "Go from your country and your kindred and your father's house to the land that I will show you (Genesis 12:1 *RSVCE*)." The land God directs Abram to is Canaan, where modern day Israel is situated. Abram was seventy-five years old when he received his mission with the promise that God would make a "great nation" for Abram. Typically, people who are given important missions are not those in their last phase of life but rather the youthfully dynamic. However, comments Miller, "the qualifications needed for God's work are very different from those of a stereotypical hero."[129]

Leaving behind the city of Haran, usually identified with the Turkish city of Harran, Abram set off for this foreign land. Abram's city of origin was not Haran but Ur, located in modern day Iraq. According to Hahn, Ur was a prosperous and powerful city.[130] By obeying God, Abram went even farther away from the comforts and security Ur offered. During his journey, which included leaving Canaan to go to Egypt and returning, Abram encountered the Priest-King of Salem, Melchizedek, who blesses Abram. In the following section we will discuss the significance of this encounter.

---

[127] "539. aman," biblehub.com, https://biblehub.com/hebrew/539.htm.

[128] Miller, 73.

[129] Miller, 72-73.

[130] Scott Hahn, *Kinship by Covenant* (New Haven: Yale University Press, 2009), 935.

Due to a famine (Genesis 12:10), Abram left Canaan for Egypt only to return to Canaan, the land that God promised Abram will possess and there have descendants that are as numerous as the stars in the sky (Genesis 15:5, 7). Since Abram is still childless, he asked God if he will be given a child and God, in a solemn manner (Genesis 15: 17-21), assured Abram that he will have an offspring.

Sarah, Abram's wife, though, grew impatient at her barrenness and encouraged Abram to have sexual intercourse with her maidservant Hagar so that she could "obtain children by her (Genesis 16:2 *RSVCE*)." Abram, points out Hamilton, in a similar way as Adam who without resistance accepted the forbidden fruit from Eve, silently agreed, had relations with Hagar who then gave birth to Ishmael.[132] This first-born son was not the one God had in mind for the fulfillment

---

[131] Rembrandt, "Abraham and Isaac (oil on canvas)," 1634, https://commons.wikimedia.org/wiki/File:Rembrandt_Abraham_en_Isaac, _1634.jpg, [Public domain], via Wikimedia Commons.

[132] Hamilton, 90.

of His prophecy. As interpreted by Pitre, Abram and Sarah sinned by trying to speed up the fulfillment of God's promise of an offspring by relying on human means, in this sexual intercourse between Abram and Hagar.[133]

Finally, when Abram was ninety-nine years old God appears to him and once again confirms Abram and Sarah will have their own offspring who, along with his descendants will possess the land of Canaan. During this appearance, God changes Abram's name from Abram (אַבְרָם), meaning in Hebrew "exalted father" to Abraham, meaning "father of a multitude."[134] Much to her surprise, and disbelieving laughter, Sarah, ninety years old, became pregnant and gave birth to Isaac, a named derived from the Hebrew verb meaning to laugh (*litz'chok*, לִצְחֹק).[135] Sarah's miraculous pregnancy at age ninety after years of barrenness points to the even more miraculous pregnancy of Mary who gave birth to Jesus while remaining a virgin.

The covenant sign that God commanded Abraham and his male descendants to perform is circumcision. Perhaps, speculates Pitre, this served as a painful reminder of Abraham's and Sarah's impatience and lack of faith in God to keep His promise to give them an heir.[136] Hamilton comments that Abraham and other notable people signaled out by Scripture as being people of faith all "have somewhere in their life a fatal flaw, and sometimes more than one."[137] He adds, "But those who at least stumble and fall forward in the direction of God's will find

---

[133] Pitre, *The Old Testament*, MP 9.

[134] "85. Abraham," "87. Abram," biblehub.com, http://biblehub.com/hebrew/85.htm, http://biblehub.com/hebrew/87.htm.

[135] "2464. Isaak," biblehub.com, http://biblehub.com/greek/2464.htm.

[136] Pitre, *The Old Testament*, MP 9.

[137] Hamilton, 92.

a divine resource and promise from God."[138] Although Abraham was flawed even in the gift of faith that he is praised for, he, nonetheless, fell forward in repentance by turning to the Lord and trusting in Him.

[139]

Years later, God tests Abraham's and Sarah's trust even more by asking them something God never asks anyone else in the Old Testament. He asks Abraham to "Take your son, your only begotten son Isaac; whom you love, and go to the land of Mor'iah, and offer him there as a burnt offering upon one of the mountains of which I shall tell you (Genesis 22: 2 *RSVCE*)." Abraham obeys even though, according to Jewish interpretation, this may have meant that Sarah would never forgive him.[140] This interpretation is based on Abraham's absence when Sarah died and subsequent travel to Hebron where he

---

[138] Hamilton, 92.

[139] James Tissot, "Sarah, 90 years old, hears that she will have a child, and laughs at the idea," c. 1900, https://commons.wikimedia.org/wiki/File: Tissot_Sarah_Hears_and_Laughs.gif, James Tissot [Public domain], via Wikimedia Commons.

[140] "Where Was Abraham at the Time of Sarah's Death?" Chabad.org, http://www.chabad.org/parshah/article_cdo/aid/1579612/jewish/Where-Was-Abraham-at-the-Time-of-Sarahs-Death.htm.

mourned and wept over her dead body (Genesis 23:2-3).

The site that God asked Abraham to sacrifice his son upon is significant because upon the site, upon Mount Moriah, King Solomon ordered the Jerusalem Temple to be built (2 Chronicles 3:1)[141] Close to this same site is where Jesus would be crucified, outside of the gates of Jerusalem (Hebrews 13:12), on Calvary, also known as Golgatha. Other spiritual connections between Abraham's willingness to sacrifice Isaac and the New Testament include the following.

According to Genesis chapter twenty-two, verse six, Abraham "took the wood of the offering and laid it on Isaac his son (*RSVCE*)" who then carried the wood up the mountain.[142] Similarly, Jesus carried the wood of the cross to the site where He was sacrificed "in atonement for our sins and the sins of the whole world." (Divine Mercy Chaplet) An essential difference between Isaac and Jesus is that Jesus was sacrificed on the wood that he carried, and Isaac was not. In the case of Isaac, Abraham was directed by an angel from heaven to take a ram

---

[141] "Then Solomon began to build the house of the Lord in Jerusalem on Mount Moriah, where the Lord has appeared to David his father, at the place that David had appointed, on the threshing floor of Ornan the Jebusite." (2 Chronicles 3:1 RSVCE)

[142] In commenting on Isaac's age Hamilton writes, "In his *Antiquities of the Jews* (1.13) Josephus states that Isaac was twenty-five at this time. Although Josephus does not explain the source of his information, the figure perhaps refers to the minimum age for active military service at the close of the Second Temple period (five years more than the minimum twenty of Scripture [Num. 1: 3, 45]). A midrash on Genesis (Genesis Rabbah 56: 8) states that Isaac was thirty-seven on this occasion! This figure is based on Sarah's age of ninety at the birth of Isaac, and her death thirty-seven years later at the age of 127 (Gen. 23: 1), precipitated by the false announcement of her son's death! In any event, the Isaac of this chapter is anything but a child." Hamilton, 97.

that was caught by its horns in possibly thorny bushes and sacrifice the ram instead of his son Isaac.

As explained by Brant Pitre, the Church Fathers interpreted the ram as a sign of Christ for rams were animals that well symbolized kingly power.[143] In addition, the bushes the ram's head and horns were caught in represent the crowns of thorns that were cruelly placed on Jesus head.

Finally, since Abraham was so obedient to God to the extent of even being willing to do the unthinkable, something never asked in the Bible of anyone else, to sacrifice a human being, to sacrifice his son, God blessed him abundantly and promised to bless Abraham's descendants (Genesis 22:17-18 *RSVCE*), and through Abraham's descendants all the nations of the earth, "and all peoples on earth will be blessed through you (Genesis 12:3 *NIV*)." This universal blessing that Abraham and his descendants received for all nations is fulfilled in Jesus Christ who by his obedience as priest-victim, as one who both offered the sacrifice and was the sacrifice, gained for us the blessing of eternal salvation.

The land and "great nation (Genesis 12:1-2)" promised to Abraham would be partially fulfilled in Moses leading his people back from Egypt to the land Abraham settled in. There, the Israelites became a great nation under King David. Only in Jesus, though, were these promises fulfilled in their fullest sense. Jesus, through his foster father Joseph's Davidic ancestry as a member of the tribe of Judah, established a Catholic Church that by its universal nature is open to and extends God's blessings to all nations. The ultimate land is the

---

[143] Brant Pitre, "The Second Sunday in Lent (Year B)," catholicproductions.com.

heavenly city of Jerusalem (Revelation 21:2). This heavenly city where the human and divine intersect is Jesus, in whom we are baptized into as members of His Mystical Body. As Benedict XVI writes:

> the interpenetration of humanity and divinity in the crucified and exalted man Jesus. Christ, the man who is in God and eternally one with God, is at the same time God's abiding openness to all men. Thus, Jesus himself is what we call "heaven"; heaven is not a place, but a person, the person of him in whom God and man are forever and inseparably one. And we go to heaven and enter into heaven to the extent that we go to Jesus Christ and enter into him.[144]

Section Questions

1. Comment on the Hebrew word *aman*, (אָמַן) used in Genesis 15:6. With specific reference to Scripture, include the following in your response: Abram, Abraham, faith, use of Amen by Catholics.

2. Comment on Abraham's and Sarah's faith and lack of faith. With specific reference to Scripture, include the following in your response: Promised a Child, Sarah and Hagar, Sarah Laughs, Circumcision, Isaac.

3. How does Abraham, Isaac, and Sarah specifically foreshadow

---

[144] Benedict XVI, *Dogma and Preaching: Applying Christian Doctrine to Daily Life*, trans. Michael J. Miller (San Francisco: Ignatius Press, 2011), 321.

Jesus and Mary? With specific reference to Scripture, include the following in your response: Virgin Birth, Wood Carried by Isaac, Ram, Thorn Bushes, Land Promised to Abraham.

Melchizedek

We now return to the mysterious King of Salem, Melchizedek, who blessed Abram and "brought out bread and wine (Genesis 14:18 *RSVCE*)." He is identified as "the priest [כֹּהֵן *kohen*] of God Most High (Genesis 14:18 *RSVCE*)." This is the first time out of 750 that the Bible explicitly uses the term *kohen* to call someone a priest.[145] Abram responds by giving "a tenth of everything." (Genesis 14:20 *RSVCE*) In interpreting this encounter, Hebrews states, "It is beyond dispute that the inferior is blessed by the superior (Hebrews 7:7 *RSVCE*)." Afterwards, it is explained that the priesthood of Jesus Christ is "according to the order of Melchizedek" and not "according to the order of Aaron (Hebrews 7:11 *RSVCE*)" for Christ's priesthood is "not according to the legal requirement concerning bodily descent but by the power of an indestructible life (Hebrews 7:16 *RSVCE*)."

Upon closer examination it is seen, as Hahn explains, that the bible explicitly identifies Salem with Jerusalem, specifically Psalm 76, verse one through two. In reference to B. Vawter, Hahn acknowledges that it is not possible to verify if the equating of Salem with Jerusalem was intended by the author of Genesis, or if it is a later development.[146]

---

[145] "3548. כֹּהֵן (kohen)," biblehub.com, http://biblehub.com/hebrew/strongs_3548.htm.

[146] Scott Hahn, *Kinship by Covenant* (New Haven: Yale University Press, 2009),133.

Even so, since the primary author of Scripture is God, such an identification is intended by Him at least for a spiritual interpretation of Melchizedek as one who prepares for the founding of Jerusalem, and for Christ the ultimate priest-king as the "king of Salem, that is, [the] king of peace (Hebrews 7:2 *RSVCE*)."

Relying on both ancient Jewish and Christian commentary, Hahn brings out another identification, Melchizedek as Noah's first-born son, Shem. In his *Letter to Evangelus*, St. Jerome concurs with Jewish commentary that Melchizedek may be a title for Shem, Noah's oldest son.[148] This identification helps to explain why Melchizedek is a priest

---

[147] ro:User:Țetcu Mircea Rareș, "An image of Melchizedek painted onto the altar side near the Royal Doors at Libotin wooden church, Maramureș County, Romania," May 2009, https://commons.wikimedia.org/wiki/File: Biserica_de_lemn_Sf.Arhangheli_din_Libotin_(13).JPG, Țetcu Mircea Rareș [CC BY 2.5 (https://creativecommons.org/licenses/by/2.5)], via Wikimedia Commons.

[148] Jerome, *The Letters of St. Jerome*, in *St. Jerome: Letters and Select Works*, eds. P. Schaff & H. Wace, trans. G, Lewis, & W.G. Martley (New York: Christian Literature Company, 1893), vol. 6, p. 154.

and is superior to Abram. He is superior because as first-born son of Noah he is older than Abram and as first-born son has inherited Noah's priesthood.[149]

Section Questions

1. Contrast the Priesthood of Melchizedek with the Levitical Priesthood. With specific reference to Scripture, include the following in your response: Salem and Jerusalem, Shem, First-Born Son, Israel, Levitical Priesthood, Jesus' Priesthood.

Jacob/Israel

The original, common priesthood of Adam, that Cain as first-born son lost, was handed to Adam's third son Seth. Generations later this common priesthood was received by Noah as the new father of all nations (Genesis 5). Many generations later the priesthood was given in a special way to the nation of Israel as the adopted "firstborn son," as a "kingdom of priests and a holy nation (Exodus 4:22; 19:6 *RSVCE*)." The reason God favored Israel, teaches the *Catechism*, was, beginning with Israel "to save humanity part by part (*CCC* 56)."[150] In other words, one nation is chosen for the sake of all nations, for all peoples are called to be adopted sons and daughters of God. The one chosen nation, Israel, and all the nations that Israel is chosen for are, in different ways, called to be adopted children of God. As Ratzinger

---

[149] Hahn, *Kinship by Covenant*,130-134.

[150] "Catechism of the Catholic Church," no. 56-63, vatican.va, http://www.vatican.va/archive/ENG0015/__PG.HTM.

explains, the adopted "firstborn" sonship of Israel is by election, after the Fall, while the adopted sonship of all other nations is by creation, prior to the Fall. To call people back to Him, God chooses elects Israel as the one nation to have a special paternal relationship with God so that gradually through time all nations will return to God.[151] God's will that all be offered salvation unfolds gradually through history, by one, or a few being chosen for many until the fullness of time when the only begotten son Jesus Christ takes on flesh.[152]

---

[151] Joseph Ratzinger, *The Meaning of Christian Brotherhood* (San Francisco: Ignatius Press, 1993), 47.

[152] Joseph Cardinal Ratzinger, "Dominus Jesus," no. 13-15, vatican.va, http://www.vatican.va/roman_curia/congregations/cfaith/documents/rc_con_cfaith_doc_20000806_dominus-iesus_en.html. In further commenting on Israel's chosen status by election and the more fundamental created chosen status of all people regardless of national identity, Benedict XVI writes:

In the normal way of things, a God who loses his land, who leaves his people defeated and is unable to protect his sanctuary, is a God who has been overthrown. He has no more say in things. He vanishes from history. When Israel went into exile, quite astonishingly, the opposite happened. The stature of this God, the way he was completely different from the other divinities in the religions of the world, was now apparent, and the faith of Israel at last took on its true form and stature. This God could afford to let others have his land because he was not tied down to any country. He could allow his people to be defeated so as to awaken it thereby from its false religious dream. He was not dependent on this people, yet nevertheless he did not abandon them in their hour of defeat. He was not dependent upon the Temple or on the cult celebrated there, as was then commonly supposed: people gave nourishment to the gods, and the gods maintained the world. No, he did not need this cult, which to some extent had concealed his real being. Thus, together with a more profound concept of God, a new idea of worship developed. Certainly, since the time of Solomon the personal God of the Fathers had been identified with the high god, the Creator, who is

The name Israel was not originally a name for a chosen nation but rather the second name of Jacob, who, although younger than his brother Esau, received, with the help of his mother Rebecca (רִבְקָה *Rivka*) a special blessing from his father Isaac. As mentioned previously, citing Hahn, God often favors the younger brother over the older brother: Abel over Cain, Isaac over Ishmael, Jacob over Esau, Perez over Zerah, Joseph over Reuben, and Ephraim over Manasseh. This contrasts with only three instances in Genesis where God favors

---

known to all religions, but in general this latter had been excluded from worship, as not being responsible for one's individual needs. This identification, which had been made in principle, although it had probably hitherto impinged little upon people's consciousness, now became the driving force for survival of the faith: Israel has no particular God at all but simply worships the one single God. This God spoke to Abraham and chose Israel, but he is in reality the God of all peoples, the universal God who guides the course of all history. The purifying of the idea of worship belongs with this. God needs no sacrifice; he does not have to be nourished by men, because everything belongs to him. The true sacrifice is the man who has become worthy of God. Three hundred years after the Exile, in the similarly severe crisis of the Hellenistic suppression of the Temple cult, the Book of Daniel expressed it thus: "At this time there is no prince, or prophet, or leader, no burnt offering, or sacrifice, or oblation,. . . no place to make an offering before thee or to find mercy. Yet with a contrite heart and a humble spirit may we be accepted" (Dan 3:38 = Prayer of Azariah 15-16). At the same time, given the failure of the present time to match up to the power and the goodness of God, the future aspect of Israel's faith emerges with correspondingly greater emphasis; or, better, we might say that the present is made relative to a wider horizon that runs far beyond the moment, indeed beyond the whole world, so that the present can be properly dealt with and understood.

Joseph Ratzinger, "Faith Between Reason and Feeling," matiane.wordpress.com, https://matiane.wordpress.com/2018/11/24/cardinal-joseph-ratzinger-faith-between-reason-and-feeling/.

the first-born son as worthy of their natural preeminence as firstborn sons: Noah, Shem, and Abraham.[153]

To signify a specific mission that Jacob is to fulfill, Jacob is renamed Israel. The renaming occurs after he wrestled at night with someone who appeared to be a man, but actually was an angelic representative of God.[154] God's representative then calls Jacob "Israel, for you have striven with God, and with men, and have prevailed (Genesis 32:28 *RSVCE*)." When studying the book of Exodus, we will see how Israel as a people also struggled with God and, due to God's fidelity to Israel, prevails with Israel's identity intact.

This prevailing identity, despite the failings of Israel, is due to God's promise to Israel, "For you are a people holy to the Lord, your God' the Lord your God has chosen you to be a people for his own possession, out of all the peoples that are on the face of the earth (Deuteronomy 7:6 *RSVCE*)." Understanding Jewish identity is important to understanding the identity of the Church since, explains the Pontifical Commission for Religious Relations with the Jews, "In spite of the historical breach and the painful conflicts arising from it, the Church remains conscious of its enduring continuity with Israel. Judaism is not to be considered simply as another religion; the Jews

---

[153] *The Ignatius Catholic Study Bible: The Book of Genesis* (San Francisco: Ignatius Press, 2010), Location 4815.

[154] Miller, 45. "… the importance of the name in ancient Israel. Decreeing the name of something is really decreeing its purpose and destiny. In Babylonian creation stories, there is a god of wisdom named Enki. And in a couple of different stories, Enki names plants, people, or regions and thus decrees their destiny, their purpose in the universe. That divine role is here given to humanity. … God will rename Abram as Abraham, he will rename Jacob as Israel, taking ownership of those people's destiny."

are instead our 'elder brothers' (Saint Pope John Paul II), our 'fathers in faith' (Benedict XVI)."[155]

156

Since Catholicism has not totally replaced the role of Judaism, the Jewish people of today and not only those before the coming of Christ are still our elder brothers and fathers in the faith. St. Paul, teaches the *Catechism,* affirms the continued status of the Jewish people as God's first chosen people with "for the gifts and the call of God are irrevocable (Romans 11:29 *RSVCE*)."[157] To understand "the message

---

[155] "The Gifts and the Calling of God Are Irrevocable," December 2015 Vatican.va., http://www.vatican.va/roman_curia/pontifical_councils/chrstuni/relations-jews-docs/rc_pc_chrstuni_doc_20151210_ebraismo-nostra-aetate_en.html.

[156] James Tissot, "Jacob and Rachel," c. 1896-1902, https://commons.wikimedia.org/wiki/File:Tissot_Jacob_and_Rachel_at_the_Well.jpg, [Public domain], via Wikimedia Commons.

[157] Cf. *Catechism of the Catholic Church* no. 839; Pope Francis, "Evangelii Gaudium," November 24, 2013, w2.vatican.va, http://w2.vatican.va/

of Jesus" properly, asserts Pope Benedict XVI, Jesus's words must not be "separated from the context of the faith and hope of the Chosen People" otherwise we risk "completely misunderstand[ing]" Jesus, his message and mission of, beginning with the Jewish people to gather all people together.[158]

The continued chosen, covenantal status, and hence unique identity of the Jewish people in relationship to the Church gathered

---

content/francesco/en/apost_exhortations/documents/papa-francesco_
esortazione-ap_20131124_evangelii-gaudium.html, "247. We hold the Jewish people in special regard because their covenant with God has never been revoked, for "the gifts and the call of God are irrevocable" (*Rom* 11:29)."

[158] Benedict XVI, "Christ and the Church: The Pope Begins a New Series of Reflections on the Relationship Between Jesus and the Church in Light of the Apostles and the Duty They Received," March 15, 2006, ewtn.com, http://www.ewtn.com/library/PAPALDOC/b16ChrstChrch1.htm.

[159] Rembrandt, "Portrait of a couple as figures from the Old Testament, known as 'The Jewish bride," c. 1665-1669, https://commons. wikimedia.org/wiki/File:Rembrandt_Harmensz._van_Rijn_-_Portret_van_ een_paar_als_oudtestamentische_figuren,_genaamd_%27Het_Joodse_brui dje%27_-_Google_Art_Project.jpg, Rembrandt [Public domain], via Wikimedia Commons.

together by Christ does not mean that there are "two parallel ways to salvation," for as an extension of Jesus's presence in time the Church proclaims that "Jesus Christ is the universal mediator of salvation, and that there is no 'other name under heaven given to the human race by which we are to be saved' (Acts 4:12)."[160] This raises the question, observes Cardinal Dulles, that if there are not two ways of salvation, one for the Jews and one for Christians, then does this mean there is only one covenant, the New Testament? Has the New Testament with its New Covenant completely replaced the Old Testament and its covenants? If so, then how can the Jewish people retain their unique chosen status?

In attempting to answer these questions, Dulles divides the Old Covenant, with its various covenants, into three ways: "as law, as promise, and as interpersonal relation with God."[161] The Old Covenant as understood from the perspective of law can be further subdivided into moral laws, purity laws, and laws of worship. With respect to moral law, as summarized in the Ten Commandments, the Old Covenant continues into the New Testament and by the Jewish people. With respect to purity laws and laws of worship, however, Catholicism believes these have found their fulfillment in Christ for they were signs pointing to Him. With respect to the promises God made to the Jewish people these also have found their fulfillment in

[160] "The Gifts and the Calling of God Are Irrevocable," December 2015 Vatican.va., http://www.vatican.va/roman_curia/pontifical_councils/chrstuni/relations-jews-docs/rc_pc_chrstuni_doc_20151210_ebraismo-nostra-aetate_en.html.

[161] Avery Cardinal Dulles, "The Covenant with Israel," November 2005, First Things, https://www.firstthings.com/article/2005/11/the-covenant-with-israel.

Christ. Dulles quotes from Paul with, "For the promises of God find there Yes in him (2 Corinthians 1:20 *RSVCE*)." However, Dulles clarifies that "human beings still have to enter fully into that fulfillment. God is still leading the elect toward the fullness of truth and life in Christ."[162]

Finally, with respect to the Old Covenant "as an interpersonal relationship," Dulles strongly argues that in this way the Old Covenant retains its validity and that Israel has not ceased "to be the People of God."[163] For as pointed out previously, "the gifts and the call of God are irrevocable (Romans 11:29 *RSVCE*)." Since God is a God of relationship "the God of Abraham, the God of Isaac, and the God of Jacob (Exodus 3:6 *RSVCE*)" the relationships God establishes and commits Himself to endure. For this reason, Dulles explains:

> Pope John Paul II…spoke of the Jews as a covenant people. In an address in Rome on October 31, 1997, he discussed the act of divine election that brought this people into existence: "This people is assembled and led by Yahweh, creator of heaven and of earth. Its existence is therefore not purely a fact of nature or of culture in the sense that the resourcefulness proper to one's nature is expressed in culture. It is a supernatural fact. This people perseveres despite everything because it is the people of the covenant, and despite human infidelities, Yahweh is faithful to his covenant. To ignore this most basic principle is to adopt a Marcionism against which the church immediately and vigorously reacted, conscious of a vital link with the Old

---

[162] Avery Cardinal Dulles, "The Covenant with Israel."
[163] Avery Cardinal Dulles, "The Covenant with Israel."

Testament, without which the New Testament itself is emptied of meaning."[164]

A related question to the ones just addressed is how is it possible that the Jewish people are still chosen, still "participants" in salvation history and yet do not explicitly believe in Jesus? The Church sees this apparent contradiction as a paradox, like Mary is a Virgin and a mother, that "is and remains an unfathomable divine mystery."[165] Due to this unique, mysterious status of the Jewish people that distinguishes them from all other non-Christians, the Church is not, teaches the Pontifical Commission, to "confront the mystery of God's work" as "a matter of missionary efforts to convert Jews, but rather [with] the expectation that the Lord will bring about the hour when we will all be united."[166]

---

[164] Avery Cardinal Dulles, "The Covenant with Israel."

[165] "The Gifts and the Calling of God Are Irrevocable," December 2015 Vatican.va., http://www.vatican.va/roman_curia/pontifical_councils/ chrstuni/relations-jews-docs/rc_pc_chrstuni_doc_20151210_ebraismo-nostra-aetate_en.html.

[166] "The Gifts and the Calling of God Are Irrevocable," December 2015 Vatican.va., http://www.vatican.va/roman_curia/pontifical_councils/ chrstuni/relations-jews-docs/rc_pc_chrstuni_doc_20151210_ebraismo-nostra-aetate_en.html. "The Church is therefore obliged to view evangelization to Jews, who believe in the one God, in a different manner from that to people of other religions and world views. In concrete terms this means that the Catholic Church neither conducts nor supports any specific institutional mission work directed towards Jews. While there is a principled rejection of an institutional Jewish mission, Christians are nonetheless called to bear witness to their faith in Jesus Christ also to Jews, although they should do so in a humble and sensitive manner, acknowledging that Jews are bearers of God's Word, and particularly in view of the great tragedy of the Shoah."

God's universal plan of salvation that includes both Gentiles and the Jewish people, began in the Old Testament, continued in the New and will be completed at the end of time. The noted theologian Hans Urs von Balthasar, while borrowing terminology from Karl Barth, explains how the two sets of chosen people, Israel and the Church, complement one another while remaining relatively distinct, and where the latter (the Gentiles) does not completely replace the former (the Jewish people).

> By virtue of Christ's death, God elects the unchosen pagans [the Gentiles] so that the chosen people, the Jews, may come to their definitive election by passing through the experience of rejection. And in this way, in this exchange of roles, all experience rejection and all experience election: God has shut up all in unbelief that he may have mercy upon all (Rom 11:32). Both groups are bound together in solidarity in Jesus Christ, who is the head of both, the chosen and the rejected:[167]

Only when, explains Paul, the "full number" of second chosen group, the once, in Balthasar's words "unchosen pagans," enter the Church and experience salvation will Israel then experience the fullness of their elected status "and so all Israel will be saved (Romans 11:25 *RSVCE*)."

---

[167] Hans Urs von Balthasar, *The Theology of Karl Barth*, trans. Edward T. Oakes (San Francisco: Ignatius Press, 1992), loc. 3760.

Section Questions

1. Why did the Pontifical Biblical Commission for Religious Relations teach that "Judaism is not to be considered simply as another religion"? Include in your response the following: Continuity, Difference, Brothers, Fathers

Twelve Tribes of Israel

168

Jacob, renamed Israel after his encounter with the angel, had 12 sons and one daughter: Reuben, Simeon, Levi, Judah, Dan, Naphtali, Gad, Asher, Issachar, Zebulun, Joseph, Benjamin, and Dinah. His first wife Leah gave birth to Reuben, Simeon, Levi, Judah, Issachar, Zebulun, and Dinah, known especially for being violated by the pagan

---

[168] "Mosaic of the 12 Tribes of Israel, from a synagogue wall in Jerusalem, From Givat Mordechai Etz Yosef synagogue facade, Ha Rav Gold street, in Jerusalem. Top row, right to left: Reuben, Judah, Dan, Asher Middle: Simeon, Issachar, Naphtali, Joseph Bottom: Levi, Zebulun, Gad, Benjamin," https://commons.wikimedia.org/wiki/File:Mosaic_Tribes.jpg, By Ori229 [Public domain], from Wikimedia Commons.

prince, Shechem, and revenged by her brothers Simeon and Levi (Genesis 34). Even though Leah was Jacob's first wife, Jacob loved Rachel, his second wife, more than Leah because Rachel was the woman he first intended to marry but was tricked by Leah's father Laban to marry Leah instead. After seven additional years of hard work, Jacob finally did marry Rachel, the woman who captured his heart (Genesis 29:30).

Out of competition to have many more children associated with her than Rachel, Leah gave Zilpah her servant girl to Jacob. Zilpah then gave birth to Gad and Asher. Partly in response to Leah's competitive attitude towards her, Rachel gave birth to Joseph and Benjamin and like Leah, gave Bilhah her servant girl to Jacob, Bilhah, who gave birth to Dan and Napthali.

Hamilton observes that providentially the lines of priests and kings fulfilled in Jesus both originate from two children of an unloved wife, from two children of the woman Jacob was deceived into having sexual relations with. This unloved woman, Leah, is mother of Levi, father of the priestly tribe, and Judah, father of the kingly tribe (Genesis 29:34-35). Quoting from Gerhard von Rad, Hamilton writes, "God's work descended deeply into the lowest worldliness and there was hidden past recognition."[169] Even though God allows human beings to exercise their freedom in evil ways, God is present as Emmanuel (Immanuel עִמָּנוּאֵל), as God with us, in the midst of human depravity and there subtly directs history towards His goodness by transforming and rectifying sinful acts in his overall plan of salvation. This redirection, rectification, and transformation may take generations to become evident.

---

[169] Hamilton, 114.

Sometimes, lists of Jacob's twelve sons include two children who are not children of either Leah and Zilpah or Rachel and Bilhah. These two children are sons of Joseph and grandsons of Jacob: Manasseh and Ephraim. When the tribe of Levi, which God did not give a portion of the land to, is not mentioned then Manasseh and Ephraim replace both Levi and Joseph, their father, and are counted as two of the twelve sons in accordance with Jacob's blessing and wish, "And now your two sons, who were born to you in the land of Egypt before I came to you in Egypt, are mine; Ephraim and Manasseh shall be mine, as Reuben and Simeon are (Genesis 48:5 *RSVCE*)."

Joseph, the father of Ephraim and Manasseh, was Jacob's eleventh biological son. Due to Jacob's preferential love for Joseph (Genesis 37:3), the firstborn son of his favorite wife Rachel, Jacob's eleven other sons grew to envy and hate Joseph. (Genesis 37:4) The envious hatred led the eleven brothers to come up with a plan to kill Joseph. Resisting this evil plan, Reuben, the eldest, counseled his brothers not to kill Joseph. Heeding their oldest brother, the eleven decide to sell Joseph to Ishmaelites. The text then becomes difficult to interpret since it is not clear in the text if the brothers sell Joseph to the Ishmaelites or if Midianites do. Some scholars attempt to clarify the text by appealing to the Documentary Hypothesis which proposes that the Pentateuch is composed by blending together various documents which differ from one another.

In Egypt, Joseph gained the trust of the Pharaoh who appointed Joseph second to the Pharaoh. Joseph gained this trust through a circuitous route of trusting in God while in prison due to a false accusation of raping the wife of Potiphar, captain of Pharaoh's guard. As a prisoner, Joseph successfully interpreted Pharaoh's dreams, and advised the Pharaoh how to prepare for a future famine. God's ability to "ordereth all things sweetly (Wisdom 8:1 *DRA*)" is evident, observes Hamilton, in Joseph's imprisonment becoming an opportunity for Joseph to encounter the Pharaoh and win his trust.[170]

While Joseph's family back home was suffering from the famine that Joseph had predicted in interpreting Pharaoh's dream, Jacob commanded his sons to "go down [to Egypt] and buy grain for us there, that we may live, and not die (Genesis 42:2 *RSVCE*)." His sons obey and ten of them travel to Egypt. There, they meet Joseph without recognizing him. Joseph, though, recognizes his brothers but does not reveal his identity. Only after the brothers return with their younger brother Benjamin does Joseph reveal, "I am your brother, Joseph, whom you sold into Egypt. And now do not be distressed, or angry with yourselves, because you sold me here; for God sent me before you to preserve life (Genesis 45:4-5 *RSVCE*)."

Interpreting his brother's sinful act of envy with eyes of faith, Joseph forgives his brothers, gives them food and invites them to return to Egypt with their families, which they do. Roy H. Schoeman interprets God's providential transformation of Joseph's rejection as fulfilled in Jesus who was rejected and crucified and yet through this crucifixion all are offered salvation by Jesus' resurrection from the dead.[171] Before Jacob, his sons, and their families relocate to Egypt, God assures Jacob, "do not be afraid to go down to Egypt; for I will there make of you a great nation. I will go down with you to Egypt, and I will also bring you up again (Genesis 46:3-4 *RSVCE*)." God

---

[170] Hamilton, 124, 127.

[171] Roy H. Schoeman, *Salvation is from the Jews* (San Francisco: Ignatius Press, 2003), 121.

fulfills this promise when a "new king over Egypt, who did not know Joseph (Exodus 1:8 *RSVCE*)" persecuted the Israelites and God raises up Moses to lead the people out of Egypt back to the Promised Land.

Section Questions

1. According to Gerhard von Rad how does God heal Leah's pain of rejection? With specific reference to Scripture, include the following in your response: Jacob, Rachel, Leah, Levi, Judah.

---

[172] James Tissot / Public domain, "Tissot Joseph Makes Himself Known to His Brethren.jpg, Joseph Makes Himself Known to His Brethren, c. 1896-1902, by James Jacques Joseph Tissot (French, 1836-1902), gouache on board, 8 13/16 x 11 7/16 in. (22.4 x 29.1 cm), at the Jewish Museum, New York," https://commons.wikimedia.org/wiki/File:Tissot_Joseph_Makes_Himself_Known_to_His_Brethren.jpg.

2. How does Joseph foreshadow Jesus? With specific reference to Scripture, include the following in your response: Egypt, Rejection, Forgiveness, Salvation.

Exodus

Essential Theme of Exodus

After covering the time of the Patriarchs and Matriarchs we will now turn to our attention to how God formed his people Israel. Regarding this period, the *Catechism* succinctly teaches:

> After the patriarchs, God formed Israel as his people by freeing them from slavery in Egypt. He established with them the covenant of Mount Sinai and, through Moses, gave them his law so that they would recognize him and serve him as the one living and true God, the provident Father and just judge, and

[1]   Edward   Poynter,   "Israel   in   Egypt,"   1867, https://commons.wikimedia.org/wiki/File:1867_Edward_Poynter_-_Israel_ in_Egypt.jpg, Edward Poynter [Public domain], via Wikimedia Commons.

so that they would look for the promised Savior.[2]

The above excerpt identifies the essential theme of exodus as entailing liberation from slavery.[3] It does not, though, define this

---

[2] "Catechism of the Catholic Church," no. 62, vatican.va, http://www.vatican.va/archive/ENG0015/__PG.HTM.

[3] How can the understanding of the Exodus as freedom from slavery be reconciled with the practice of slavery by the Israelites, since God as a God of all desires all to be free from evil forms of domination and not just the Israelites? In answering this delicate question, it is important to define the use of the term slavery according to its biblical context. In clarifying the terms biblical context, Miller writes:

Most slavery in ancient Israel was private. There was no state slavery or corporate slavery, and most slaves were fellow Israelites, they were not foreigners. Most people became slaves through debt.

So, a man who wants to plant wheat goes to guy to buy the seed, and doesn't have enough money, so he says, "I will pay you when the wheat harvest comes in." And the seller says he needs some kind of collateral. What happens if the wheat harvest doesn't come in? "It always comes in. That's not to be a problem. I don't have any collateral." The seller: "I will take your house." The buyer: "I don't own my house. I just rent; how about my clothes?" The seller: "All your clothes aren't worth enough. How about your son?" The buyer: "Okay, fine, my son is the collateral. But the wheat harvest will come in, it always comes in." Then there's a famine, there's a plague of locusts, and the wheat harvest doesn't come in and little Johnny has to go away as a slave. He is not born into slavery. It's never anything to do with race or ethnicity."

Exodus 21, says, "When someone strikes his … slave…so the slave dies under his hand, the act shall certainly be avenged." You could not have passed a law like that in the early 1800s in the Southern states of the US. The

liberation as a primarily a political liberation from a tyrannical pharaoh. Instead, Exodus depicts the liberation that Israel experienced as first being a spiritual liberation in two primary ways: freedom to worship the one, true God, freedom from Egyptian idolatrous and immoral practices so as to live in accordance with the gift of the law given on Mount Sinai. In describing this law, Pope Francis teaches, "Law is itself a gift of God which points out the way, a gift for everyone without exception; it can be followed with the help of grace, even though each human being 'advances gradually with the progressive integration of the gifts of God and the demands of God's definitive and absolute love in his or her entire personal and social life.'"[4]

The freedom to worship God and the freedom to live in accordance with our created natures as images of the holiness of God, which the law on Sinai provides essential direction for, are significantly more important than the land promised to Israel "And I will bring you into the land which I swore to give to Abraham, to Isaac, and to Jacob; I will give it to you for a possession (Exodus 6:8 *RSVCE*)." In explaining that the Mosaic Covenant given on Mount Sinai is a

---

Code of Hammurabi does not forbid you killing your own slave. Israelite law does. But the owner could not even unintentionally kill his own slave without—well, it says the act will certainly be avenged, that means death penalty. It means slaves are within the purview of justice and slavery has certain rights. If a man punches his male slave and the slave loses an eye, the slave is now a free man, it says in verse 26: all sorts of qualifications on slavery.

[4] Francis, "Post-Synodal Apostolic Exhortation: Amoris Laetitia," w2.vatican.va, https://w2.vatican.va/content/dam/francesco/pdf/apost_exhortations/documents/papa-francesco_esortazione-ap_20160319_amoris-laetitia_en.pdf, no. 296.

more important end than even the Promised Land Benedict XVI writes that the, "goal of the Exodus was freedom. But one must add that the figure of freedom is the covenant and that the form in which freedom is realized is the right relation of men to one another described in the Law of the covenant, and this relation is derived from the right relation to God."[5] In contrasting the end of the Promised Land with the gift of the Law on Mount Sinai Benedict XVI writes:

> one can understand that the "land" was definitely numbered among the goals of the Exodus. For, no doubt it is part of the freedom of a people to possess a land of its own. But at the same time, it becomes evident that in a certain respect Sinai remains superior to the land. For if Israel loses Sinai in its land, that is, if it destroys the Law and the covenant and dissolves the order of freedom through the disorder of caprice, then it has returned to its pre-Exodus condition; it then lives in its own land and yet is still in Egypt, because it destroys its freedom from within. The Exile makes visible in a merely external, political way the prior inner loss of freedom through the loss of justice. One must thus say that what is truly liberating in the Exodus is the institution of the covenant between God and man, which is concretized in the Torah, that is, in the ordinances that are the form of freedom. Accordingly, the Exodus is made possible, not by the particular boldness or industry of Moses, but by a religious event, the paschal sacrifice, which anticipates an essential ingredient of the

---

[5] Joseph Ratzinger, *Church, Ecumenism and Politics: New Endeavors in Ecclesiology* (San Francisco: Ignatius Press, 2008), 248-250.

Torah. In this is expressed a primordial knowledge of humanity, one encountered ever again in the history of religion, that freedom and the formation of community are ultimately to be obtained, not through the use of force or through mere industry, but through a love that becomes sacrificial and that first binds men together in their depths because it lets them touch the dimension of the divine. Thus, at the core of the Old Testament liberation event, there is incipiently present that which later emerges openly in the figure of Jesus Christ and from him becomes the means to a new history of freedom."[6]

In Exodus chapter four, God emphasizes the more important end of divine worship by commanding Moses to "say to Pharaoh, Thus says the Lord, Israel is my first-born son, and I say to you, Let my son go so that he might serve me (Exodus 4:22-23 *RSVCE*)." God, in chapter three and five, further clarifies His request by commanding Israel to leave Egypt, journey into the desert for three days, and there offer sacrifice (Exodus 3:17; 5:3). Israelites were also to bring animals from their flocks and herds with which to offer "sacrifices and burnt offerings to the Lord (Exodus 10:25 *RSVCE*)." The animal sacrifices explains Pitre, were requested by God as a way of purifying the Israelites from their years of captivity in Egypt where animals such as these were worshiped.[7] For example, the Egyptian goddess Hathor was often portrayed in the form of a cow; Amon was typically represented

---

[6] Ratzinger, *Church, Ecumenism and Politics*, 248-250.

[7] Brant Pitre, *Genesis and the Books of Moses: Unlocking the Mysteries of the Pentateuch,* MP3, 14.

with ram features, Bastet as a cat, Thoth as a baboon or ibis, Anubis as a jackal etc.[8]

Secondarily, liberation from Egypt did entail political freedom from a tyrant. Often this consequence that flowed from being spiritually liberated to freely worship the true God is presented without reference to the more essential spiritual liberation. Over emphasizing the political liberation the Israelites experienced, obscures the relationship that Israel was intended by God to have with Egypt and all other nations. Israel, as explained previously, was chosen by God to be the "first-born son (Exodus 4:22 *RSVCE*)" so that, beginning with Israel as a "priestly people," as a mediator of salvation, God may "part by part"[9] (*CCC* 56) gather all the nations scattered by sin back to Himself.[10] Israel, however, often failed in her God given mission to be a "kingdom of priests and a holy nation (Exodus 19:6 *RSVCE*)" that leads the nations out of idolatry to worship of the true God (Exodus 19:6).

This failure entailed falling into the idolatrous practices of those nations Israel was called to free from idolatry.[11] God responded to Israel's repeated regressions into idolatry by making concessions to the law He originally gave to them so that Israel would not be totally lost and assimilated into pagan cultures. For example, points out Pitre, before the worship of the golden calf there is no mention of God

---

[8] "11 Egyptian Gods and Goddesses," britannica.com, https://www.britannica.com/list/11-egyptian-gods-and-goddesses.

[9] "Catechism of the Catholic Church," no. 56, vatican.va, http://www.vatican.va/archive/ENG0015/__PG.HTM.

[10] Pitre, *Genesis and the Books of Moses,* MP3, 14.

[11] Brant Pitre, *The Old Testament-A Historical and Theological Journey through Jewish Scripture,* MP 15.

stating he will separate the Israelites from the other nations by driving out these nations before Israel or God commanding Israel to eliminate these people. Instead the emphasis is on Israel being a priestly nation to the pagan nations, on Israel's role of mediating God's salvific will.[12]

After the worship of the golden calf, after Israel had demonstrated its weakness towards pagan ways, after eleven of the Twelve Tribes had lost their priesthood and was replaced by the remaining Levitical priesthood, God then decrees a separation from these people that God will bring about: "Observe what I command you this day. Behold, **I** will drive out before you the Am'orites, the Canaanites, the Hittites, the Per'izzites, the Hi'vites, and the Jeb'usties. Take heed to yourself, lest you make a covenant with the inhabitants of the land where you go, let it become a snare in our midst (Exodus 34:11-12 *RSVCE*)." In the verses that immediately follow, God also commands the Israelites to "tear down the altars (Exodus 34:13 *RSVCE*)" of the inhabitants and forbids the Israelites from making "a covenant with the inhabitants (Exodus 34:15 *RSVCE*)."

Pitre interprets these passages as indicating that now that eleven tribes have lost their priestly status, they have, in a sense, also lost their ability to be priests who lead pagan nations back to the one true God as in the early days of Noah (Genesis 9:16; *CCC* 56-58, 71). In its place they are tasked with a non-priestly, "secular task," states Pitre, of destroying pagan items and ensuring a separation takes place between Israel and the other nations.[13]

When Israel fails in her call to be a holy nation by being seduced by the sexual and idolatrous practices of the Moabites and Midianites

---

[12] Pitre, *The Old Testament,* MP 15.

[13] Pitre, *Genesis and the Books of Moses,* MP 3 25.

(Numbers 25:1-6), God intensifies the requirement of separation between Israel and the pagan nations by requiring Israel actively drive the inhabitants away: "[Y]ou shall drive out all the inhabitants of the land (Numbers 33:52 *RSVCE*)." Previously, in Exodus, this separation would take place by God, "I will drive out," according to His providential designs without explicit mention that the Israelites would take an active part in driving out the inhabitants. In addition, the Israelites are commanded to destroy idolatrous images, altars and figures that they come across (Numbers 33:52),

Finally, in Deuteronomy God decrees that not only are the Israelites to be separated from the six mentioned nations, but they are to eliminate these people: "[I]n the cities of these peoples that the Lord your God gives you for an inheritance, you shall save alive nothing that breathes, but you shall destroy them, the Hittites, and the Am'orites, the Canaanites and the Per'izzites, the Hi'vites, and the Jer'usites, as the Lord your God has commanded; that they may not teach you to do according to all their abominable practices which they have done in the service of their gods, and so to sin against the Lord your God (Deuteronomy 20:16-18 *RSVCE*)."

As is evident, this warfare of total destruction (herem חֵרֶם), is an example of later concessionary law, law made because of Israel's weakness. The reason for the concessionary law, according to Pitre, is that the Israelites demonstrated to God that if they mingle with people of other nations, they will very likely adopt these people's idolatrous practices. Therefore, although not the original intention of God, God commands in certain cases, by way of concession, a total warfare. This helps to ensure the Israelites will one day fulfill their fundamental vocation to be a "light to the nations (Isaiah 49:6 *RSVCE*)" by leading other nations to the worship of God.[14]

Section Questions

1. How is the Mosaic law understood as a gift? With specific reference to Scripture, include the following in your response: Freedom From and Freedom To, Law of Mount Sinai, Animal Sacrifices and Egyptian Idolatry, Israel's Status as Older Son, Divine Concessions, Grace

Moses

The leader of Israel as a priestly nation was Moses. A key characteristic of Moses was humbleness, or meekness (*anav*, עָנָו):[15] "Now the man Moses was very meek, more than all men that were on the face of the earth (Numbers 12:3 *RSVCE*)." How Moses led his people and listened to advice demonstrates his meekness. Although Jethro, Moses father-in-law, was not an Israelite, Moses took to heart Jethro's advice to delegate authority (Exodus 18). Hamilton comments that Moses' humility of listening to advice reflects Proverbs that teaches "a wise man listens to advice (Proverbs 12:15 *RSVCE*)." In addition, adds Hamilton, the wise decision Moses took to delegate authority is repeated by Jesus's disciples whom Acts describes as delegating their authority to deacons so that the Apostles could focus on prayer and preaching (Acts 6:1-6). Humbly delegating authority is often difficult for those in ministry since, explains Hamilton, there is

---

[14] Pitre, *The Old Testament,* MP 15.

[15] "6035. Anav," biblehub.com, http://biblehub.com/hebrew/6035.htm.

a tendency for Christian leaders to develop "a messianic complex and feel the urge to monopolize ... to be involved in every issue."[16] One way to resist this tendency is to realize that delegation of a spiritual ministry of leadership does not diminish the gift of leadership, "any more than one candle loses any of its flame when it lights another candle," writes Hamilton.[17]

In writing on this distinguishing feature of Moses John Chrysostom describes it as kind of gentleness: "What distinguished the first Moses? *Moses,* Scripture tells us, *was more gentle than all who dwelt upon the earth.* We can rightly say the same of the new Moses, for there was with him the very Spirit of gentleness, united to him in his inmost being."[18] In describing Christ as the new Moses who fulfills actions of the old Moses, Chrysostom adds:

> In those days Moses raised his hands to heaven and brought down manna, the bread of angels; the new Moses raises his hands to heaven and gives us the food of eternal life. Moses struck the rock and brought forth streams of water; Christ touches his table, strikes the spiritual rock of the new covenant and draws forth the living water of the Spirit. This rock is like a fountain in the midst of Christ's table. so that on all sides the flocks may draw near to this living spring and refresh

---

[16] Victor P. Hamilton, *Handbook on the Pentateuch, Second Edition* (Grand Rapids: Baker Academic, 2005), 182.

[17] Hamilton, 324.

[18] Second Reading, *From the Catecheses by Saint John Chrysostom*, in *The Liturgy of the Hours*, vol. 2 (New York: Catholic Book Publishing Col, 1976), 160-161.

themselves in the waters of salvation.[19]

[20]

As a new Noah, Moses also points to Jesus who will fulfill both the old Noah and new Noah. One indication that Moses is presented as a New Noah is that Moses, like Noah, was saved out of water. As pointed out be Hahn, the Hebrew word used for an ark made out of gopher wood and the Hebrew word used for a basket made out of papyrus is the same word (תֵּבָה, *tebah* of gopher wood in Genesis 6:14 and תֵּבַת of papyrus in Exodus 2:3).[21] In both cases, a floating box, or chest saved

---

[19] Second Reading, *From the Catecheses by Saint John Chrysostom*, in *The Liturgy of the Hours*, vol. 2 (New York: Catholic Book Publishing Col, 1976), 160-161.

[20] James Tissot, "Pharaoh's Daughter Has Moses Brought to Her," c. 1896-1902, https://www.wikiart.org/en/james-tissot/pharaoh-s-daughter-has-moses-brought-to-her/, [Public domain], via Wikimedia Commons.

[21] "8392. Tebah," Strong's concordance, Brown-Drover-Briggs, biblehub.com, http://biblehub.com/hebrew/8392.htm; Scott Hahn, and

its inhabitant, Noah in the gopher box and Moses in the papyrus box.

Moses, explains Hahn, also points forward to Christ in a way that Noah does not. An important similarity that Moses and Jesus share is that a powerful, envious ruler tried to kill them when they were infants. In the case of Moses, the Pharaoh ordered the midwives of the Hebrew people to kill immediately after birth all babies that were male (Exodus 1:16). Similarly, King Herod ordered all male children who were two years old and younger to be killed (Matthew 2:16).[22]

Among still other ways that Christ is a new Moses, the fulfillment of Moses, is Christ being a law giver by teaching on a mountain the Beatitudes. This action resembles Moses who gave Ten Commandments on Mount Sinai. Also, comments Hahn, Christ's face shining "like the sun" when transfigured on a "high mountain (Matthew 17:2 *RSVCE*)" resembles Moses whose "face shone because he had been talking with God (Exodus 34:29 *RSVCE*)" on Mount Sinai.[23] A difference, as pointed out by theologians, is that while Moses' face merely reflected the light of God, the light of God shone through Jesus face, from His Sacred Heart since Jesus is divine.

Because Moses was abundantly blessed by God even to the extent

---

Curtis Mitch, *Ignatius Catholic Study Bible: The Book of Exodus* (San Francisco: Ignatius Press, 2012), loc. 2756.

[22] Scott Hahn, and Curtis Mitch, *Ignatius Catholic Study Bible: The Book of Exodus*, loc. 2756.

[23] Hahn and Mitch, *Ignatius Catholic Study Bible: The Book of Exodus*, loc. 3871. In its translation of Exodus 34:29, points out Hahn, the Vulgate mistakenly translates the Hebrew verb shine with the Hebrew word for horn. "And when Moses came down from the mount Sinai, he held the two tables of the testimony, and he knew not that his face was horned from the conversation of the Lord. And Aaron and the children of Israel seeing the face of Moses horned, were afraid to come near." (Exodus 34:29-30 DRA)

of having divine light shine forth from his face, he faced the danger of falling into pride by attributing his gifts to himself rather than from God. Perhaps to help Moses retain his meekness God providentially ordained that Moses suffer from a speech impediment. In Exodus chapter four, Moses refers to his difficulty in speaking by protesting that he is not the right person to speak on the Lord's behalf. "But Moses said to the Lord, 'Oh, my Lord, I am not eloquent, either heretofore or since you have spoken to your servant; but I am slow of speech and of tongue." (Exodus 4:10 *RSVCE*) In anger, God responds to Moses' multiple protests that indicate Moses's lack of faith in God's power to overcome our limitations. Aaron, Moses' brother, then becomes Moses's spokesperson, "He shall speak for you to the people; and he shall be a mouth for you, and you shall be to him as God (Exodus 4:16 *RSVCE*)."

Later in this same chapter God once again becomes angry with Moses to the extent of even wanting to kill Moses (Exodus 4:24) for not having circumcised his son Gershom. Fortunately, Gershom's mother Zipporah saved her husband's life by quickly circumcising her son. We will see in the Book of Numbers that God again in anger wants Moses to die. This time Moses does die and, consequently, does not enter the Promised Land. The reason for this punishment provided by Numbers is, once again, Moses' lack of faith. (Numbers 20:12)

Section Questions

1. How was Moses meek (*anav*, עָנָו)? With specific reference to Scripture, include the following in your response: Leadership, Delegation, Gentleness.

2. How does Moses foreshadow Jesus? With specific reference to Scripture, include the following in your response: Killing of Babies, Manna, Rock, Water, 10 Commandments, Shining Face, Promised Land.

God's Name

Standing before a burning bush, Moses receives his mission to lead the Israelites out of Egypt to worship in the desert and from there to bring them to "a land flowing with milk and honey (Exodus 3:17 *RSVCE*)." Although on fire, the bush that Moses saw "was not consumed (Exodus 3:2 *RSVCE*)." In commenting on this passage, Bishop Barron explains that the fire represents God's life, God's uncreated existence, God as being who is not in competition with our created being, who does not want to destroy created being but rather who desires not only to sustain the existence of all creation but also to transform and elevate all of creation.[24] According to Revelation, this transformation, this perfection of creation, will be fully realized at the end of time when divine fire will bring about a New Heavens and a New Earth by not replacing the old heavens and earth but rather by actualizing all its potential. (Rev. 21:1; cf. Is. 65:17; 2 Peter 3:13)

When assigning Moses to the role of leader and mediator God reveals His name in two ways: personally, as related to us, and as existence itself. Pitre distinguishes these two ways as God revealing himself immanently, and God revealing himself transcendentally.[25]

---

[24] Robert Barron, *Catholicism: The New Evangelization*, DVDs (Word on Fire).

[25] Pitre, *The Old Testament,* MP 11.

The first personal and immanent revelation is when God tells Moses, "I am the God of your father, the God of Abraham, the God of Isaac, and the God of Jacob (Exodus 3:6 *RSVCE*)." Here God is defined in relationship to the patriarchs, to the originating father figures of the Hebrew people.

The second transcendent revelation of the divine name brings out how God is totally different from any other originating father. God reveals this to Moses with, "I am who I am (Exodus 3:14 *RSVCE*)." These words, writes St. Thomas Aquinas, teach that "the existence of God is His essence itself, which can be said of no other."[27] As

---

[26] Sébastien Bourdon, "Burning Bush, Painting from Hermitage Museum, Saint Petersburg," 17th century, https://commons.wikimedia.org/wiki/File:Bourdon,_S%C3%A9bastien_-_Burning_bush.jpg, Sébastien Bourdon [Public domain], via Wikimedia Commons.

[27] Thomas Aquinas, "Summa Theologiae: The names of God (Prima Pars, Q. 13), art. 11, newadvent.org, http://www.newadvent.org/summa/1013.htm#article11.

understood by Aquinas, the essence of something is what it is, while the existence of something is that it is. No created being can rightly claim to have an existence that is equivalent to its essence since it once was in the mind of God as an idea and not yet existing.

The Hebrew words for God's essential name is "*eh-yeh aser eh-yeh* אֶהְיֶה אֲשֶׁר אֶהְיֶה (Exodus 3:14)." Translating these words accurately is difficult since Biblical Hebrew, unlike Modern Hebrew, only has two tenses: a perfect tense signifying a completed action and an imperfect tense signifying uncompleted action. Often imperfect tenses are translated into future tense, perfect tenses are translated into past tense. Sometimes, depending on the context, the imperfect tense will be translated into present tense, a tense that does not exist in Biblical Hebrew. For this reason, the imperfect tense of the verb to be in Exodus 3:14 is usually translated into the present tense. Some English translations though, translate, Exodus 3:14 into a future tense, or to be fair, in both tenses, "I am/will be what I am/will be (Exodus 3:14 *CJB*)."

The various ways of translating this verse all can be seen as complementary of one another and not in contradiction since the essential teaching is that only God can say I am in an unqualified sense, as someone who has no beginning and no end. For this reason, explains Miller, God's essential name of "I am (*Ehhey*)" is only used once in the Bible, since only God can say he exists in a totally unqualified sense with "I am." All other times in the Bible God is referred to as Yahweh, "He is" which is often, out of respect for God, substituted with the all capitalized LORD, or in Hebrew by substituting the vowels of LORD (*Adonai*) for the vowels of Yahweh that lie underneath the consonants, the origin of the mispronunciation of the name as Jehovah.[28]

Section Questions

1. What does the burning bush reveal about God's relationship to creation? Include the following in your response: not a destroying fire but perfecting fire.

2. Describe the two complementary ways God revealed his identity to Moses in Exodus 3:6, and 3:14.

---

[28] "[I]in the 9th century CE, Christians and Jews had not been talking to each other for a very long time. So, with the arrival of the early Renaissance, and the humanist era that began in the 13th century, Western Europe rediscovered Hebrew. And Christian scholars learned the Hebrew language that was really unknown for many centuries.

Around the year 1250, a Christian scholar says something like, "The Jews know the name of God. Now that we can read their letters, we can see what God's name is." And God's name is Yodh, that's Y, except there is no Y in Latin, so they write I or J. Then comes the vowel. Now, remember he's reading the vowels of Adonai. So, the first vowel is A. Then comes Hey, H. And the second vowel of Adonai, O. And then comes Vav, V. Then the third vowel of Adonai, AI, and a final Hey, H. And when you put it all together, you get Jehovah.

The Jewish community must've been doubled over laughing. He's read a word that doesn't exist. They've read the consonants of Yahweh and the vowels of Adonai, which are not meant to be read together. Jehovah is not God's name; it's not even a word. It's based on a Christian misunderstanding of what the Jews had done with the text, and it originates with an obscure 13th-century Dominican. Of course, it's all over the place now. It's not any god's name." Robert D. Miller II, *Understanding the Old Testament* (Chantilly: The Teaching Company, 2019), 89-91.

Plagues

The one, true, transcendent and personal God that Moses was the spokesperson of punished the Egyptians primarily because as worshippers of false Gods the Egyptians refused to allow Israel to worship the true God. The divine judgment over the false Gods of the Egyptians (Exodus 12:12) was expressed by punishing the Egyptians with ten plagues.

Pitre, reflecting Talmudic interpretation, proposes that each of these plagues be interpreted as a specific divine response to at least one

---

[29] Charles Sprague Pearce, "Lamentations over the Death of the First-Born of Egypt," 1877, https://commons.wikimedia.org/wiki/File:Lamentations_over_the_Death_of_the_First-Born_of_Egypt_by_Charles_Sprague_Pearce.JPG, Charles Sprague Pearce [Public domain], from Wikimedia Commons.

of the false Gods of the Egyptians.[30] Below is a chart,[31] based on Pitre's explanation, that associates nine of the ten plagues with specific Egyptian gods.

Plagues	Egyptian Gods
1. River Water turns to Blood	River God of the Nile - Hapi
2. Over Population of Frogs	Frog Goddess - Heket
3. Swarm of Gnats	Insect God - Kepher
4. Swarm of Flies	Same as above
5. Death of Cattle	Cow God and Goddess – Amon and Hathor
6. Boils	Healing God - Sekhmet
7. Hail	Sky Goddess - Nut
8. Locusts	Protector from Locusts God - Serapia
9. Darkness	Sun God - Re

Pitre not only shows how the plagues are a response to Egyptian idolatry, by demonstrating to the Egyptians that their Gods are false since they do not help them in time of need, he also brings out the typological dimension of the plagues both with the Old Testament itself and in relationship to the New Testament.

---

[30] The text seems to imply this connection, comments Hamilton. "Indeed, Exod. 12:12 has the Lord saying, 'And on all the gods of Egypt I will execute judgments' (*RSVCE*). See also Num. 33: 4b: 'For the LORD had brought judgment on their gods' (*NIV*). That does apply to some of the plagues: … We should note that the biblical text gives no indication that the plagues are to be associated with Egyptian religion and deities. The similarities may, therefore, be coincidental." Hamilton, 159-160.

[31] Pitre, *Genesis and the Books of Moses,* Outline, 47.

With respect to the Old Testament, the plagues are a mirror image, a kind of reverse typology, of how God created the world. In creating the world, God first creates light, and in one of his final punishments of the Egyptians God prevents light from shining in the dark. Similarly, in Genesis God fills the waters, the land and the sky with a multitude of life forms. In Exodus, however, God punishes the Egyptians by sending agents of death throughout water, land and the sky.[32]

The first plague where Moses acts on God's behalf by turning river water into blood, explains Pitre, anticipates an even greater miracle to come when Jesus turns water at the Wedding of Cana into wine, and then turns wine at the Last Supper into life giving blood, containing His supernatural life. According to Pitre, John hints at this typology by using the phrase "the first of His signs (John 2:11 *RSVCE*)" to signal to Jewish hearers and readers that Jesus fulfills the role of Moses whose first miraculous of the ten plagues was turning water into blood.[33]

Some modern Biblical scholars interprets all the ten plagues as describing not divine miraculous interventions but rather as descriptions of unusual natural events. This "naturalistic explanations of the Ten Plagues of Exodus" writes Miller, "go all the way back to 2nd century BCE Jewish authors such as Artapanus of Alexandria and Philo of Alexandria." Miller argues that this interpretation is not as reasonable as interpreting the concerned text as intentionally describing miraculous occurrences:

---

[32] Hahn and Mitch, *Ignatius Catholic Study Bible: The Book of Exodus*, loc. 2981.

[33] Pitre, *Genesis and the Books of Moses*, MP3, 14; Pitre, *The Old Testament*, MP 9.

First and most important is that if these are natural events, even weird ones, you lose the entire meaning of the passage: that these plagues demonstrate the mighty hand of God delivering his people. The same thing happens with naturalistic explanations for the manna: there's some insect in the Sinai Peninsula, and it eats some plant, and this crust comes out, and that was the manna. The second problem is that these readers are taking the text completely literally. Everything that's described is thought to have happened—it just wasn't miraculous. This reflects a bizarre sort of fundamentalism. Everything that's in the Bible might have happened, but there's nothing supernatural about it.[34]

Section Questions

1. How does Miller argue that explaining the ten plagues in a purely naturalistic manner is less reasonable than interpreting the text as intentionally describing miracles. With specific reference to Scripture, include the following in your response: overly literalistic interpretation that is self-contradictory.

Passover

The tenth plague is the origin of Passover, a Jewish holyday on which liberation by God from Egypt is celebrated. The word Passover is related to the Hebrew verb *pasah* (פָּסַח) meaning skip over or pass

---

[34] Miller, 92.

over.[35] On a midnight designated by God the Israelites marked the lintels and doorposts with the blood of an unblemished lamb so that, upon seeing this blood, the "destroyer (Exodus 12:23 *RSVCE*)" sent by God would pass over the Israelites dwelling places without killing the first-born. However, when the destroyer passed over the Egyptian houses, which did not have this cross like mark of lamb's blood, he would kill the first-born humans and animals within the house.

36

God also commanded the Israelites to eat the sacrificed, Passover lamb, "roasted; with unleavened bread and bitter herbs (Exodus 12:8 *RSVCE*)." Every year, the Israelites were to relive this saving, Passover by eating on one day the flesh of a roasted, unblemished lamb

---

[35] "Strong's Concordance, 6452. pacach," biblehub.com, http://biblehub.com/hebrew/6452.htm.

[36] James Tissot, "The Jews' Passover," c. before 1902, https://commons.wikimedia.org/wiki/File:Tissot_Passover.jpg, James Tissot [Public domain], via Wikimedia Commons.

according to the ritual set forth by God and by eating unleavened bread for seven days (Exodus 12:14-15, 46).

As Pitre points out, the ritualistic eating of bread and flesh is repeated in another, complementary way during the Israelites journey through the desert when they ate *Manna*, bread sent by God and flesh of quail (Exodus 16).[37] The various types of flesh and bread that God has the Israelites to eat are fulfilled in Jesus:

> Truly, truly, I say to you, it was not Moses who gave you the bread from heaven; my Father gives you the true bread from heaven. For the bread of God is that which comes down from heaven and gives life to the world. ... I am the living bread which came down from heave; if anyone eats of this bread, he will live forever; and the bread which I shall give for the life of the world is my flesh." (John 6:32-51 *RSVCE*)

According to the *Catechism*, Jesus fulfills his promise to give himself as an unblemished, sinless "lamb," and as supernatural bread and flesh by instituting the Eucharist during a Passover meal:

> By celebrating the Last Supper with his apostles in the course of the Passover meal, Jesus gave the Jewish Passover its definitive meaning. Jesus' passing over to his father by his death and Resurrection, the new Passover, is anticipated in the Supper and celebrated in the Eucharist, which fulfills the Jewish Passover and anticipates the final Passover of the

---

[37] Pitre, *Genesis and the Books of Moses,* Outline, 48.

Church in the glory of the kingdom (1340 *CCC*).[38]

Paul explicitly indicate that Jesus gives the Passover meal its ultimate meaning by being the paschal lamb. "For Christ, our Paschal Lamb, has been sacrificed (1 Corinthians 5:7 *RSVCE*)."

Section Questions

1. How does the tenth plague foreshadow Jesus? With specific reference to Scripture, include the following in your response: Passover, Unblemished Lamb Blood, Paschal Lamb, Unleavened Bread.

Crossing the Red Sea

St. Paul refers to the crossing of the Red Sea[39] as a type of baptism "into Moses (1 Corinthians 10:2 *RSVCE*)" that prefigured baptism into Christ.

---

[38] "Catechism of the Catholic Church," vatican.va, http://www.vatican.va/archive/ccc_css/archive/catechism/p2s2c1a3.htm, no. 1340.

[39] According to Hamilton, a better translation of Red Sea may be Reed Sea, "The crossing of the Reed Sea (to be preferred to 'Red Sea,' which is based not on the Hebrew but on the Greek *erythra thalassa* and the Latin *mare rubrum*) is described miraculously. Reading the Hebrew yām sûp as 'Reed Sea' rather than 'Red Sea' reflects the fact that sûp, when used alone, refers to reeds or rushes, as in Exod. 2: 3, 'She placed the child in it and put it among the reeds [sûp] along the bank of the Nile' (NIV), or Exod. 2: 5, 'She saw the basket among the reeds.'" Hamilton, 171. Miller counters this "scholarly construct" arguing that while the Hebrew word *yām* means sea, *sûp* can be translated in a variety of ways including end and reeds. Although,

Early Christians, such as the Church Father Gregory of Nyssa, also interpreted the Israelites' crossing of the Jordan River under the leadership of Joshua as yet another type of baptism. "The people of the Hebrews," writes Gregory of Nyssa, "… did not enter the land of promise until it had first been brought, with Joshua for its guide and the pilot of its life, to the passage of the Jordan. But it is clear that Joshua also, who set up the twelve stones in the stream, was anticipating the coming of the twelve disciples, the ministers of Baptism."[40]

Building upon and refining this spiritual interpretation, Thomas Aquinas distinguishes the crossing of the Red Sea from the crossing of the Jordan River with:

> The crossing of the Red Sea foreshadowed baptism in this—that baptism washes away sin: whereas the crossing of the Jordan foreshadows it in this—that it opens the gate to the heavenly kingdom: and this is the principal effect of baptism and accomplished through Christ alone. And therefore, it was fitting that Christ should be baptized in the Jordan rather than in the sea.[41]

---

sûp sounds like the Egyptian word *choofee* for reed, no specific Egyptian body of water is named in historical records as the *pa choof*, reed sea. Miller, 93-94.

[40] Gregory of Nyssa, "On the Baptism of Christ: A Sermon for the Day of the Lights," newadvent.org, http://www.newadvent.org/fathers/2910.htm.

[41] Thomas Aquinas, "Summa Theologiae," III, art. 4, ad. 1, newadvent.org, http://www.newadvent.org/summa/4039.htm.

According to Aquinas, the crossing of the Red Sea and the crossing of the Jordan River foreshadows Baptism since the crossings signify beginnings. For the Israelites, the crossing of the Rea Sea represents the beginning of their pilgrimage with Moses to the Promised Land, and in crossing the Jordan River, their entrance into the Promised Land. These two crossing foreshadow the Christian beginning his pilgrimage on earth after being washed clean from sin and entrance into heaven in being united to Christ.

The crossing of the Jordan River is distinguished from the crossing of the Red Sea in that it takes place at the end of the Israelites' forty-year journey through the desert. This crossing, led by Joshua, is fulfilled by Jesus as the new Joshua, whose name Jesus, (יְהוֹשֻׁעַ *Yehoshua*), shares with Joshua. The name Joshua, or Jesus, literally means, "The Lord is salvation."[43] Joshua saves the Israelites by leading them into an earthly promised land. Jesus, as the new Joshua, saves us by leading us through the waters of death into the promised land of

---

[42]   James Tissot, "The Waters are Divided," c. 1896-1902, https://commons.wikimedia.org/wiki/File:Tissot_The_Waters_Are_Divide d.jpg, James Tissot [Public domain], via Wikimedia Commons.

[43]   "Strong's Concordance, 3091. Yehoshua," biblehub.com, http://biblehub.com/hebrew/3091.htm.

heaven.

These two spiritual crossings are similar in that, according to Aquinas, they both are due to the unmerited "help of grace."[44] In the first, Baptism, we receive the unmerited, initial, or first, grace that begins our journey. In the second, death, which corresponds to the crossing of the Jordan River, we may receive another unmerited grace, the grace of final perseverance.[45] The Sacrament though which Jesus ordinarily, but not exclusively, gives this grace of final perseverance is, specifies Pitre, the Anointing of the Sick.[46]

Section Questions

1. How does the crossing of the Red Sea and the Crossing of the Jordan River relate to the Catholic faith? With specific reference to Scripture, include the following in your response: Sacraments, Jesus Baptized, Initial and Final Grace.

Miriam

The New Testament's name Mary (Μαρία) is the Greek version of the Hebrew name Miriam, Moses's sister. Miriam (Mir-yām מִרְיָם) serves as a type of Mary, according to early Church interpretation of Scripture. Exodus identifies Miriam as a prophetess (Exodus 15:20)

---

[44] Thomas Aquinas, "Summa Theologiae," I-II, q. 114, art. 2 and reply to objection 1, [Cf. I-II, 109, 10, II-II, q. 137, art. 4], newadvent.org, http://www.newadvent.org/summa/2114.htm#article9.

[45] Thomas Aquinas, "Summa Theologiae," I-II, q. 114, art. 5 and art. 9, [Cf. I-II, 109, 10, II-II, q. 137, art. 4].

[46] Pitre, *Genesis and the Books of Moses,* MP3, 15.

who accompanies her people and assists her brothers. According to the Talmud, which contains ancient Jewish oral tradition, the three leaders of the Israelites in the desert were Moses, Aaron, and Miriam, each of whom were given a gift by God for their people.

[47]

Moses was given Manna to feed his people. Aaron was given a pillar of cloud to guide his people, and Miriam's gift was a well, which mysteriously accompanied the Israelites' journey through the desert. Miriam's death is referred to in the beginning verses of Numbers chapter twenty. Her death is followed by Moses miraculously obtaining water from a rock. According to the Talmud, the rock he obtained water from was the rock of the well that Miriam looked over and dried up after she died.[48]

---

[47]   Anselm   Feuerbach,   "Miriam   the   Prophetess,"   1862, https://commons.wikimedia.org/wiki/File:Feuerbach_Mirjam_2.jpg, Anselm Feuerbach [Public domain], via Wikimedia Commons, {{PD-1923}} – published anywhere before 1923 and public domain in the U.S.

[48] "Talmud, Tract Taanith (Fasting)," Chapter 1, sacred-texts.com, http://www.sacred-texts.com/jud/t04/taa06.htm. "An objection was raised: R. Jose the son of R. Jehudah said: Three good leaders were given to Israel, and they are: Moses, Aaron, and Miriam; and three good gifts were given

St. Paul in his letter to the Corinthians explicitly refers to the miraculously water giving rock by identifying the rock as Christ, "I want you to know, brethren, that our fathers were all under the cloud, and all passed through the sea, and all were baptized into Moses in the cloud and in the sea, and all ate the same supernatural food and all drank the same supernatural drink. For they drank from the supernatural Rock which followed them, and the Rock was Christ (1 Corinthians 10:1-4 *RSVCE*)." This typological association well suits the role of Miriam who accompanies the rock and Mary who accompanies her son Jesus who provides us with living water of eternal life (John 4:14; 7:38).

Gregory of Nyssa (c. 330-c. 395) presents Miriam as "a type of Mary the mother of God" since not only was Miriam a prophetess but also, according to Gregory, a virgin. In presenting this as a possibility Gregory writes:

---

through them, namely: the well of water which the Israelites had along with them in the desert was given them for the sake of Miriam; the 'pillar of cloud which led them by day was given them on account of Aaron, and the Manna was given them for Moses' sake. When Miriam died, the well vanished, as it is written [Numbers, xxi. 1]: "Miriam died there and was buried there"; and immediately afterwards it says: "And there was no water for the congregation." Still, the well was again given to the children of Israel through the prayers of Moses and Aaron.

When Aaron died, the pillar of cloud left. Still, both the well and the pillar of cloud were returned for the sake of Moses; but when Moses died, everything vanished, as it is written [Zechariah, xi. 8]: "And I removed the three shepherds in one month." Did then Moses, Aaron, and Miriam die in the same month? Did not Moses die in Adar, Aaron in Abh, and Miriam in Nissan? Therefore, infer from that passage that the three gifts which were given to Israel vanished in the same month that Moses died."

[I]t is perhaps not very far removed from the bounds of probability that Miriam was a virgin. However, we can but guess and surmise, we cannot clearly prove, that this was so, and that Miriam the prophetess led a dance of virgins, even though many of the learned have affirmed distinctly that she was unmarried, from the fact that the history makes no mention either of her marriage or of her being a mother; and surely she would have been named and known, not as "the sister of Aaron," but from her husband, if she had had one; since the head of the woman is not the brother but the husband.[49]

Section Questions

1. How does Miriam foreshadow Mary, the Mother of Jesus? Include the following in your response: Exodus, Virgin, St Paul on the Rock and Water as Christ (1 Corinthians 10:1-4).

Manna

The gift God gave to Moses to feed the Israelites with, as mentioned above, was "bread from heaven," also known as Manna, along with quail. The name Manna is a transliteration of the Israelite response upon seeing the heavenly bread for the first time. Seeing the bread, they said (Exodus 16:15), "Mon hu." (מָן הוּא) This is often

---

[49] Gregory of Nyssa, "NPNF2-05. Gregory of Nyssa: Dogmatic Treatises, etc." Ascetic and Moral, chap xix, ccel.org, http://www.ccel.org/ccel/schaff/npnf205html, (accessed June 5, 2016).

translated as, "What is it?"[50]

According to Hahn, St. Paul implicitly associates the heavenly bread of "Manna" with Christ, in this case with Christ's heavenly, Eucharistic presence. One indication that St. Paul implies this connection is that almost immediately after referring to the "supernatural drink" from the "Rock" which "was Christ" St. Paul then refers to the celebration of the Eucharist which is "a participation in the blood...and body of Christ (1 Corinthians 10:2-16 *RSVCE*)."[51]

Jesus explicitly link the Eucharist with Manna in John chapter six:

> I am the bread of life. Your fathers ate the manna in the wilderness, and they died. This is the bread which comes down from heaven, that a man may eat of it and not die. I am the living bread which came down from heaven; if any one eats of this bread, he will live forever; and the bread which I shall give for the life of the world is my flesh (John 6:48-51 *RSVCE*).

Since the liturgy, especially the celebration of the Eucharist, is a principle means through which the Holy Spirit inspires the Church to develop her theology, in accordance with the Latin phrase *Lex orandi, ex credendi* (the law of praying is the law of believing), it is important also to look to the liturgy when interpreting Scripture. Eucharistic Prayer II, points out Pitre, refers to the Old Testament Manna with the word "dewfall" as a foreshadowing of the Holy Spirit's descent, since Exodus describes the Manna forming after "the dew had gone up

---

[50] Scott Hahn, *Catholic Bible Dictionary* (New York: Doubleday, 2009), 571.

[51] Hahn, *Catholic Bible Dictionary*, 572.

(Exodus 16:14 *RSVCE*)". The specific place in which this connection is made is in the Epiclesis of Eucharistic Prayer II where the priest calls down the Holy Spirit with, "Make holy, therefore, these gifts, we pray, by sending down your Spirit upon them like the dewfall, so that they may become for us the Body + and Blood of our Lord, Jesus Christ."[52]

[53]

The Eucharist is the Catholic heavenly manna that sustains those who are nourished by it during their earthly pilgrimage. Reverent reception of the Eucharist greatly aids Catholic to, in the words of Jesus, "not to labor for food that perishes, but for the food which endures to eternal life (John 6:27 *RSVCE*)." Interestingly, Hamilton observes, God commands the Israelites to only collect a day's portion

---

[52]   "Eucharistic   Prayers   I-IV,"   catholic-resources.org, http://www.catholic-resources.org/ChurchDocs/RM3-EP1-4.htm.

[53] James Tissot, "The Gathering of the Manna (color)," c. 1896-1902, https://commons.wikimedia.org/wiki/File:Tissot_The_Gathering_of_the_Manna_(color).jpg, James Tissot [Public domain], via Wikimedia Commons.

of Manna and no more except on the sixth day, since on the Sabbath, the seventh day, Manna is not sent down (Exodus 16:4-5, 26). With this command, God taught the Israelites to trust in Divine Providence by living in the present moment and not excessively preparing for and worrying about the future. Reflecting this wisdom Jesus, comments Hamilton, told his disciples "do not be anxious about your life, what you shall eat or what you shall drink, nor about your body, what you shall put on. Is not our life more than food, and the body more than clothing? … your heavenly Father knows that you need them all. But seek first his kingdom … Therefore, do not be anxious about tomorrow, for tomorrow will be anxious for itself (Matthew 6:25, 32-34 *RSVCE*)."[54]

Section Questions

1. How does the Manna and Quail foreshadow the Eucharist? With specific reference to Scripture, include the following in your response: Manna, Quail, Heaven, John Chapter Six.

Cloud of Fire

In the Old Testament, God sometimes chooses to appear through the form of fire, and other forces of nature such as strong winds and earthquakes (Exodus 119:18; Numbers 16:31-32, Judges 5:5, 2 Samuel 22:8, 11; 1 Kings 19:12-12; Job 38:1; Psalm 18:7, 10; Isaiah 24:19-20, 29:6, 59:16; Nahum 1:3, 5). In the New Testament God similarly

---

[54] Hamilton, 179.

manifests Himself in tongues of fire at Pentecost (Acts 2:3). This specific continuity between the New Testament and the Old Testament is often lost sight of. In continuity with the Old Testament image of divine fire Jesus said, "I came to cast fire upon the earth: and would that it were already kindled. … Do you think that I have come to give peace on earth? No, I tell you, but rather division (Luke 12:49-51 *RSVCE*)." The division that Jesus brings is always directed towards greater unity, dividing us from our disordered loves so as to reorder us in true unity ordered by love of God and neighbor.

55

In clearly bringing this continuity out Benedict XVI writes, "Jesus does not come to make us comfortable; rather he sets fire to the earth; he brings the great living fire of divine love, which is what the Holy

55 Paul Hardy, The Art Bible," 1896, https://commons.wikimedia.org/wiki/File:The_pillar_of_fire,_by_Paul_Hardy.jpg, By Internet Archive Book Images [No restrictions], via Wikimedia Commons.

Spirit is, a fire that burns."[56] Hamilton similarly writes, that in Jesus "God himself has not changed. He has not transformed himself from a holy God into a 'consumer-friendly' God."[57] In asserting this, Hamilton references Hebrews chapter twelve which describes the "terrifying (Hebrews 12:21 *RSVCE*)" appearance of God in fire at Mount Sinai, then shifts our attention to Jesus until finally concluding with, "our God is a consuming fire (Hebrews 12:29 *RSVCE*)." Understood in this way, Jesus is a fire that purifies, transforms, and reorders all our desires, priorities and goals in accordance with our ultimate end, union with His Heavenly Father in communion with the saints.

God's fiery, transformative presence appears in Exodus chapter thirteen as a "pillar of cloud by day and [a] pillar of fire by night (Exodus 13:22 *RSVCE*)." This may be interpreted as the same reality that looks different depending if it is night or day. According to Exodus, the miraculous pillar of fire guided the Israelites to the Promised Land. Church Fathers interpreted this guiding pillar as a symbol of Holy Spirit leading the Israelites for forty years (Exodus 16:35) into and through the desert. St. Ambrose writes, "the pillar of cloud went before the people of the Jews by day, and the pillar of fire by night, that the grace of the Spirit might protect His people."[58]

Similarly, the synoptic gospels describe Jesus as "led up by the

---

[56] Benedict XVI, *Benedictus: Day by Day with Pope Benedict XVI* (San Francisco: Ignatius Press, 2012), 105.

[57] Hamilton, 187.

[58] Ambrose of Milan, *Three Books of St. Ambrose on the Holy Spirit*, in P. Schaff & H. Wace eds, *St. Ambrose: Select Works and Letters*, trans. H.T.F. Duckworth (New York: Christian Literature Company, 1896), vol. 10, pp. 138–139.

Spirit into the wilderness to be tempted by the devil" for "forty days and forty nights (Matthew 4:1-2 *RSVCE*)." Unlike the Israelites who were tempted in the wilderness, in the desert for forty years and sinned, Jesus was tempted and did not sin. Immediately afterwards, Jesus begins his public ministry in the lands of Zebulun and Naphtali, the very lands where the first Israelite tribes were deported in 733 B.C. by the Assyrian conquerors.[59] Here, explains Pitre, Jesus began his ministry in order to begin reversing the breakup of Israel where it first began with the goal of gathering the Twelve Tribes into a New Covenant. By so doing, Jesus fulfilled the prophecy of Isaiah that one day these lands, despite being "brought into contempt (Isaiah 9:1 *RSVCE*)," will be made glorious.[60]

Jesus fulfills the prophecy of a future time where the Twelve Tribes of Israel will be reunited by not, explains Pitre, duplicating the Twelve Tribes as they existed previously but rather by building upon this structure and transforming it. It is transformed by having Jesus as its center, by having Jesus as the new Jacob, the new father of the Twelve Tribes and the Twelve Apostles, who do not represent by their genealogies the Twelve Tribes. Instead the Twelve Apostles are a New Israel that is in continuity with the Israel of old but also is different, and their lack of full representation of the Twelve Tribes indicates this difference of being open to all in a manner that the Israel of old was not.[61]

---

[59] 2 Kings 15:29.

[60] *The Ignatius Catholic Study Bible New Testament*, (San Francisco: Ignatius Press, 2010), loc. 2746.

[61] Pitre, *The Old Testament*, 56.

Section Questions

1. How is God's Old Testament appearances in fire, strong wind, and earthquakes fulfilled in Jesus? Include in your answer Luke 12:49-51, division, unity, purifying, transforming, perfecting, destroying.

Mosaic Law

[62]

Before reaching the Promised Land, the miraculous cloud guided the Israelites to Mount Sinai where God established a covenant with Israel and gave them the gift of the Ten Commandments, a gift greater than even the Promised Land since following these laws ensures right

---

[62] James Tissot, "Moses and the Ten Commandments," c. 1896-1902, https://commons.wikimedia.org/wiki/File:Tissot_Moses_and_the_Ten_Co mmandments.jpg, [Public domain], via Wikimedia Commons.

relationship with God. Along with the Ten Commandments, the Sinai Covenant also bound the Israelites to observe an additional set of less important laws, liturgical and non-liturgical laws (Exodus 21-31).

As the essence of the moral law the Ten Commandments are presented as the most important laws in the Old Testament. This is evident, argues Miller, in the Biblical Hebrew terminology for the Ten Commandments. Biblical Hebrew classifies the Ten Commandments as "Ten Words, *'ă·śe·reṯ had·də·ḇā·rîm* עֲשֶׂרֶת הַדְּבָרִים (Exodus 34:28; Deuteronomy 4:13, 10:4)." This unique way of naming the laws as words distinguishes the Ten Commandments from other laws in the Old Testament that are named, writes Mark F. Rooker, "commandments (*miswa*), statutes (*hoq*), and regulations (*mispat*)."[63] In addition, no other laws in the Old Testament are "written with the finger of God (Exodus 31:18 *RSVCE*)." As Miller explains, by describing God's finger as writing the Ten Commandments, "the Israelites were saying that unlike the other commandments, which were written down by Moses, this commandment set was— metaphorically speaking—inscribed by God. In other words, it was something directly divine in a way that the other commandments were not."[64] Finally, Miller appeals to a second century B.C. ancient non-biblical text, the Nash Papyrus, which contain the Ten Commandments and nothing else, indicating that the Jewish people understood these Commandments as the most important of the

---

[63] Mark F. Rooker, *The Ten Commandments: Ethics for the Twenty-First Century* (Nashville: B&H Publishing Group, 2010), 3.

[64] Robert D. Miller II, *Understanding the Old Testament* (Chantilly: The Teaching Company, 2019), 104.

traditionally referred to 613 laws.[65]

Exodus chapter thirty-one ends this detailed list of laws with God giving "to Moses, when he had made an end of speaking with him upon Mount Sinai, the two tables of the covenant, tables of stone, written with the finger of God (Exodus 31:18 *RSVCE*)." These words clearly affirm the divine origin of the Ten Commandments. Modern Scripture scholars have indicated that some aspects of the Ten Commandments are likely influenced by non-Israelite cultures, but this does not mean that their divine origin is negated as Benedict XVI responds:

> the fact that particular elements of the Ten Commandments can be traced to non-Israelite origins tells us nothing about whether or not they can be separated off from the core of covenant faith. Such a view can only be maintained if one assumes that there is no analogy between the nations' reason and God's revelation, and that the two phenomena confront each other in a pure paradox; that is, if one has a particular concept of the relationship between revelation and reason, a concept that is not verified by the biblical texts, but rather is

---

[65] Miller, *Understanding the Old Testament*, 104. "A final reason I think there's something special about the Ten Commandments is that we know they circulated independently of copies of the book of Exodus. In other words, we have a text called the Nash Papyrus, which is a copy of the Ten Commandments on their own; or rather, it's the Ten Commandments plus Deuteronomy 6: the prayer called the Shema in Judaism. The Nash Papyrus is from about the 2nd century BCE, it was found in Egypt. It's not a fragment of the Bible. It's a complete text that contains the Shema plus the Ten Commandments. So already by the 100s BCE, people considered the Ten Commandments to be something different from the rest of the laws."[65]

falsified by them.[66]

To properly interpret the Ten Commandments, it is necessary to read them in light of the additional laws that were given in chapters twenty-one through thirty-one. For example, the Ten Commandments prohibition of making "a graven image (Exodus 20:4 *RSVCE*)" is to be understood in light of God commanding the Israelites in Exodus chapter twenty-five to make two graven images by fashioning angels of gold (cherubim), and attach them on the two ends of the "mercy seat" which is to be placed upon the Ark of the Covenant (Exodus 25:18-21).

According to St. Augustine's commentary on Exodus, the prohibition of graven images is intended by God to be part of the commandment against idolatry, against not having false gods.[67] This is a reasonable interpretation since God as truth does not contradict himself. Therefore, the apparent contradiction between what God commands in Exodus chapter 20, where He forbids graven images, with what He commands in Exodus chapter twenty-five by commanding graven images of cherubim is resolved when it is realized that the command against graven images is part of the command against idolatry. As Pitre explains, the commandment is not against all graven images but only against graven images of false gods that the Israelites may be tempted to worship.[68]

---

[66] Joseph Ratzinger, *Principles of Christian Morality*, trans. G. Harrison (San Francisco: Ignatius Press, 1986), 58.

[67] St. Augustine, "Questionum in Heptateuchum Libri Septem, Liber Secundus, Questiones in Exodum," no. 71, augustinus.it, http://www.augustinus.it/latino/questioni_ettateuco/index2.htm.

[68] Pitre, *The Old Testament,* MP 12.

Another misconception of the Ten Commandments, provided by Pitre, is the belief that the Old Testament law is only about external behavior in contrast with the New Testament law that simplifies and interiorizes the Old Testament laws.[69] This is quickly seen as false when the Ten Commandments are carefully looked at, especially the last set of commands: "You shall not covet (*tahmod* תַחְמֹד) your neighbor's house; you shall not covet your neighbor's wife, or his manservant, or his maidservant, or his ox, or his ass, or anything that is your neighbor's (Exodus 20:17 *RSVCE*)." The word used in Hebrew *tahmod* is based on the Hebrew root verb for desiring is *chamad* (חָמַד) and also means to greatly desire in a disordered manner.[70] Since, coveting and desiring are interior actions, these commandments prohibit not simply external acts but also internal ones. In the New Testament, Jesus intensifies and builds upon the interior dimension of the Old Law and gives us a relationship with God, gives us grace that enables to fulfill the law's demands (Romans 8:4).

This intensification of the interior demand of the law is particular evident in Matthew chapter five. Here, Jesus is described as going up a mountain, in a similar way that Moses went up a mountain. As a new Moses, Jesus gives his disciples laws, specifically the Beatitudes and similar commandments that further interiorize the Law. In interiorizing the Law, Jesus, Pitre comments, prohibits not only excessive willed attraction by coveting our neighbor's goods and wife but also forbids excessive willed anger, "You have heard that it was said to the men of old, 'You shall not kill; and whoever kills shall be

---

[69] Pitre, *The Old Testament*, MP 12.

[70] "2530. חָמַד (chamad)," biblehub.com, http://biblehub.com/hebrew/strongs_2530.htm.

liable to judgment.' But I say to you that everyone who is angry with his brother shall be liable to judgment (Matthew 5:21-22 *RSVCE*)."[71]

Jesus also intensifies the demands of the Mosaic Law intended to restrain violence. According to Exodus, "If any harms follows, then you shall give life for life, eye for eye, tooth for tooth, hand for hand, foot for foot, burn for burn, wound for wound, stripe for stripe (Exodus 21:23-25 *RSVCE*)." In contrast, Jesus teaches, "You have heard that it was said, 'An eye for an eye and a tooth for a tooth.' But I say to you, do not resist one who is evil. But if anyone strikes you on the right cheek, turn to him the other also (Matthew 5:38-39 *RSVCE*)."

While the law as presented by Moses and the law as presented and lived out by Jesus differ they are essentially motivated by the same reason stated in Leviticus that we are to be holy, we are to be moral because God is holy, because God is absolutely moral and good (Leviticus 19:2-3; 1 Peter 1:16). Jesus personifies the holiness of God. For this reason, Jesus commands, "love one another; even as I have loved you (John 13:34 *RSVCE*)." With these words, Jesus invites us to love by participating in His holiness, in His divine life for as St. Peter explains, through Christ, we have "become partakers of the divine nature (2 Peter 1:4 *RSVCE*)

The more we participate in divine life the more we are capable of living in accordance with the law and the more we recognize the law, the Ten Commandments as a gift (Psalm 19[18]), a structure that both reflects the structure of creation which in turns reflects the nature of its creating God who is social reality since God is Triune in one. The very number ten hints at the Ten Commandments reflection of created order since, as Benedict XVI explains:

---

[71] Pitre, *The Old Testament*, MP 13.

The words "God said" appear ten times in the creation account. In this way the creation narrative anticipates the Ten Commandments. This makes us realize that these Ten Commandments are, as it were, an echo of the creation; they are not arbitrary inventions for the purpose of erecting barriers to human freedom but signs pointing to the spirit, the language, and the meaning of creation; they are a translation of the language of the universe, a translation of God's logic, which constructed the universe.[72]

The structure provided by the Ten Commandments can be understood as a home in which we are created by God to live in as a community of people. Only by following the Ten Commandments can we live harmoniously under the one roof provided by the Ten Commandments. The ability to live in accordance with the Ten Commandments is the New Law which "is the grace of the Holy Spirit given to the faithful through faith in Christ (*CCC* 1965)."[73] When we live by the Holy Spirit the law no longer is burdensome but becomes a joy since we realize that the law exists only so that we can love relationally as a reflection of the relational love of our Triune God. Those who truly love relationally respect their parents and do not steal, kill, lie, or commit adultery since all of these actions destroy

---

[72] Pope Benedict XVI, *In the Beginning: A Catholic Understanding of the Story of Creation and the Fall,* trans. Boniface Ramsey (Grand Rapids: William B. Eerdmans Publishing Company, 1986), Kindle Locations 266-269.

[73] "Catechism of the Catholic Church," vatican.va, http://www.vatican.va/archive/ccc_css/archive/catechism/p3s1c3a1.htm, no. 1966.

relationships in our common home and prevent us from being capable of living together under one roof.

Sadly, though, the Ten Commandments, the Covenant given on Sinai, is often seen not as a gift that provides us with a framework that we have been created to live according to since the framework reflects God's social nature as Triune. Instead the Ten Commandments, "the law" is often seen, writes Benedict XVI:

> as a straitjacket that prevents one from enjoying the real promises of life. It is so easy to convince people that this covenant is not a gift but rather an expression of envy of humankind and that is robbing human beings of their freedom and of the most precious things of life. With this doubt people are well on their way to building their own worlds. In other words, it is then that they make the decision not to accept the limitations of their existence; it is then that they decide not to be bound by the limitations imposed by good and evil, or by morality in general, but quite simply to free themselves by ignoring them.[74]

When we choose selfish forms of love over love that is relational as governed by the Ten Commandments, we always will feel frustrated and never truly happy since we are not living in accordance with our created natures that are created to be images of God's social, relational nature. May we look to Jesus who is the way to truly satisfying peace and happiness since Jesus as the Son of the Father in the eternal love

---

[74] Benedict XVI, *Day by Day with Pope Benedict XVI*, ed. Peter John Cameron (San Francisco: Ignatius Press, 2006), 53.

of the Holy Spirit, writes Benedict XVI, "is by nature relationship and relatedness, reestablishes relationships. His arms, spread out on the cross, are an open invitation to relationship, which is continually offered to us."[75] The relationships Jesus calls us to are structured by the Ten Commandments.

Section Questions

1. What are the arguments that support the Ten Commandments as the most important laws of the Mosaic Code? With specific reference to Scripture, include the following in your response: Words, Finger, Nash Papyrus, Non-Israelite Moral Codes.

2. Since the First Commandment prohibits "graven images (Exodus 20:4)" why were graven images of angels placed upon the Ark (Exodus 25:18-21)? Include in your response the following: image and idolatry.

---

[75] Benedict XVI, *Day by Day with Pope Benedict XVI*, ed. Peter John Cameron (San Francisco: Ignatius Press, 2006), 56. The greater context of this quotation is: ""The One who is truly like God does not hold graspingly to his autonomy, to the limitlessness of his ability and his willing. He does the contrary: he becomes completely dependent, he becomes a slave. Because he does not go the route of power but that of love, he can descent into the depths of Adam's lie, into the depths of death, and there raise up truth and life. Thus Christ is the new Adam, with whom humankind begins anew. The Son, who is by nature relationship and relatedness, reestablishes relationships. His arms, spread out on the cross, are an open invitation to relationship, which is continually offered to us. The cross, the place of his obedience, is the true tree of life."

3. Why is it inaccurate to depict the Ten Commandments as concerned only with external behavior? With specific reference to Scripture, include the following in your response: Commandments 9 and 10, Ultimate Reason for Following the Law (Leviticus 19:2), Role of Number 10 in Genesis.

Modification of the Mosaic Law

The Mosaic Law is modified, and a new set of Ten Commandments are made after Moses comes down with the first set of Ten Commandments and is shocked upon seeing his people drinking, eating and "playing" around a golden calf. This golden calf was likely a depiction of the Egyptian God Apis, which the Egyptians portrayed as a bull calf.[76] The depiction of an animal known for its sexual virility and power in gold, explains Pitre, is indicative of the people's excessive love for money, power, and pleasure. The three-fold temptation the Israelites fell into of being overly possessive, overly desirous for sensual pleasure, and, out of pride, wanting to be powerful were the same temptations that Adam and Eve gave into, and Jesus resisted in his forty days and nights in the Judean desert. Only Jesus emerged from these temptations unscathed.[77] Moses responds to the Israelites falling into adulterous idolatry by breaking the Ten Commandments apart, grinding the golden calf into powder, mixing the golden power with water and then commanding the Israelites to drink this concoction (Exodus 32: 20).

---

[76] Hahn, *Catholic Bible Dictionary*, 796.

[77] Pitre, *Genesis and the Books of Moses*, 50.

He then goes back up Mount Sinai, pleads that God will be merciful and is reissued a new set of Ten Commandments along with a longer list of additional commandments. These additional laws are listed Deuteronomy, which in Greek literally means second law, and in Leviticus. In addition, the priesthood that had been shared by all the tribes was restricted to the tribe of Levi, the tribe that Moses, Aaron and Miriam belonged to. Moses' tribe was the only tribe of the twelve that rallied around Moses when Moses in anger at the idolatry around the golden calf, asked "Who is on the Lord's side? Come to me (Exodus 32:26 *RSVCE*)."

The Levites then gather around Moses who commands them to punish the Israelites. They do so by killing three thousand men. Upon demonstrating that their loyalty to God surpasses loyalty to their people, Moses then asserts the Levites have ordained themselves as priests. With these words, Moses inaugurates a new priesthood, the Levitical priesthood. According to the Letter to the Hebrews, Jesus as

---

[78] James Tissot, "The Golden Calf, as in Exodus 32:4," c. 1903, https://commons.wikimedia.org/wiki/File:Tissot_The_Golden_Calf.jpg, James Tissot [Public domain], via Wikimedia Commons.

a non-Levite, as a member of the tribe of Judah, returns to the original priesthood that was not restricted to one tribe. The priesthood of Jesus is "according to the order of Melchizedek" (Hebrews 7:11 *RSVCE*)." Melchizedek, as explained earlier had blessed Abraham, was believed to be Shem, Noah's oldest son.

In acknowledgement of the Levites replacing the priesthood of the first-born sons, Exodus commands that all the first-born sons are to be redeemed (Exodus 34:20). The act of freeing themselves from the role of the priests consists of paying five coins (shekels) to a Levitical priest, specifically to a male descendent of Aaron (Numbers 3:47-48).

This practice of redeeming the first-born sons is still practiced today by Jewish people and is called in Hebrew *Pidyon Haben* (פדיון הבן).[79] During Jesus' time the Jewish people also redeemed their first-born sons by paying five coins to a Levitical priest. Following Jewish law, Mary fulfilled this law when she presented Jesus in the Temple (Luke 2:23).

Before leaving Mount Sinai, God commands Moses to take Israel's first census which entails determining which men are "able to go forth to war (Numbers 1:3 *RSVCE*)." Hamilton points out that this phrase is used fifteen time in this chapter. He comments, "The presence of God over/among/at the head of his people as they march on does not render the need for a prepared army superfluous. God works not outside of his people, but through his people, to see them realize his

---

[79] "The History of Pidyon Haben," Chabad.org, https://www.chabad.org/library/article_cdo/aid/928156/jewish/The-History-of-Pidyon-Haben.htm.

destination for them."[80]

Section Questions

1. When and how was original, patriarchal priesthood modified? With specific reference to Scripture, include the following in your response: Melchizedek, Levitical, Golden Calf, First-Born Sons, Redemption Payment.

Tabernacle

The Levitical priesthood's central duty was to serve in the movable tabernacle, and later to serve in the Jerusalem Temple. The last six chapters of Exodus (35-40) are on the construction of the tabernacle, the items within the tabernacle, priestly vestments, and the erection of the tabernacle. According to St. Paul, these features of the tabernacle and the consequent worship that developed around the tabernacle and later the Temple, "are only a shadow of what is to come" (Colossians 2:17 *RSVCE*). What they foreshadow, Paul adds, is Christ. Ratzinger, in reference to St. Gregory the Great, points out that although Old Testament Jewish worship foreshadows the worshipping Church, the Church is not the reality that is signified in its fullness. Rather, as Gregory the Great explains, the Church represents the beginning of dawn that gradually "yields" to the fullness of day, representing Christ's coming at the end of time when all of creation will be

---

[80] (Numbers 1:3, 18, 20, 22, 24, 26, 28, 30, 32, 36, 38, 40, 42, 45) Victor P. Hamilton, *Handbook on the Pentateuch, Second Edition* (Grand Rapids: Baker Academic, 2005), 306.

transformed into a New Heavens and New Earth (Revelation 21:1):

Since the daybreak or the dawn is changed gradually from darkness into light, the Church, which comprises the elect, is fittingly styled daybreak or dawn. While she is being led from the night of infidelity to the light of faith, she is opened gradually to the splendor of heavenly brightness, just as dawn yields to the day after darkness. … Holy Church, inasmuch as she keeps searching for the rewards of eternal life, has been called the dawn. While she turns her back on the darkness of sins, she begins to shine with the light of righteousness.[82]

Salvation history, therefore, is comprised of three basic phases that Benedict XVI identifies as shadow, image, and reality.[83]

---

[81] "Model of the Tabernacle in Timna Valley Park, Israel," 2 April 2011, James Tissot [Public domain], via Wikimedia Commons, By Ruk7 [GFDL (http://www.gnu.org/copyleft/fdl.html) or CC BY-SA 3.0 (https://creativecommons.org/licenses/by-sa/3.0)], from Wikimedia Commons.

[82] First Reading, *From the Moral Reflections on Job by Saint Gregory the Great (Lib. 29, 2-4: PL 76, 478-480)*, in *The Liturgy of the Hours*, vol. 3 (New York: Catholic Book Publishing Col, 1975), 308.

[83] Joseph Ratzinger, *The Spirit of the Liturgy*, trans. J. Saward (San Francisco: Ignatius Press, 2000), 54. "That is why the Church Fathers

Pitre applies these three stages to Genesis by defining the tabernacle as the shadow of the Church, representing the dawn, and the Church as the image of the fully reality that is to come when Christ comes once again in time to judge and perfect creation by bringing about the identification of the Church on earth with its heavenly reality.[84]

The Hebrew word for the Latin-based word tabernacle is *mishkan* (מִשְׁכָּן). *Mishkan* evokes the sense of a heavenly reality residing on earth. *Mishkan* comes from the Hebrew verb *lishkan* (לִשְׁכֵּן) meaning to dwell, or to house. The word literally means, consequently, the dwelling place,[85] and signifies the dwelling place of God on earth. For this reason, God commands Moses to construct His earthly dwelling place in a way that symbolizes heaven on earth, in a such a way, explains Pitre, that both creation and heaven are represented by the tabernacle.

The reflection of earthy creation of heavenly realities is evident in

---

described the various stages of fulfillment, not just as a contrast between Old and New Testaments, but as the three steps of shadow, image, and reality. In the Church of the New Testament the shadow has been scattered by the image: '[T]he night is far gone; the day is at hand' (Rom 13:12). But, as St. Gregory the Great puts it, it is still only the time of dawn, when darkness and light are intermingled. The sun is rising, but it has still not reached its zenith. Thus, the time of the New Testament is a peculiar kind of 'in-between', a mixture of 'already and not yet'. The empirical conditions of life in this world are still in force, but they have been burst open, and must be more and more burst open, in preparation for the final fulfillment already inaugurated in Christ."

[84] Pitre, *The Old Testament*, MP3.

[85] "4908. Miskan, Strong's Concordance," biblehub.com, http://biblehub.com/hebrew/4908.htm.

the comparison between God creating the world and Moses making the tabernacle. God creating the world, observing the world in admiration (Genesis 1:31), blessing and consecrating creation (Genesis 2:3) are analogous to Moses's actions of creating the tabernacle, admiring creation (Exodus 39:43), blessing (Exodus 39:43) and consecrating it (Exodus 40:9). These and other similarities between God creating the world and Moses, heeding God's commands, building the tabernacle indicate that creation itself, Hahn writes, is "a Cosmic Temple"[86] that is intended by God to worship Him. In addition, Pitre affirms, these similarities demonstrate that the tabernacle, and later the Temple and Eucharistic worship by the Church, liturgically represent all of universe where heavenly worship joins with earthly worship.[87]

God reveals his plans for the heavenly dwelling place on earth in a vision to Moses (Exodus 25:9). Both Acts and Hebrews refers to this divine blueprint that God communicated to Moses in a vision. "Our fathers had the tent of witness in the wilderness, even as he who spoke to Moses directed him to make it, according to the pattern that he had seen (Acts 7:44 *RSVCE*)." "[F]or when Moses was about to erect the tent, he was instructed by God, saying, "See that you make everything according to the pattern which was shown you on the mountain (Hebrews 8:5 *RSVCE*)." Hebrews also explicitly states that the vision given to Moses of how the tabernacle was to be constructed served as "a copy and shadow of the heavenly sanctuary (Hebrews 8:5 *RSVCE*)."

---

[86] Scott W. Hahn, *A Father Who Keeps His Promises* (Ann Arbor, Mich: Charis, 1998), 52-53.

[87] Pitre, *The Old Testament*, MP3.

The tabernacle and the items within it are, consequently, visible signs of an invisible heavenly reality. The ark with the two golden cherubim affixed on top clearly is a visible sign of the heavenly angelic court that surrounds God. The contents of the ark also act as sacred signs of heaven. According to Hebrews, in the ark were the Ten Commandments, a jar of manna, and staff of Aaron (Hebrews 9:3; cf. Exodus 16:34, Numbers 17:10). All three items were means through which God was intensely present to his people. The Ten Commandments are a revelation of God's words. The manna, believed by ancient tradition to be stored in heaven by God, was a sign of God's sustaining and intervening presence, especially in time of need.[88] Aaron's staff which miraculously sprouted to indicate the Levites had been chosen by God to replace the first-born son's priesthood also

---

[88] Mishnah describes manna as one of ten items created by God on the seventh day. "Ten things were created at twilight of the eve of Sabbath: the mouth of the earth and the mouth of the well, and the mouth of the ass, and the bow, and the manna, and the rod, and the Shomir worm, and the character and the writing, and the tables." "Tractate Avot: Chapter 5," jewishvirtuallibrary.org, http://www.jewishvirtuallibrary.org/tractate-avot-chapter-5.

The apocryphal work 2 Baruch states, "8 And it shall come to pass at that self-same time that the treasury of manna shall again descend from on high, and they will eat of it in those years, because these are they who have come to the consummation of time. 30 1 And it shall come to pass after these things, when the time of the advent of the Messiah is fulfilled, that He shall return in glory." "2 Baruch," pseudepigrapha.com, http://www.pseudepigrapha.com/pseudepigrapha/2Baruch.html. Cf. Brant Pitre, *Jesus and the Jewish Roots of the Eucharist*, 86-91.

signified God's saving, intervening presence. The Ten Commandments, the Manna, and Aaron's "virgin" staff which budded were
interpreted by Church Fathers as fulfilled in Jesus who is the New Law,
the heavenly "bread of life," and was born of a virgin.[89]

The bread of presence affirmed God's special presence as well
(Exodus 25:30). This sacred sign consisted of a table on which was
placed an offering of bread called in Hebrew *lechem panim* (לֶחֶם פָּנִים)
literally meaning the bread of the face (*panim*).[90] According to
Leviticus, the bread of the face consisted of twelve loaves of bread
placed on a gold table and represented an eternal covenant (Leviticus
25:9). From a Catholic perspective, this presence is fulfilled in the
Eucharistic presence of the risen Lord Jesus.

The fire, especially on the Golden Lampstand, and water in the
laver of bronze also can be understood as representing God's presence.
Pitre points out that typically both fire and water signify in the bible
the presence of the Holy Spirit.[91] In the first chapter of Genesis, God's
spirit is described hovering over the primordial waters (Genesis 1:2).
Similarly, when Jesus was baptized a dove, representing God's
presence as Holy Spirit, hovered above the waters of the Jordan River
(Matthew 3:16). Fire signifies God's protective, guiding, transforming

---

[89] Luigi Gambero, *Mary in the Middle Ages* (Kindle Edition: Ignatius
Press, 2010), loc. 987. The following source was cited. Rabanus Maurus,
Enarrationes in librum Numerorum 2, 20; PL 108, 688B; Luigi Gambero,
Mary in the Middle Ages (Kindle Edition: Ignatius Press, 2010), loc. 1208.
The following source was cited. Fulbert of Chartres, *Sermo* 4; PL 141, 321C;
TMPM 3:849-50.

[90] "3899. Lechem, 6440. panim or paneh" biblehub.com,
http://biblehub.com/hebrew/3899.htm,
http://biblehub.com/hebrew/6440.htm.

[91] Brant Pitre, "The Easter Vigil (Year B)," catholicproductions.com.

presence, among others, in the form of the Burning Bush, Cloud of Fire, and Fire descending on Mount Sinai. In the New Testament, the Holy Spirit descends upon the Mary and the Apostles gathered around her in the form of tongues of fire (Acts 1:14; 2:3), and St. Peter in his second letter states that "heaven and earth that now exist have been stored up for fire, being kept until the day of judgment and destruction of ungodly men (2 Peter 3:7 *RSVCE*)."

Even the priestly vestments served as signs of God's presence. Aaron the high priest was commanded to wear upon his forehead a turban with a plate of gold that is engraved with the words, "Holy to the Lord (Exodus 28:36 *RSVCE*)." This is immediately followed by the explanation that "and Aaron shall take upon himself any guilt incurred (Exodus 28:38 *RSVCE*)." As Pitre clarifies, Aaron, in his office as high priest stands between his people and God as a bearer of the people's

---

[92] Illustrators of the 1890 Holman Bible, "The Holy of Holies; illustration from the 1890 Holman Bible," https://commons.wikimedia.org/wiki/File:Holman_The_Holy_of_Holies.jpg, By illustrators of the 1890 Holman Bible [Public domain], via Wikimedia Commons.

sins.[93]

According to ancient Jewish tradition, Aaron and the Levites could not act as priests unless they are wearing their priestly garments. As the Talmud states, "When wearing their [appointed] garments, they are invested with their priesthood; when not wearing their garments, they are not invested with their priesthood."[94] In reference to Ezekiel, Pitre demonstrates that this is, in a way, explicit in Scripture, for Ezekiel states that the priestly garments "communicate holiness (Ezekiel 44:19 *RSVCE*)." In continuity and fulfillment of the Old Testament understanding of priestly vestments, Benedicts XVI writes, that "Liturgical vestments are direct reminder of those texts in which St. Paul speaks of being clothed with Christ "For as many of you as were baptized into Christ have put on Christ" (Gal 3:27)." He continues:

> For St. Paul, there is no question any more of masks and rituals, but of a process of spiritual transformation. … Vestments are a reminder of all this, of this transformation in Christ, and of the new community that is supposed to arise from it. Vestments are a challenge to the priest to surrender himself to the dynamism of breaking out of the capsule of self and being fashioned anew by Christ and for Christ. They remind those who participate in the Mass of the new way that began with Baptism and continues with the Eucharist, the way

---

[93] Brant Pitre, *Genesis and the Books of Moses: Unlocking the Mysteries of the Pentateuch,* MP 3, 18.

[94] "Zevachim, 17b," halakhah.com, http://halakhah.com/rst/kodoshim/41a%20-%20Zevochim%20-%202a-27b.pdf.

that leads to the future world already delineated in our daily lives by the sacraments.[95]

Not only was it believed that priestly garments communicate holiness, communicate the priesthood to the wearer but also that the garments stand for the entire universe, as the ancient Jewish historian Flavius Josephus testifies.[96] These vestments reflect the universal symbolism of three-part division of the temple. The Holy of Holies is a sign of heaven, while the other two temple divisions represent the sky, sea and land.[97]

---

[95] Joseph Cardinal Ratzinger, *The Spirit of the Liturgy*, trans. John Saward (San Francisco: Ignatius Press, 2000), 216-217.

[96] Flavius Josephus, "Antiquities of the Jews-Book III," chapter 7, 7, sacred-texts.com,   http://www.sacred-texts.com/jud/josephus/ant-3.htm. "And for the ephod, it showed that God had made the universe of four elements; and as for the gold interwoven, I suppose it related to the splendor by which all things are enlightened. He also appointed the breastplate to be placed in the middle of the ephod, to resemble the earth, for that has the very middle place of the world. And the girdle which encompassed the high priest round, signified the ocean, for that goes round about and includes the universe. Each of the sardonyxes declares to us the sun and the moon; those, I mean, that were in the nature of buttons on the high priest's shoulders. And for the twelve stones, whether we understand by them the months, or whether we understand the like number of the signs of that circle which the Greeks call the *Zodiac,* we shall not be mistaken in their meaning. And for the mitre, which was of a blue color, it seems to me to mean heaven; for how otherwise could the name of God be inscribed upon it? That it was also illustrated with a crown, and that of gold also, is because of that splendor with which God is pleased."

[97] Flavius Josephus, "Antiquities of the Jews-Book III," chapter 7, 7,

The Church Father Clement Alexandria affirmed the Jewish belief in the Temple and the vestments of the priest as representing the created universe and heaven. He does so in chapter six of the Stromata, titled *The Mystic Meaning of the Tabernacle and its Furniture.*[98]

---

sacred-texts.com,   http://www.sacred-texts.com/jud/josephus/ant-3.htm. "When Moses distinguished the tabernacle into three parts, and allowed two of them to the priests, as a place accessible and common, he denoted the land and the sea, these being of general access to all; but he set apart the third division for God, because heaven is inaccessible to men."

[98] Clement of Alexandria, The Stomata, or Miscellanies, in A Roberts, J. Donaldson & A. C. Coxe, *Fathers of the Second Century: Hermas, Tatian, Athenagoras, Theophilus, and Clement of Alexandria (Entire)* (Buffalo, NY: Christian Literature Company, 1885), Vol. 2, 452-254.

"chap. vi.—the mystic meaning of the tabernacle and its furniture It were tedious to go over all the Prophets and the Law, specifying what is spoken in enigmas; for almost the whole Scripture gives its utterances in this way. It may suffice, I think, for any one possessed of intelligence, for the proof of the point in hand, to select a few examples. Now concealment is evinced in the reference of the seven circuits around the temple, which are made mention of among the Hebrews; and the equipment on the robe, indicating by the various symbols, which had reference to visible objects, the agreement which from heaven reaches down to earth. And the covering and the veil were variegated with blue, and purple, and scarlet, and linen. And so, it was suggested that the nature of the elements contained the revelation of God. For purple is from water, linen from the earth; blue, being dark, is like the air, as scarlet is like fire. In the midst of the covering and veil, where the priests were allowed to enter, was situated the altar of incense, the symbol of the earth placed in the middle of this universe; and from it came the fumes of incense. And that place intermediate between the inner veil, where the high priest alone, on prescribed days, was permitted to enter, and the

Building upon this understanding of priests as sin bearers when they are wearing their priestly vestments, the letter to the Hebrews asserts that Christ is the high priest in the fullest sense who truly is the sin bearer, and as such atones for our sins as both priest and victim, as both priest and the sinless victim that is offered on our behalf (Hebrews 8-10). By taking on flesh in the Incarnation, Christ became the perfect priest who is a mediating bridge between God, Christ's divine nature, and man, Christ's human nature, united in the Divine Person of Jesus. Analogously, the clothing that Jesus assumed was human flesh, which unlike garments cannot be taken on and off at will.

As the vestments of the high priest Aaron represent all of creation that Aaron interceded for, especially on the yearly Day of Atonement when Aaron went into the Holies of Holies, representing heaven on earth, (Leviticus 16; 23:26-32) Christ, explains the Letter to the Hebrews "entered, not into a sanctuary made with hands, a copy of the true one, but into heaven itself (Hebrews 9:24 *RSVCE*)." The sacrifice He offered, adds Hebrews, was Himself, and the entire created world

---

external court which surrounded it—free to all the Hebrews—was, they say, the middlemost point of heaven and earth. But others say it was the symbol of the intellectual world, and that of sense. The covering, then, the barrier of popular unbelief, was stretched in front of the five pillars, keeping back those in the surrounding space. ... Now the high priest's robe is the symbol of the world of sense. The seven planets are represented by the five stones and the two carbuncles, for Saturn and the Moon. ... And they say that the robe prophesied the ministry in the flesh, by which He was seen in closer relation to the world. So, the high priest, putting off his consecrated robe (the universe, and the creation in the universe, were consecrated by Him assenting that, what was made, was good), washes himself, and puts on the other tunic—a holy-of-holies one...."

was represented not by physical garments but Christ's humanity, which Christ clothed himself in at the Incarnation. By His Incarnation, Death and Resurrection, Jesus perfectly interceded for the entire created, fallen world, by the flesh He assumed, by bearing human flesh as the one High Priest, and as victim, by his death on the cross where Christ offered himself on behalf of all creation to God.[99]

In describing Christ as the reconciler of all creation, as one who came to save all of creation, in particular human beings who are made in God's image and likeness, St. Paul writes:

> He is the image of the invisible God, the first-born of all creation; for in him all things were created, in heaven and on earth, visible and invisible, whether thrones or dominions or principalities or authorities—all things were created through him and for him. He is before all things, and in him all things hold together. He is the head of the body, the church; he is the beginning, the first-born from the dead, that in everything he might be pre-eminent. For in him all the fullness of God was pleased to dwell, and through him to reconcile to himself all things, whether on earth or in heaven, making peace by the blood of his cross. (Colossians 1:15-20 *RSVCE*)

Reflecting Paul's inspired teaching, the *Catechism* describes all of creation as in need of salvation. Due to Original Sin the "[h]armony with creation is broken: visible creation has become alien and hostile

---

[99] Brant Pitre, *Genesis and the Books of Moses: Unlocking the Mysteries of the Pentateuch*, MP 3 23.

to man (*CCC* 400)."[100] The original harmony of creation will be fully restored when Christ comes to judge the living and the dead. Christ initiated the restoration of creation by assuming flesh at the Incarnation as a "new creation," writes the Church Father St. Ephraim.[101] In becoming incarnate and rising from the dead Christ became "new leaven," writes Ephraim, who calls forth fallen creation to be harmonized and re-ordered according to the truth of Jesus Christ and God the Father in the love of the Holy Spirit.[102] By his passion, death, resurrection, and ascension to the Heavenly Father Christ acted as the perfect priest who atones for all of creation wounded by sin, thereby bringing to perfection the atoning sacrifices, and Day of Atonement of the Old Testament which, notes Hamilton, not only atoned for the high priest, and the people but also "inanimate objects as well by atoning for the sanctuary" specifically the Holy Place, the altar, and the tent of meeting which represent the entire universe in miniature (Leviticus 16:20).[103]

When Catholic priests celebrate the Mass, they participate in *persona Christi* in this reordering of fallen creation back to God. This does not mean that the priests by celebrating mass add anything essential to the saving action of Jesus Christ the High Priest. Rather,

---

[100] "Catechism of the Catholic Church, no. 400," vatican.va, http://www.vatican.va/archive/ccc_css/archive/catechism/p1s2c1p7.htm.

[101] Ephraim Syrus, "The Nisibene Hymns, Hymn XXXV, Concerning Our Lord, and Concerning Death and Satan 5," ccel.org, http://www.ccel.org/ccel/schaff/npnf213.txt.

[102] Ephraim Syrus, "The Nisibene Hymns, Hymn IX, 10," ccel.org, http://www.ccel.org/ccel/schaff/npnf213.txt.

[103] Victor P. Hamilton, *Handbook on the Pentateuch, Second Edition* (Grand Rapids: Baker Academic, 2005), 273.

the celebration of masses throughout history and across the world is the Church's sacramental way of applying the restored relationship of all of creation with God in time that Jesus obtained by his Incarnation, death and Resurrection. The Church applies Christ's saving grace as the extension of Christ's mystical body in time.

Along this line of thought, Fr. Menard, the founder of my religious society, affirms that God intends not only the Mass, which is to be, in the words of *Lumen Gentium*, the "font" and "summit"[104], but all "our being, our activities and our apostolate all continue the incarnation of the Son of God."[105] This means that, continues Menard, "We must love the world in order to save the world; believe in the same Father who created the world and who saved the world and collaborate with Him in order to complete this creation and this redemption."[106] "In addition," Menard teaches:

> since the body of Christ belonged to this creation, lived and was rooted in it, and is now transfigured and glorified, we can say that the whole world is associated to him and is likewise called to glorification and transfiguration. So that with the resurrection of Christ the entire cosmos finds all its beauty in the original plan of God. It's already done; it's a sure thing. But

---

[104] "Sacrosanctum Concilium, chap. 1, no. 10," vatican.va, http://www.vatican.va/archive/hist_councils/ii_vatican_council/documents /vat-ii_const_19631204_sacrosanctum-concilium_en.html.

[105] Eusebe Menard, *Authority as Service in the Society of the Missionaries of the Holy Apostles*, 1975, 4.

[106] Eusebe Menard, *Revolution of Love* (New Hope: St. Martin de Porres, 2016), 36.

it is for man, made lord of creation by God, to give his free assent to this.

It is the vocation of a priest to carry this deep yearning in his prayer and to help men and women to leave behind their sinful mentality in order to render themselves to God; then nature's own transfiguration can commence, bringing the whole of nature, animal, vegetable and mineral, all technical and scientific advances under the reign of God. Creation, instead of being at the service of evil, being used for the destruction and sabotage of true values, for the loss of minds and hearts, will serve the good – to the honor of God, the salvation of men, and the fulfillment of the whole universe.

This is then the priest's struggle as well. Far from leaving behind the world, creation, and progress, he must do everything to snatch them from the domination of evil. And his is confident, because Christ has risen. Easter is assured for the entire universe. When the priest celebrates the Eucharist, he celebrates with the universe itself.[107]

---

[107] Eusebe Menard, *At All Times in Every Age*, trans. Paul Schwartz (Chicago: Franciscan Herald Press, 1977), 78-79. Menard similarly wrote, "And it is a sublime vocation of the priest to immerse this anguish in his prayer and help men to discard their sinful mentality, in order to give themselves up to the divine action: in this way, the very transfiguration of men will have repercussions in Nature and will attract the material world, be it vegetal or animal, be it the world of scientific realizations, or technical ones, into the line of the Kingdom of God… So as to attain that Creation, instead

of serving evil and being used for destruction, for the sabotage of the true values, for the loss of intelligence and heart, shall end up serving good, for the glory of God, the salvation of mankind and the triumph of the Universe. This, then is the priest's struggle. It is not that of someone who complains of the world, Creation, or Progress, but rather the struggle of one who does all in his power to save them from evil. And he performs this task in total confidence … Since Christ has risen, the Easter Resurrection is ensured for the entire Cosmos. Yes, when the priest celebrates Mass, he celebrates it over the entire world." Menard, *The Charism*, 9; "This varied scenario of celebrations of the Eucharist has given me a powerful experience of its universal and, so to speak, cosmic character. Yes, cosmic! Because even when it is celebrated on the humble altar of a country church, the Eucharist is always in some way celebrated *on the altar of the world*. It unites heaven and earth. It embraces and permeates all creation. The Son of God became man in order to restore all creation, in one supreme act of praise, to the One who made it from nothing. He, the Eternal High Priest who by the blood of his Cross entered the eternal sanctuary, thus gives back to the Creator and Father all creation redeemed. He does so through the priestly ministry of the Church, to the glory of the Most Holy Trinity. Truly this is the *mysterium fidei* which is accomplished in the Eucharist: the world which came forth from the hands of God the Creator now returns to him redeemed by Christ." John Paul II, *Encyclical Letter Ecclesia de Eucharistia*, 2003, vatican.va, http://www.vatican.va/holy_father/special_features/encyclicals/documents/hf_jp-ii_enc_20030417_ecclesia_eucharistia_en.html, no. 8. "The Eucharist joins heaven and earth; it embraces and penetrates all creation. The world which came forth from God's hands returns to him in blessed and undivided adoration: in the bread of the Eucharist, [quoting Benedict XVI, Homily for the Mass of Corpus Domini (15 June 2006)] "creation is projected toward divinization, toward the holy wedding feast, toward unification with the Creation himself." Francis, *Encyclical Letter Laudato Si'*, 2015, vatican.va,

Section Questions

1. According to Gregory the Great and Benedict XVI how are the following correlated with one another? Heaven, Church, Night, Dawn, Day, Shadow, Image, Reality, Old Testament Times

2. As explained by Pitre, what are biblical indicators that the Tabernacle Moses constructed is a sign of Heaven? With specific reference to Scripture, include the following in your response: Comparison of Genesis 1 with Exodus 39-40, Hebrews 8:5, Gold Angels, Meaning of the Hebrew Word *Mishkan* (מִשְׁכָּן)

3. How are the three items housed in the Ark fulfilled by Jesus Christ? In your response include the following: names of the three items stored in the Ark - How each item is fulfilled by Jesus in a specific sense.

4. What is the symbolism associated with the Old Testament priestly vestments? With specific reference to Scripture, include the following in your response: Turban, Holiness, Creation, Sin, Bearer of Sin, Fulfillment in Jesus Christ.

---

http://www.vatican.va/content/francesco/en/encyclicals/documents/papa-francesco_20150524_enciclica-laudato-si.html, no. 236.

Leviticus

The priesthood is the focus of the Pentateuch's third book, Leviticus. According to Hebrews, when Christ established His priesthood, he did not ground it in the Levitical priesthood but rather in the more ancient, original priesthood of Melchizedek, in the priesthood of the Patriarchs, and renewed it as His one high priesthood (Hebrews 7). This more ancient priesthood was shortly lost after the worship of the Golden Calf. In establishing his new priesthood, Christ not only went back to an older priesthood but also fulfilled the newer Levitical priesthood above all their sacrifices by being the one, true sacrifice, the Lamb of God who takes away the sins of the world.

---

[1] James Tissot, "The Two Priests Are Destroyed," c. 1896-1900, https://commons.wikimedia.org/wiki/File:Tissot_The_Two_Priests_Are_D estroyed.jpg, James Tissot [Public domain], via Wikimedia Commons.

Section Questions

1. Place the following it their proper chronological order as revealed in time: Priesthood of Jesus Christ, Levitical Priesthood, Golden Calf, Order of Melchizedek

Sacrifice

Pitre pithily defines biblical sacrifice as "ritualized self-offerings which express communion with God or ... restore communion with God."[3] A clear example of communion with God being restored through sacrifice is the commandment of a yearly day of atonement "made for the sons of Israel once in the year because of all their sins (Leviticus 16:34 *RSVCE*)." On this day the high priest sacrificed and offered a bull both for his sins and a goat for the sins of the people (Genesis 16:11).

---

[2] James Tissot, "Noah's Sacrifice," c. 1896-1902, https://www.wikiart.org/en/james-tissot/noah-s-sacrifice/, James Tissot [Public domain], via Wikimedia Commons.

[3] Brant Pitre, *The Old Testament-A Historical and Theological Journey through Jewish Scripture,* MP 13.

An the yearly Day of Atonement, the blood of the sacrificed animals was sprinkled on the ark's mercy seat.[4] In addition, the high priest was to take another goat, "lay both his hands upon the head of the live goat and confess over him all the iniquities of the sons of Israel (Leviticus 16:21 *RSVCE*)." Afterwards, the goat was released into the wilderness where it symbolically carried the sins of people into the desert. These atoning actions were understood as restoring communion with God. Jewish tradition, Hamilton states in reference to Jubilees, related the scapegoat released into the desert to Joseph who was similarly rejected by his brothers and taken to across the Egyptian dessert by Ishmaelites. As Joseph brothers later beg Joseph for forgiveness so too are the Israelites on the Day of Atonement to seek God's mercy.[5]

---

[4] Victor P. Hamilton, *Handbook on the Pentateuch, Second Edition* (Grand Rapids: Baker Academic, 2005), 275.

[5] Hamilton, *Handbook on the Pentateuch*, 276. "And they dealt treacherously with him, and formed a plot against him to slay him, but changing their minds, they sold him to Ishmaelite merchants, and they brought him down into Egypt, and they sold him to Potiphar, the eunuch of Pharaoh, the chief of the cooks, priest of the city of 'Elew. And the sons of Jacob slaughtered a kid, and dipped the coat of Joseph in the blood, and sent (it) to Jacob their father on the tenth of the seventh month. And he mourned all that night, for they had brought it to him in the evening, and he became feverish with mourning for his death, and he said: 'An evil beast hath devoured Joseph'; and all the members of his house [mourned with him that day, and they] were grieving and mourning with him all that day. And his sons and his daughter rose up to comfort him, but he refused to be comforted for his son. And on that day Bilhah heard that Joseph had perished, and she died mourning him, and she was living in Qafratef, and Dinah also, his daughter, died after Joseph had perished. And there came these three mournings upon Israel in one month. And they buried Bilhah over against

According to another ancient Jewish tradition recorded in the Talmud, observes Pitre, a crimson thread was tied "to the gate of the Temple, and as the he-goat had reached the desert, the wool used to become [by miracle] white [with some exceptions]; as it is said: 'Though your sins be scarlet, they shall be as white as snow; though they be red as crimson, they shall become like wool' [Isaiah 1:18]."[6] The Talmud adds that, "The rabbis taught: Forty years before the Temple was destroyed, the lot never came into the right hand, the

---

the tomb of Rachel, and Dinah also his daughter, they buried there. And he mourned for Joseph one year, and did not cease, for he said, 'Let me go down to the grave mourning for my son'. For this reason it is ordained for the children of Israel that they should afflict themselves on the tenth of the seventh month -on the day that the news which made him weep for Joseph came to Jacob his father- that they should make atonement for themselves thereon with a young goat on the tenth of the seventh month, once a year, for their sins; for they had grieved the affection of their father regarding Joseph his son. And this day has been ordained that they should grieve thereon for their sins, and for all their transgressions and for all their errors, so that they might cleanse themselves on that day once a year. And after Joseph perished, the sons of Jacob took unto themselves wives." "The Book of Jubilees, From "The Apocrypha and Pseudepigrapha of the Old Testament" R.H. Charles Oxford: Clarendon Press, 1913," wesley.nnu.edu, http://wesley.nnu.edu/sermons-essays-books/noncanonical-literature/noncanonical-literature-ot-pseudepigrapha/the-book-of-jubilees/, chapter 34.

   [6]   Babylonian   Talmud: Tractate   Yoma: Chapter   6," jewishvirtuallibrary.org, http://www.jewishvirtuallibrary.org/tractate-yoma-chapter-6; Brant Pitre, *Genesis and the Books of Moses: Unlocking the Mysteries of the Pentateuch*, MP 3, 21.

red wool did not become white."[7] Since the Temple was destroyed in 70 A.D., the red thread that was tied to the Temple gate did not turn white at or around the time of Jesus' death and resurrection.

The two sacrificed goats, one offered in the Temple, representing heaven on earth, and the other sent into the isolating reality of the desert, representing hell, are, interprets Pitre, fulfilled by Jesus who both "descended into hell" and "ascended into heaven." (Apostles Creed) By His death outside of the Temple area in Jerusalem, Jesus takes upon all the sins of the world, perfectly atones for them, and

---

[7]   Babylonian   Talmud: Tractate   Yoma: Chapter   4," jewishvirtuallibrary.org, http://www.jewishvirtuallibrary.org/tractate-yoma-chapter-4; Pitre, *Genesis and the Books of Moses,* MP 3, 21.

[8] Internet Archive Book Images / No restrictions, "The art Bible, comprising the Old and new Testaments : with numerous illustrations," https://commons.wikimedia.org/wiki/File:The_art_Bible,_comprising_the_Old_and_new_Testaments_-_with_numerous_illustrations_(1896)_(14596068067).jpg.

fulfills the role of the second goat. By His ascension into heaven, where he intercedes as high priest before the Father (Hebrews 5:10), Jesus fulfills the first goat's role which was offered directly in the Temple. In this way, Jesus is both the high priest who atones for our sins by offering sacrifice and is the sacrifice itself as the innocent lamb, in other words the one who offers and the one who is offered.[9]

A sacrifice that represents communion with God entails eating a portion of what is offered. These communion sacrifices included cereal offering, where grain was offered and eaten (Leviticus 2:1-16; 6:14-23) and peace offerings, where an animal would be sacrificed, offered to God and parts of it would be eaten (Leviticus 3:1-17; 7:11-36). The book of Numbers adds the detail of a cereal offering that would also entail offering wine that would be mixed with the cereal to be offered (Numbers 15:4-10).

These sacrifices act as a substitution for those who are sacrificing, and they allow, explains Pitre, those who are offering the sacrifice to participate in the sacrifice.[10] This two-fold dimension of Old Testament sacrifice (substitution and participation) is fulfilled by Christ who both substitutes as the sinless one who takes our place and who invites us to participate in His one, perfect sacrifice. Christ does not merely offer a sacrifice that substitutes for us, but sacrifices so that our imperfect sacrifices can be joined to his perfect sacrifice.

The second letter of Peter affirms that Christ invites us to participate in salvation history with the assertion that we "participate in divine nature (2 Peter 1:4 *NIV*)." Christ's infinite, perfect sacrifice makes it truly possible to actualize the natural desire to participate in

---

[9] Pitre, *Genesis and the Books of Moses,* MP 3, 21.

[10] Pitre, *Genesis and the Books of Moses,* MP 3, 18.

sacrifice. As Pitre puts it, Christ did not sacrifice himself "so that we don't have to." Instead, He sacrificed himself so that we can also sacrifice in union with Him, so that our finite sacrifices that can never atone for an infinite sinful offense, due to God being offended, can be taken up into by the perfect, infinite atoning sacrifice of the Lord Jesus.[11] St. Paul in his letter to the Colossians explicitly affirms the Catholic teaching that we are invited by Christ to join our sacrifices with Christ's perfect sacrifice with "Now I rejoice in what I am suffering for you, and I fill up in my flesh what is still lacking in regard to Christ's afflictions, for the sake of his body, which is the church (Colossians 1:24 *RSVCE*)."

Reflecting St. Paul's teaching on participating in Christ's sacrifice the *Catechism* teaches:

> The cross is the unique sacrifice of Christ, the "one mediator between God and men". But because in his incarnate divine person he has in some way united himself to every man, "the possibility of being made partners, in a way known to God, in the paschal mystery" is offered to all men. He calls his disciples to "take up [their] cross and follow [him]," for "Christ also suffered for [us], leaving [us] an example so that [we] should follow in his steps." In fact, Jesus desires to associate with his redeeming sacrifice those who were to be its first beneficiaries. This is achieved supremely in the case of his mother, who was associated more intimately than any other person in the mystery of his

---

[11] Pitre, *Genesis and the Books of Moses*, MP 3, 18.

redemptive suffering (*CCC* 618).[12]

As Aquinas teaches in his commentary on Colossians, St. Paul and our participation in the redemptive sufferings of Christ do not mean that Christ's redemptive suffering was not perfect and needed to be added to. Rather, St. Paul is referring to the application of Christ's perfect act of redemptive suffering in Christ's mystical body extended through time.[13] As Dr. Dawn Goldstein pithily states, summarizing Aquinas, "Christ has completed His suffering for us, but He has not yet completed His suffering in us."[14] This later part, the application, takes place in time in the Mystical Body of Christ.

The sacrifices of the Old Testament not only pointed forward to Christ for fulfillment but also served as a way to purify the Israelites of their undue attachment to the goods of this world. Aquinas and St. Justin Martyr, comment Pitre, both explain this additional reason by pointing out that when sacrifice is offered to God the sacrifice is offered not because God is "in need of them." God specifically teaches, Aquinas observes, that "I desire not holocausts of rams, and fat of fatlings, and blood of calves, and lambs, and buck goats (Isaiah 1:11 *DRA*)." Sacrifices are offered not because God is need of them but because we are in need of sacrifice since offering to God that which we

---

[12] "Catechism of the Catholic Church," no. 618, vatican.va, http://www.vatican.va/archive/ccc_css/archive/catechism/p122a4p2.htm.

[13] Thomas Aquinas, "Super Epistolam B. Pauli ad Colossenses lectura Commentary on the Epistle to the Colossians," no. 61, dhspriory.org, http://dhspriory.org/thomas/SSColossians.htm.

[14] Dawn Eden Goldstein, *The Mystical Body and its Loving Wounds: Redemptive Suffering in Magisterial Teaching, Pre-Papal Writings, and Pope's Teachings as Private Theologians*, 1939-2015 (Mundelein: 2016), 76.

are attached to helps us to become progressively detached from what we excessively and idolatrously desire. As previously stated, during the Old Testament era, sheep, rams and oxen were sacrificed, since these animals were worshipped by the Egyptians whose idolatrous practices influenced the Jewish people who were living under Egyptian rule. The Jewish people, therefore, needed to be purified of these idolatrous practices. In part, the purification included sacrificing to God animals the Egyptians believed were sacred.[15] St. Justin Martyr writes, "God, accommodating Himself to that nation [Israel], enjoined them also to offer sacrifices, as if to His name, in order that you [the Israelites] might not serve idols."[16]

Section Questions

1. What do the bull and two goats in Day of Atonement ritual symbolize? With specific reference to Scripture, include the following in your response: Sin, Communion, Heaven, Hell, Fulfillment in Jesus.

2. With reference to Leviticus 11:45, how are sacrifices externalization of self-offering?

---

[15] Thomas Aquinas, "Summa Theologica," I-II, q. 103, art. 3, ad. 1-2, newadvent.org, http://www.newadvent.org/summa/2102.htm#article3.

[16] Justin Martyr, "Dialogue with Trypho," chap. 19, newadvent.org, http://www.newadvent.org/fathers/01282.htm.

Laws

Leviticus chapters 11-27 are on laws that are intended to form a holy people who are to be holy because God is holy. "[Y]ou shall be therefore be holy, for I am holy (Leviticus 11:45 *RSVCE*)." To the extent the people were striving for holiness their sacrifices were genuine externalization of offering themselves to God. The holiness laws included liturgical laws, moral laws, laws specific to the priesthood, and purity laws. The laws that often are the most misunderstood are the laws dealing with purity. For this reason, we will focus our attention on the purity laws.

Purity laws include legislation on food, purification of women, skin diseases, and bodily discharges. These laws on purity, Pitre explains, are not to be confused with moral laws. The reason they are enacted is for proper liturgical worship in which what is done has a sign value on various levels: as a sign of Eden, as pointing to future

---

[17]   Oren   Neu   Dag,   "Ten   Commandments,"   28   June   2007, https://commons.wikimedia.org/wiki/File:Lukhot_Habrit.svg, By Oren neu dag [CC BY-SA 3.0 (https://creativecommons.org/licenses/by-sa/3.0)], from Wikimedia Commons.

fulfillment, and as a sign of heaven. In connecting purity laws to worship Leviticus states, "Thus you shall keep the sons of Israel separate from their uncleanness, lest they die in their uncleanness by defiling my tabernacle that is in their midst (Leviticus 15:31 *RSVCE*)."

The various explanations for these laws, including their sign value, are multiple. Pitre provides six reasons for the food legislation: ethical, aesthetic, morphological, hygienic, theological, and ecclesiological.[18] These various explanations can be seen as complementary of one another.

According to the ethical interpretation of food laws these laws help the observer to be moral by restraining desire. Unrestrained desire, points out Shmuly Yanklowitz, led to Adam and Eve's first sin. In addition to restraining desire, the laws also encourage respect for animals and the environment. Respect for animals is evident in the laws that developed from God's command to Moses on slaughtering an animal, "you may kill any of your herd or your flock…as I have commanded you (Deuteronomy 12:21 *RSVCE*)."[19]

The aesthetic interpretation shifts the understanding of the food laws away from a moral concern. It does so by showing a correlation of animals considered clean and proper to eat with appealing animals and by correlating animals considered unclean and unfit to eat with animals deemed ugly. Consequently, toads, frogs and other reptiles are deemed unclean because of their lack of aesthetic appeal.

---

[18] Pitre, *Genesis and the Books of Moses*, 52.

[19] Schmuly Yanklowitz, "What is 'Ethical' Kashrut?" myjewishlearning.com, https://www.myjewishlearning.com/article/ethical-kashrut/; Rabbi Gersion Appel, " Kosher Slaughter: An Introduction," myjewishlearning.com, https://www.myjewishlearning.com/article/kosher-slaughtering-an-introduction/.

An interpretation related to the aesthetic is the morphological. According to this interpretation, out of respect of the natural order created by God that which does not naturally combine ought not to be.[20] "You shall not let your cattle breed with a different kind; you shall not sow your field with two kinds of seed; nor shall there come upon you a garment of cloth made of two kinds of stuff (Leviticus 19:19 *RSVCE*)." Similarly, animals that appear to be anomalies due the combination of that which is not ordinary in nature are classified as unclean and not to be eat. For example, a water creature that does not have both fins and scales, (Leviticus 11:10) since this is the norm, is considered an anomaly, deformed and impure, not to be eaten.

Another natural based explanation identified by Pitre is the hygienic interpretation. According to this interpretation some of the classification is explained by some creatures being classified as pure due to a belief that they are healthy to eat in contrast with impure, unhealthy to eat creatures. Sometimes, this interpretation can be problematic, comments Miller, since, he writes, "you're more likely to get sick eating undercooked chicken, which is always kosher, than undercooked pork."[21]

A subcategory of this hygienic interpretation categorizes creatures that are associated with life from creatures associated with death. Examples of creatures associated with death included vultures, which eat dead animals, and the carcasses of any dead animal (Leviticus 11:18, 39). Since God is life itself, He who is, touching that which is

---

[20] *New Collegeville Bible Commentary, Old Testament* (Collegeville: Liturgical Press, 2015), 362.

[21] Robert D. Miller II, *Understanding the Old Testament* (Chantilly: The Teaching Company, 2019), 141.

associated with death can render the Israelite impure and in need of ritual purification so as to best represent being images and likenesses of God who is life.

The last two interpretations that Pitre discusses are more directly spiritual interpretations: theological and ecclesiological. The theological, god-centered, interpretation helps to explain the classification of pure and impure creatures in relationship to the First Commandment that forbids idolatry. According to a theological interpretation, the Semitic people, the descendants of Noah's son Shem, were allowed to eat pork. Included among the Semitic people are the Hebrew people, whose Father is Abraham. The Hebrew also were allowed to eat pork. However, the Israelites, the descendants of Jacob/Israel, were forbidden by the Mosaic law to eat pork (Deuteronomy 14:8). From the perspective given by the theological interpretation this prohibition of eating pork is because God wants the Israelites to detach themselves from pagan practices, specifically idolatry, and in this case the Egyptian God associated with pigs, Seth.

In Egyptian mythology, Seth, in the "form of a black pig," injured Horus, another Egyptian god. Due to this injury, for Horus sake, "That is how the pig became an abomination to the [other Egyptian] gods, as well as men, for Horus' sake."[22] Although ancient Egyptians typically did not eat pigs for a variety of reasons, including its association with the violent God Seth, once a year an exception was made, states Buffie Johnson, when pigs were sacrificed on a full moon and then eaten. In addition, the female pig, the sow, was associated in a positive sense

---

[22] "Ancient History Sourcebook: Coffin Text: The Tale of Horus and the Pig, c. 1900 BCE," sourcebooks.fordham.edu, https://sourcebooks. fordham.edu/Halsall/ancient/1900horuspig.asp.

with the Nut, the Sky Goddess, who was explicitly even called "the Sow" and depicted as a sow.[23]

The second spiritual interpretation, the ecclesiological interpretation, is very similar to the theological interpretation, but in this interpretation greater emphasis is given to the Israelites as a people in relationship to the true God, as distinct from other people who worshipped false gods. The various food prohibitions, which distinguished the Israelites from their neighbors, helped to remind the Israelites of this important distinction, explains Pitre.[24] In accordance with the ecclesiological interpretation, Miller writes, "People who are called to a higher perfection—as the Israelites believed they were— were guided to eat according to categories deemed morally fit. They were urged to eat the more perfect animals."[25] By eating distinctly different food from people from surrounding cultures, the Israelites were constantly reminded that of their calling to a higher perfection as the first-born adopted son of God who are to lead the other nations back to God. Eating food unique to them as a group also helped to naturally strengthen their unity with one another.[26]

---

[23] Buffie Johnson, *Lady of the Beasts: The Goddess and Her Sacred Animals* (Rochester: Inner Traditions International, 1994), 266.

[24] Pitre, *The Old Testament*, MP 13.

[25] Miller, *Understanding the Old Testament*, 141. Miller cites the anthropologist Mary Douglas.

[26] Miller, *Understanding the Old Testament*, 141. "What I mean is brought out in an article called 'Matzah, Meat, Milk and Manna' from the 2011 Journal of Cross-cultural Psychology. It states: "Religions will often have common foods …to establish group membership and group solidarity. These common foods may also be unique foods or require distinct preparation rituals that serve to distinguish one religio-cultural group from another, especially in areas with multiple religio-cultural groups. These

From a salvation-historical understanding, further explains Pitre, the separation of the Israelites from the Gentiles, from the pagan nations, was done by God with the end of later uniting in Christ the Gentiles with the Israelites in the New Israel, the Catholic, universal Church. The unification, though, took place after the Israelites had become sufficiently detached from the idolatrous practices of the pagan nations.

A way God drew the Israelites to Himself and away from false Gods was by enacting temporary legislation that restricted the Israelites from eating certain foods and commanded them to act and dress in a distinctive manner. Jesus reminds his people that these regulations and related concessionary laws were temporary and not from the beginning, "from the beginning it was not so (Matthew 19:8 *RSVCE*)." After Jesus rises from the dead, ascends into heaven, and sends the Holy Spirit down upon his disciples, He reveals to Peter in a vision that the temporary legislation regarding food and, by implication, circumcision was no longer in force since the time of unification of God's children in the Catholic Church had come.[27] For this reason Peter, points out Pitre, states that "God has shown me that I should not call any man common or unclean (Acts 10:28 *RSVCE*)." By Jesus' blood on the cross all people, Gentile and Jew, have been cleansed, thus bringing an end to the separation of Israel from the Gentiles that the Mosaic law required.[28]

---

traditional and sometimes ancient socio-functional food practices persist because people also hold beliefs about divinely ordained fixed biological categories."

[27] Pitre, *The Old Testament,* MP 13.

[28] Pitre, *Genesis and the Books of Moses,* MP 3, 19.

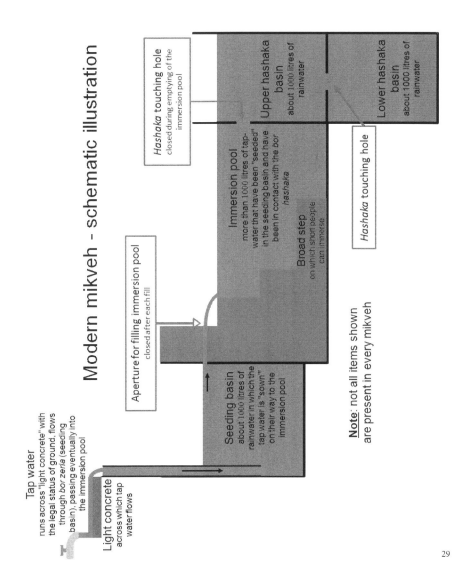

Modern mikveh - schematic illustration

Hashaka touching hole
closed during emptying of the immersion pool

Upper hashaka basin
about 1000 litres of rainwater

Lower hashaka basin
about 1000 litres of rainwater

Immersion pool
more than 1000 litres of tap-water that have been "seeded" in the seeding basin and have been in contact with the *bor hashaka*

Broad step
on which short people can immerse

Hashaka touching hole

Aperture for filling immersion pool
closed after each fill

Seeding basin
about 1000 litres of rainwater in which the tap water is "sown" on their way to the immersion pool

Note: not all items shown are present in every mikveh

Tap water
runs across "light concrete" with the legal status of ground, flows through *bor zeria* (seeding basin), passing eventually into the immersion pool

Light concrete
across which tap water flows

29

──────────

[29] ויקיגמדון "modern mikveh - schematic illustration," 16 November 2011, https://commons.wikimedia.org/wiki/File:Modern_mikveh.PNG, By ויקיגמדון [Public domain], from Wikimedia Commons.

The distinction between clean and unclean is not restricted in Leviticus to food and Gentiles. Certain actions and conditions also determine whether an Israelite is considered clean or unclean. These actions and conditions include, leprosy, nocturnal emissions, certain sexual relations, menstruation, and touching a dead body. To properly understand purity laws it is essential, asserts Pitre, not to confuse cultic purity with moral laws, especially moral laws, such as concerning adultery, that prohibit intrinsically evil acts.

This distinction, explains Pitre, becomes clear when it is pointed out that God never commands a person to commit what is deemed as essentially morally disordered. However, God does command certain actions that require a person to contract ritual impurity, such as touching a dead body. Afterwards, the impure person is to undergo a

---

[30] (File Upload Bot (Magnus Manske ויקישיתוף, " בור טבילה עם הדגשה על," חור ההשקה https://commons.wikimedia.org/wiki/File: %D7%94%D7%A9%D7%A7%D7%942.jpg, By (File Upload Bot (Magnus Manske ויקישיתוף) (ויקישיתוף) [CC BY-SA 3.0 (https:// creativecommons.org/licenses/by-sa/3.0)], via Wikimedia Commons.

time of purification.[31]

An explanation that can be applied to virtually all the ritual purity laws, provided by Pitre in reference to ancient Jewish tradition, is impure actions and conditions are associated with death, dying and decay. In the Old Testament, God, interprets Pitre, is revealed as a giver of life, a God who promotes life, a God who time and again inspires and supports a culture of life against a culture of death. God also is repeatedly revealed as one who calls his people out of a culture of death into a civilization of life.

Why sexual relations bring about impurity in both the husband and the wife can be explained in this life-death manner. When copulating, a man loses his semen, his seed, which represents life. Loss of life is an act of death. Since in marriage two are "one flesh (Genesis 2:24 *RSVCE*)," what the man experiences is participated by his wife. Consequently, both the man and the woman are deemed sexually impure after they engage in sexual intercourse since the sexual union entails loss of life. Hamilton, quoting B. Levine, observes that by deeming sexual intercourse as an act that causes ritual impurity distinguishes Israel from "most other ancient Near Eastern religions where 'everything that pertained to sexuality had a role in cult and ritual.'"[32] This distinction is present since Revelation teaches that God is life while creation only participates in life as an unmerited gift. By not ritualizing sexual intercourse into sacred rites, such as temple prostitution, as other Near Eastern religions typically did, the religion of the Old Testament makes a clear distinction even within the act whereby men and women bring forth new life, between life

---

[31] Pitre, *The Old Testament,* MP 13.

[32] Hamilton, 267.

participated in by creation and God as life itself (Exodus 3:14).

Right from the first chapters of Genesis God is revealed in this manner, as life and as one who creates a vast variety of life forms. Man and woman are created as the crown of created life forms by being related to the spiritual world of angels with their immortal souls and to the physical creation with their bodies. Sadly, Adam and Eve chose to sin, but are not consequently completely destroyed or corrupted by so doing. This is indicated by Eve being named the Mother of the Living even after she had sinned (Genesis 3:20). As pointed out by Ratzinger, this naming of Eve indicates that she has retained her dignity in relationship to life and needs healing from the wound of sin which brings forth misery, decay, and death.[33]

Sin, and its promoter the devil, is expressed corporately in the fourth chapter of Genesis which describes the beginning of a violent, polygamous, proud civilization whose father is Cain, guilty of fratricide. This civilization of man, as explained by St. Augustine in the *City of God*, with its desire for power and murderous inclinations tries to defeat by force or seduction the city of God, a civilization that promotes life, is God centered, signified by worship of the true God being at the heart of its life.

The founders of the city of God are multiple, since the citizens of this city of life at times are seduced by the contrary city of death with its violence, excitement, and power. Those identified as founders of the city of life include, according to Augustine, Abel, murdered by his brother, Seth, the third son of Adam, and Shem, the son of Noah, from which came forth the Semitic people, including the Hebrews, and later

---

[33] Joseph Ratzinger, *Daughter Zion: Meditations on the Church's Marian Belief*, trans. J.M. McDermott (San Francisco: Ignatius Press, 1983), 16.

the Israelites.

As a way to serve as a constant reminder to the Israelites that they are to be a people of life, a civilization that worships the God of life they are to refrain from certain actions that although not necessarily immoral are associated with death. If they perform actions that bring them into contact with death, such as touching a dead body, then, when required, they are to ritually purify themselves so as to be the most fitting signs of people who reflect God and life which God promotes. An idea that would, of course be almost unthinkable for the Israelites was to build a place to worship the God of life over graves since graves are connected with decay and death, precisely opposite of who God is. And yet, early Christians, comments Hahn, deliberately built Churches over the tombs of martyrs. They did so in the belief they were in continuity with the Old Testament affirmation of life by their belief that the bones of these martyrs are life giving due to their participation in the life of Christ who died and rose from the dead.[34]

The great care to affirm life since God is life is especially evident in the life of Old Testament priests who are more restricted by purity laws since they will be serving in the Tabernacle, and later the Temple, in which the presence of the God of life is particularly intense as contrasted with constant manifold loss of life, and cycles of death outside of the Tabernacle/Temple. The Tabernacle/Temple animal sacrifices, where an animal is killed, is explained by Leviticus in relationship to life since, "[L]ife of the flesh is in the blood; and I have given it for you upon the altar to make atonement for your souls; for it is the blood that makes atonement, by reason of the life (Leviticus

---

[34] Scott Hahn, *Signs of Life: 40 Catholic Customs and Their Biblical Roots* (New York: Doubleday, 2009), 179.

17:11 *RSVCE*)." The life of the animal is offered to God in the Temple which represents heaven on earth, a place where God, as described by Revelation, in reference to Isaiah, "will wipe away every tear from their eyes, and death shall be no more, neither shall there be mourning nor crying nor pain any more, for the former things have passed away (Revelation 21:4 *RSVCE*; cf. Isaiah 25:8)."

When the impurity laws are interpreted in relationship to life, it becomes evident that actions and conditions that are deemed as impure are related to the loss of life, or at least the decay of life: the loss of blood is deemed impure, for example in menstruations,[35] since life is in the blood (Leviticus 17:11), the loss of semen by nocturnal emissions since a man's semen contains life, the decay of flesh in leprosy etc. To even better represent the need to restore a person who has experienced a loss of life, such as emission of semen or menstruation where a woman loses blood, it is required to be purified in what Jewish oral tradition defines as "living water (Leviticus 15:13)," water that is spring feed or is part of a natural well.[36]

It may be objected that if Leviticus teaches that life is in the blood then why is it prohibited to "eat blood (Deuteronomy 12:16)," isn't this the eating of life, "do not eat blood; for the blood is the life, and you shall not eat the life with the flesh (Deuteronomy 12:23 *RSVCE*)"? Pitre addresses this objection by pointing to the New Testament in which

---

[35] Pitre applies this principle to explain why it took longer for a mother to be purified when giving birth to a baby girl as compared to giving birth to a baby boy. According to ancient rabbinical commentary, the reason is that a mother loses more blood, and hence life, when giving birth to a female than when giving birth to a male. Pitre, *The Old Testament*, MP 13.

[36] Mishhah – Ma. Mikva'oth Chapter 1," no. 8, Halakhah.com, http://halakhah.com/pdf/taharoth/Mikvaoth.pdf.

Jesus commands the drinking of his blood and the eating of his flesh, "he who eats my flesh and drinks my blood has eternal life (John 6:54 *RSVCE*)." Since human beings have been created to participate in the life of God and are, consequently, to develop civilizations centered around this worship of divine life, they are not to eat flesh with natural blood whose life is already in a state of decline, decay and death but rather only drink the supernatural blood, the blood of the risen Christ by which we participate in eternal life. In this sense, argues Pitre, Jesus fulfilled and did not reject the Old Testament law prohibiting the eating of natural blood.[37]

The life affirming reason for the purity laws greatly helps to explain why these laws were commanded. From this life perspective, and before moving on to the next section, I would like to briefly reflect why tattoos are prohibited (Leviticus 19:28). Pitre explains this with respect to belonging. People often mark something to indicate that it belongs in a certain place, or to someone.

For example, I may write my name on the inside of a book as a way of telling another that this book belongs to me. Similarly, tattoos both at the time of Leviticus and today indicate that a person belongs to a particular culture. To ensure that the Israelites see themselves as principally to God and his life affirming ways, Leviticus forbids the Israelites from tattooing themselves. The Sacraments of the Church, further explains Pitre, deeply fulfill the human desire to belong and fulfill God's covenant with Israel in which He binds himself to His chosen people.[38]

In affirming the indelible, permanent nature of Baptism,

---

[37] Pitre, *Genesis and the Books of Moses*, MP 3, 20.

[38] Pitre, *Genesis and the Books of Moses*, MP 3, 20.

Confirmation and Holy Orders the *Catechism* states, "As in the case of Baptism and Confirmation this share in Christ's office is granted once for all. The sacrament of Holy Orders, like the other two, confers an *indelible spiritual character* and cannot be repeated or conferred temporarily (*CCC* 1582)."[39]

Section Questions

1. Distinguish between purity laws and moral laws. Then, explain the purity laws according to at least three of the following reasons: ethical, aesthetic, morphological, hygienic, theological, ecclesiological, association with life and death.

Love

[40]

When asked by the Pharisees which of the many laws is the most

---

[39] "Catechism of the Catholic Church," no. 1582, vatican.va, http://www.vatican.va/archive/ccc_css/archive/catechism/p2s2c3a6.htm.

[40] Bagande, "Red-Outline Heart Icon," 16 May 2009, https://commons.wikimedia.org/wiki/File:Heart_icon_red_hollow.svg, By Heart_left-highlight_jon_01.svg: Jon Phillipsderivative work: Bagande (Heart_left-highlight_jon_01.svg) [CC0 or CC0], via Wikimedia Commons.

important Jesus responded, "You shall love the Lord your God with all your heart, and with all your soul, and with all your mind. This is the great and first commandment. And a second is like it, You shall love your neighbor as yourself. On these two commandments depend all the law and the prophets (Matthew 22:37-38 *RSVCE*)."

With these words Jesus quoted, with a difference, Deuteronomy chapter six, verse five, and Leviticus chapter nineteen, verse eighteen, and verse thirty-four.[41] As presented in the Greek and later English translation of Matthew's Gospel, Jesus slightly modified the Deuteronomy verses he quotes.

Deuteronomy commands the love of God in three ways: with the whole heart, soul, and **might** (מְאֹדֶךָ mə·'ō·ḏe·ḵā)[42]. Jesus, however, commands the love of God with the whole heart, soul, and **mind** (διανοίᾳ, dianoia), as pointed out by Pitre. An obvious textual reason is that Biblical Hebrew, which Deuteronomy was written in, does not have a separate word for mind. Instead, Biblical Hebrew uses the word *lev* (לֵב) for mind, heart, and will.[43]

However, the 250 B.C. Septuagint Greek translation of the Old Testament that was used by the New Testament writers translates the three Hebrew words in Deuteronomy 6:5 (לְבָב *levab*; *nephesh* נֶפֶשׁ; *meod* מְאֹד) with three Greek words (καρδίας, heart; ψυχῆς, soul;

---

[41] "...you shall love the Lord your God with all your heart, and with all your soul, and with all your might." (Deuteronomy 6:5 RSVCE) "You shall love your neighbor as yourself... The stranger who sojourns with you shall be to you as the native among you, and you shall love him as yourself; for you were strangers in the land of Egypt." (Leviticus 19:18; 34 RSVCE)

[42] "Deuteronomy 6:5," biblehub.com, http://biblehub.com/interlinear/deuteronomy/6-5.htm.

[43] "3820. leb," biblehub.com, https://biblehub.com/hebrew/3820.htm.

δυνάμεώς, might), and does not translate the Hebrew word *meod*, with the Greek work for mind, (διανοίᾳ) that is distinct from heart.

The reason for the difference could be, Pitre speculates, that Jesus, through the Greek translation, wants to further emphasize the interiorization of the law and therefore replaces the command to love with all our might, or strength, with a term that is more closely associated with the interior dimension of the person, the mind.[44]

Jesus does not change the command of "loving our neighbor as yourself" but rather give us the ability to fulfill this law. The ability to fulfill the law is by relying on the relationship Jesus offers us, by relying on the grace Jesus gives to us that we are to participate in with our hearts, souls, and minds.

The term "neighbor," further comments Pitre, is defined both in Leviticus and by Jesus in the same way. Both define neighbor as any person living near us, regardless if there are Jewish or non-Jewish. This is evident in Leviticus since after commanding that "You shall love your neighbor as yourself," Leviticus then includes with the term neighbor a non-Israelite stranger with the words, "The stranger [or immigrant] who sojourns with you shall be to you as the native among you, and you shall love him as yourself; for you were strangers in the land of Egypt (Leviticus 19:18; 34 *RSVCE*)."

Here, comments Miller, God cautions Israel not to become like their Egyptian oppressors by becoming oppressive themselves, for God has preferential love, but not exclusive, love for the widow, the orphan, and the stranger "foreign guest worker," in Miller's words.[45]

---

[44] Pitre, *Genesis and the Books of Moses,* MP 3 24.

[45] Miller, 127. "The specific term for foreigners here is translated as resident alien, which means a guest worker, or a foreigner who does not plan

Building upon this universal law of love that cares especially for those on the margins of society and providing us with the means to fulfill the law, Jesus commands to love all our neighbors as an expression of our love of God.[46]

Hamilton also demonstrates Jesus' Two Great Commandments are in continuity with the Old Testament. According to Hamilton, the Two Great Commandments are a summary of the Ten Commandments. Jesus' first commandment is a condensation of commandment one through three of the Ten Commandments that deal with human being's relationship with God, and Jesus' second commandment is a condensation of the remaining commandments that are on how humans relate to one another.

Furthermore, adds Hamilton, Jesus' response to the rich young man who asked him, "Teacher, what good deed must I do, to have eternal life (Matthew 19:16 *RSVCE*)?" indicates that the Two Great Commandments are to be integrated with one another and, consequently, are to inform one another. If this is not the case than either the display of loving God is false and merely a show or the act of loving one's neighbor is false since it is not formed by love, worship and belief in God. The goal of eternal life at the end of the rich young man's question implies that the rich man is concerned with love of God since God is eternal life. For this reason, Jesus responds by

---

on—and really could not become an Israelite citizen—but who is living there for an extended time. This is not about tourists; there weren't any. It's a guest worker without any rights or title. They didn't really have borders, so the difference between one nationality and another was about language, family, and a belief system."

[46] Pitre, *Genesis and the Books of Moses,* MP 3, 20.

encouraging him to follow commands four through ten which regulate human relations since these indicate that love of God is genuine and not hypocritical.[47]

Section Questions

1. With respect to one key word, how does Matthew 23:37-38 differ from Deuteronomy 6:4-5? Regarding interiorization, why is this difference important?

Liturgical Calendar

In a similar way as the Old Testament laws may be viewed as anticipations of Jesus as the living law, the Old Testament liturgical calendar may be interpreted typologically. We will reflect on the daily, weekly, and annual Israelite liturgy from this perspective.

---

[47] Hamilton, 191.

[48] "The National Library of Israel, Jewish New Year cards C HL 12," 23 July 2012, This file of Jewish New Year cards was donated to Wikimedia Commons by the National Library of Israel

as part of a collaboration project with Wikimedia Israel.

According to Exodus (29:38-46) and Numbers (28:1-8) twice daily, once in morning and the once in the evening, a lamb was to be sacrificed. This perpetual or continual sacrifice (Exodus 29:38), is called by in the *Mishnah* the *Tamid* (תָּמִיד) which means perpetual or daily.[49]   The early Jewish historian Flavius Josephus identifies the second sacrifice of the day as offered at ninth hour, or around 3 P.M.[50] From a Catholic perspective, even though the Temple was destroyed in 70 A.D., and, as a consequence, the Tamid sacrifices in the Temple ended, the perpetual sacrifice commanded by Exodus and Numbers continues in the Eucharist, the application of Jesus' "9th hour" perfect sacrifice on the Cross (Matt. 27:45; Mark 15:34). This one, perfect sacrifice of Jesus (Hebrews 10:12) is celebrated every time a mass is offered. Each celebration of the mass re-presents Christ's one, perfect sacrifice, and in so doing, enables us to truly participate in Christ's one sacrifice by joining our finite sacrifices with his infinite sacrifice.

Along with required daily sacrifices, the Israelites were also commanded to keep holy the Sabbath, the seventh day of the week. Sabbath observance recalls the day God "and hallowed (Genesis 2:2-

---

[49] "Mishnah Tamid," sefaria.org, https://www.sefaria.org/Mishnah_Tamid?lang=bi.

[50]   Josephus, "Jewish Antiquities," Book 14.65, attalus.org, http://www.attalus.org/old/aj_14a.html. "And any one may hence learn how very great piety we exercise towards God, and the observance of his laws, since the priests were not at all hindered from their sacred ministrations by their fear during this siege, but did still twice a-day, in the morning and about the ninth hour, offer their sacrifices on the altar; nor did they omit those sacrifices, if any melancholy accident happened by the stones that were thrown among them…."

3)" and rested (*shabath*, שָׁבַת).[51] The Hebrew word Sabbath contains the idea of resting since it comes from the Hebrew verb meaning rest (*shabath*, שָׁבַת). Leviticus (23:3) reaffirms what the Third Commandment requires, to keep holy the Lord's day. Numbers further states that during the Sabbath rest and celebration, "two male lambs a year old without blemish" are to be sacrificed and offered to God along with flour, oil, and "a drink offering (28:9-10 *RSVCE*)."

In Christianity, as attested in Acts (20:7),[52] the weekly celebration and sacrifice ceased being observed on the seventh day. Instead, God was weekly worshipped, and the sacrificial meal of the Eucharist was celebrated in a special way on the first day of the week, the day that Genesis describes God as creating. This is because Jesus rose "on the first day of the week" (Mark 16:9 *RSVCE*), signaling a new creation had begun, a creation springing forth from the grace given to us through Jesus. This grace, received by Baptism, restores human beings to the intimate relationship Adam and Eve had before falling into sin. Christians, therefore, fulfill the Third Commandment to keep holy the Lord's day by resting and abstaining from unnecessary labor on the first day of the week and not the last day of the week. Because Christ rose from the dead, Christians, asserts the Church Father Ignatius of Antioch, "no longer obser[ve] the [Jewish] Sabbath," in other words the Jewish day of rest, but rather "obser[ve] the Lord's Day."[53]

---

[51] "7673. Shabath," biblehub.com, http://biblehub.com/hebrew/7673.htm.

[52] Cf. 1 Cor. 16:2

[53] "The Epistle of Ignatius to the Magnesians," Chapter 9, newadvent.org, http://www.newadvent.org/fathers/0105.htm.

Interestingly, according to Leviticus, and other books of the Pentateuch, there are seven yearly feasts, three in the Spring, one in the Summer, and three in the Fall. The Spring feasts are Passover, Unleavened Bread, First Fruits. The Summer feast is Pentecost. The Fall Feasts are Trumpets, the Day of Atonement, and Tabernacles. In the Catholic faith, these seven feasts are believed to be fulfilled in Christ.

Passover, as explained earlier, comes from the Hebrew verb *pasah* (פָּסַח), meaning to pass over. This feast day remembers, and in a certain sense relives, the night shortly before the Exodus out of Egypt, when God sent a "destroyer," tasked with killing the first born. The destroyer, though, was commanded to pass over the Israelite houses and spare their first born provided that the Israelites marked their doorposts and lintels with the blood of an unblemished lamb. So as not to forget this momentous day, the Israelites were commanded to

---

[54] Baruch Zvi Ring, "Memorial Tablet and Omer Calendar - Google Art Project," 1904, https://commons.wikimedia.org/wiki/File:Baruch_Zvi_Ring_-_Memorial_Tablet_and_Omer_Calendar_-_Google_Art_   Project.jpg, Jewish Museum [Public domain], via Wikimedia Commons.

relive the first Passover by eating an unblemished lamb (Exodus 12:46). This meal anticipated the sacrificial meal of the Eucharist when Christians eat the risen body of Jesus, "the Lamb of God, who takes away the sins of the world (John 1:29 *RSVCE*)."

In describing Jesus' resurrection from the dead as a fulfillment of the Old Testament Passover, of the Exodus liberation from death by the destroying angel, Benedict XVI writes:

> On the night of Passover, the angel of death now passes over Egypt and strikes down the firstborn. Liberation is liberation for life. Christ, the firstborn from the dead, takes death upon himself and, by his Resurrection, shatters death's power. Death no longer has the last word. The love of the Son proves to be stronger than death because it unites man with God's love, which is God's very being.[55]

The annual, one day feast day of Passover, during which liberation from death is celebrated, was immediately followed by yet another yearly feast day, the feast of Unleavened Bread. According to the Pentateuch, for seven days the Israelites are to eat unleavened bread as a way to remember and relive the unrisen "bread of affliction" their ancestors ate when fleeing Egypt. (Deuteronomy 16:3 *RSVCE*)[56] "When Jesus instituted the Eucharist" states the *Catechism* "he gave a

---

[55] Benedict XVI, *Benedictus: Day by Day with Pope Benedict XVI*, ed. John Cameron (San Francisco: Ignatius Press, 2012), 120.

[56] See also: Exodus 12:15; Leviticus 23:5-8; Numbers 28:17; Deuteronomy 16:8.

new and definitive meaning"[57] to the unleavened bread that the Israelites eat during this feast day.

The third Spring feast day is First Fruits. During this liturgical celebration, the first sheaves are given to the priests who offer them to the Lord along with an unblemished lamb, and a cereal offering (Leviticus 23:9-14; Deuteronomy 26:1-4). In his First Letter to the Corinthians, St. Paul refers to Christ as a type of first fruit of all creation, "Christ has been raised from the dead, the first fruits of those who have fallen asleep. For as by a man came death, by a man has come also the resurrection of the dead (1 Corinthians 15:20-21 *RSVCE*)." As interpreted by Pitre, Jesus fulfills this feast as the New Creation's first fruit by his rising from the dead and ascending to his Father. Interestingly, the day the Old Testament priests offered the first fruits of the harvest corresponds to the day Jesus rose from the dead. According to Leviticus, First Fruits, is to be celebrated on the day after the Sabbath, or the first day of the week. (Leviticus 23:11) This is very same day that Jesus rose from the dead, points out Pitre.[58]

The Summer feast day of Pentecost is directly related to the previous Spring feast of First Fruits. According to the Pentateuch, Pentecost is to be observed seven weeks after First Fruits. More precisely, it is to be observed exactly fifty days after First Fruits. The Greek derived term of this feast day, Pentecost, is used in the Septuagint Greek translation of the Old Testament and means fiftieth to signify the fiftieth day after First Fruits.[59] The Hebrew word for this

---

[57] "Catechism of the Catholic Church," no. 1334, vatican.va, http://www.vatican.va/archive/ccc_css/archive/catechism/p2s2c1a3.htm.

[58] Pitre, *Genesis and the Books of Moses*, MP 3, 20.

[59] "Pentecost," etymonline.com, https://www.etymonline.com/word/Pentecost/

feast is Shavuot (שָׁבֻעוֹת) and simply means weeks to signify the seven weeks that make up the fifty days.

On Pentecost/Shavuot "a cereal offering of new grain (Leviticus 23:16 *RSVCE*)" is offered to God in thanksgiving for the harvest. On this day, as the Israelites thank God for His countless blessings they are commanded to "rejoice before the Lord (Deuteronomy 16:11 *RSVCE*)." The fulfillment of what this feast day spiritually promises, interprets Pitre, will be take place on Judgment Day when, stated St. Paul "there will be a resurrection of both the just and unjust (Acts 24:15 *RSVCE*)." This collective resurrection of the body will take place since Christ as "first fruit" has been raised from the dead (1 Corinthians 15:20).[60] On this day of harvest Jesus will say to the sound grain, or good sheep, "Come, O blessed of my Father, inherit the kingdom prepared for you from the foundation of the world." These will rejoice. To the rest, the weeds/bad goats, Jesus will say "Depart from me, you cursed, into the eternal fire prepared for the devil and his angels (Matthew 25:34, 41 *RSVCE*)." Judgment Day will be, in a certain sense, the final Pentecost in time as we know it. On Judgment Day the good will rejoice while the wicked will depart in misery and sadness. This Old Testament's manner or relating happiness with holiness which the New Testament builds upon often is unfortunately overlooked, comments Hamilton.[61]

The first Christian Pentecost took place on the Jewish feast of Pentecost (Acts 2:1). On that day, "three thousand souls (Acts 2:41 *RSVCE*)" were harvested for the Lord in preparation for their final

---

[60] Pitre, *Genesis and the Books of Moses,* MP 3, 20. Pitre cites Exodus 23:16, Leviticus 23:15-22, Numbers 28:26-31, and Deuteronomy16:9-12.

[61] Hamilton, 289.

harvest at the end of time when their bodies will be reunited to their souls.

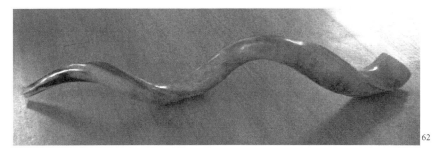

---

[62] Photo taken by Olve Utne., original. https://creativecommons.org/licenses/by-sa/2.5CC BY-SA 2.5 Creative Commons Attribution-Share Alike 2.5 truetrue / CC BY-SA (https://creativecommons.org/licenses/by-sa/2.5) "Yemenite-style shofar," https://commons.wikimedia.org/wiki/File:Jemenittisk_sjofar_av_kuduhorn.jpg.

[63] Matson Photo Servide / Public domain, "Yemenite Jew blowing the shofar, late 1930s," https://commons.wikimedia.org/wiki/File:

The three Spring feasts, and one summer feast, are followed by three Fall Feasts: Trumpets, Day of Atonement, and Tabernacles. Trumpets beings on the first day of the seventh month of a twelve-month calendar (Leviticus 23:23). According to Jewish tradition, this celebration marks the beginning of the liturgical New Year, as distinct from the beginning of the first calendar month (Exodus 12:2).[64] As the name indicates, the New Year begins with the blowing of trumpets (Leviticus 23:23-25; Numbers 29:1-6). Nine days later, on the tenth day of the seventh month, Trumpets is followed by the Day of Atonement (Yom Kippur, יום הכיפורים, Leviticus 23:27).[65]

According to Leviticus, on the Day of Atonement the High Priest, the successor of Aaron the first High Priest, is to "once a year with the blood of the sin offering of atonement he shall make atonement (Exodus 30:10 *RSVCE*)." Leviticus chapter sixteen further describes two goats and one bull that the High Priest was to offer to God. After one of the goats and the bull were killed, the High Priest sprinkled some of their blood on the mercy seat in the inner sanctuary of the Temple, called the Holy of Holies (*Kodesh Hakodashim*, קֹדֶשׁ הַקֳּדָשִׁים Exodus 26:33). The other goat, as explained previously, was to be sent out into the desert after the priest laid "both his hands (Leviticus 16:21 *RSVCE*)" on its head.

According to the Letter to the Hebrews, Jesus fulfilled the rituals that took place on the Day Atonement by entering into the reality that the Holy of Holies of the Temple signified. He did so by presenting as

---

Shofar_for_the_Sabbath_from_the_Matson_Collection,_ca._1934-39_ (LOC).jpg.

[64] "Jewish Calendar," Judaism 101, http://www.jewfaq.org/ holiday2.htm#NewYear.

[65] See also Leviticus 16 and Numbers 29:7-11.

the one true High Priest His crucified and risen self in Heaven, the Holiest of Holies, the fulfillment of the Holy of Holies (Hebrews 9:24). As explained by Pitre, Jesus fulfills the Old Testament sacrifices on the Day of Atonement in a variety of ways. Through his Ascension and glorification in Heaven Jesus as priest-victim fulfilled the role of the Old Testament High priest, and the sacrificed goat and bull.

In addition, in his role as priest-victim who was crucified outside of the gates of Jerusalem (Hebrews 13:12), outside of the city that represents life, Jesus fulfills the role of the scapegoat of the Old Testament who was banished into the desert, representing death, while symbolically carrying the sins of the people. Jesus, in contrast, actually bore the sins of all people and made atonement for all by his perfect sacrifice[66] whose salvific application is applied by the Church sacramentally as Christ's presence to human beings in time.[67]

The third Fall feast is Tabernacles, also called the Feast of Booths, (*Sukkot* סוכות), or, in Exodus, "the feast of ingathering at the year's end" since it takes place at the end of the agricultural season (Exodus 43:22 *RSVCE*; cf. 23:16). The other titles for this feast, Tabernacles and Booths, refer to stipulation for the Israelites to celebrate this feast by living for seven days in a temporary shelter that is to resemble the tent like structures the Israelites under the leadership of Moses dwelt in during their pilgrimage through the desert to the Promised Land (Leviticus 23: 42-43; Deuteronomy 16:13). Numbers describes in a

---

[66] Pitre, *Genesis and the Books of Moses,* MP 3, 20.

[67] Dawn Eden Goldstein, *The Mystical Body and its Loving Wounds: Redemptive Suffering in Magisterial Teaching, Pre-Papal Writings, and Pope's Teachings as Private Theologians*, 1939-2015 (Mundelein: 2016), 37. Dr. Goldstein refers to Pius XII's *Mystici Corporis* and Walter Kasper, *Jesus the Christ*: New Edition (London: T&T Clark, 2011), 192.

detailed manner the sacrifices that are to be offered to God during the seven-day observance of Booths (Numbers 29:12-39).

This feast can be spiritually interpreted as fulfilled by Catholicism in two ways. First, it serves as a reminder that in this life we are pilgrims who, in the words of an early Christian letter, "dwell in their own countries, but simply as sojourners. As citizens, they share in all things with others, and yet endure all things as if foreigners. Every foreign land is to them as their native country, and every land of their birth as a land of strangers."[68] In addition, the agriculture dimension of the feast may be seen as spiritually referring to the end of time when Christ with a "winnowing fork is in his hand …. will clear his threshing floor and gather his wheat into the granary, but the chaff he will burn with unquenchable fire (Matthew 3:12 *RSVCE*)." The Israelite joyful gathering in the harvest and remembering that God has liberated them from slavery is ultimately fulfilled in heaven as described by Revelation chapter seven, where a multitude of people from every nation are depicted happily praising and worshiping God (Revelation 7:9-10).

Section Questions

1. How did Jesus fulfill the Tamid sacrifices and the Sabbath? With specific reference to Scripture, include in your response the following: Perpetual, Resurrection, Creation

2. Choose two of the following feasts and explain how Jesus

---

[68] "The Epistle of Mathetes to Diognetus," chapter V, Roberts-Donaldson English Translation, Early Christian Writings, http://www.earlychristianwritings.com/text/diognetus-roberts.html.

fulfilled the feast in a specific Scripturally based sense. Passover, Unleavened Bread, First Fruits, Pentecost, Trumpets, Day of Atonement, Tabernacles.

Numbers

The fourth book of the Pentateuch is named by the Greek Septuagint Numbers (*Arithmoí* Ἀριθμοί) since chapter one begins with the first official counting of the number of Israelites, the first census. This section will focus on the following four aspects of Numbers: the Levitical Priesthood, the Nazarite vow, rebellion, and faithlessness.

[1] Henri Félix Emmanuel Philippoteaux, "The Numbering of the Israelites (engraving by Henri Félix Emmanuel Philippoteaux)," before 1894, https://commons.wikimedia.org/wiki/File:Philippoteaux_The_Numbering _of_the_Israelites.jpg, Henri Félix Emmanuel Philippoteaux [Public domain], via Wikimedia Commons.

Levitical Priesthood

As mentioned previously, the biblical notion of priesthood is traceable to Adam who was commanded by God to guard the garden in a similar way as, points out Hahn, the Levitical priesthood was to guard the tabernacle and later the Temple.[3] This is evident in that the Hebrew root verb, meaning guard (שָׁמַר, *shamar*) is used in both Genesis 2:15, with respect to Adam's responsibilities, and in Numbers 8:26, with respect to the Levitical priesthood's responsibilities.[4]

Adam's high priesthood remained after the Fall but in a wounded sense that Jesus healed, restored, and transformed in his one high priesthood as the Son of God. Between Adam's and Jesus's priesthood, the Old Testament describes, Hahn explains, the priesthood in two basic manners: patriarchal and Levitical. Genesis focuses on the

---

[2] "High Priest Offering a Sacrifice of a Goat (illustration from Henry Davenport Northrop. Treasures of the Bible. International Pub. Co., 1894.)," https://commons.wikimedia.org/wiki/File:High_Priest_Offering_Sacrifice_ of_a_Goat.jpg, By Illustrator of Henry Davenport Northrop's "Treasures of the Bible," 1894 [Public domain], via Wikimedia Commons.

[3] Scott Hahn, *Catholic Bible Dictionary* (New York: Doubleday, 2009), 302.

[4] Hahn, *Catholic Bible Dictionary*, 302.

patriarchal priesthood of Abraham, while Exodus, Leviticus, Numbers, and Deuteronomy focus on the Levitical priesthood.[5]

An essential difference between these two is that priests of the Patriarchal era included all fathers whose role in leading their families entailed a priestly dimension. Firstborn sons inherited their father's priesthood in a special way (Deuteronomy 21:15-17; 2 Kings 2:9). In contrast, beginning at Mount Sinai with the establishment of the Levitical priesthood, priests were limited to only one tribe, the tribe of Levi.[6] Because the Israelites fell into idolatry by worshipping around golden calf God decrees, "Behold, I have taken the Levites from among the sons of Israel instead of every first-born that opens the womb among the sons of Israel (Numbers 3:12 *RSVCE*)."

The Book of Numbers distinguishes within the tribe of Levites three clans: the Kohathites, the Gershonites, and the Merarites. The Kohathites served as priests, while the Gershonites and Merarites served as assistants to the priests (Numbers 4: 1-33). A high priest oversaw the service of both the priests and their assistants. The first Levitical high priest was Aaron. Aaron's high priesthood was passed down to his descendants and was a life-long ministry (Numbers 3:5-10; 35:25, 28).

All of these kinds of priests (high, ordinary, and assistants) are understood as being set apart from the people (Exodus 29:1). The Hebrew root word used for this distinction is *kadesh* (קָדֵשׁ) to consecrate, set aside, make holy.[7] Building upon this concept of

---

[5] Hahn, *Catholic Bible Dictionary*, 725.

[6] Hahn, *Catholic Bible Dictionary*, 725. Hahn references Job 1:5 as representative of patriarchal priesthood where fathers were naturally priests of their families.

[7] "6942. Qadash," biblehub.com, http://biblehub.com/hebrew/6942.htm.

priesthood of being set aside, comments Pitre, Jesus consecrated his disciples and set them apart from others, "Sanctify them in the truth (John 17:19 *RSVCE*)."[8] The Greek New Testament word (*hagiazo*, ἁγιάζω) that is translated by "sanctify" is also, observes Pitre, used in Exodus (*hagiasai*, ἁγιάσαι) for when priests are ordained (Exodus 29:1), which in turn is a translation of the Hebrew infinitive to consecrate, *likadesh* (לְקַדֵּשׁ).[9]

Another indication of the establishment of a New Testament priesthood that is in continuity, but with a difference, from the Old Testament priesthood is evident in the process by which another person was chosen to replace Judas's role among the Twelve Apostles. The Apostles cast lots to determine who would replace Judas (Acts 1:26). According to Old Testament practice, explains Pitre, (1 Chronicles 24) the various priestly roles were likewise determined by sacred lots being cast. The practice of casting lots to determine priestly roles was also used to determine when Zechariah, the father of John the Baptist, would serve in the Temple (Luke 1:8).[10]

In continuity with the Old Testament priesthood, but also with difference, the Church gradually developed the New Testament new priesthood. As the Church progressed in time the Holy Spirit inspired early Christians to explicitly interpret the three-fold order of high priest, priests, and servants of the priests as fulfilled by a corresponding three-fold order of bishop, priests, and deacons. One ancient witness of this interpretation is from Christian text the

---

[8]   Brant   Pitre,   "The   Seventh   Sunday   of   Easter   (Year   B),"
catholicproductions.com.

[9] Pitre, "The Seventh Sunday of Easter (Year B)."

[10] Pitre, "The Seventh Sunday of Easter (Year B)."

Didascalia Apostolorum, "For they are your high priests [cf. Did 13.3]; but the priests and Levites now are the presbyters and deacons… but the Levite and high priest is the bishop."[11]

[12]

Once the Church was sufficiently distanced in time from the Old Testament priesthood there was less of a need to use terminology that would confuse people's understanding of the New Testament priesthood that uses the terms *diakonos* (διάκονος) meaning servant, presbyter (πρεσβύτερος), meaning elder, and *epískopos* (ἐπίσκοπος), meaning overseer, with the Old Testament priesthood of *cohen* (כֹּהֵן)

---

[11] "Didascalia Apostolorum," chapter ix, earlychristianwritings.com, http://www.earlychristianwritings.com/text/didascalia.html.   Also,   see Clement's *Letter to the Corinthians* chapters 32, 36, 40, 41, 43, 44.

[12] Needham, George C. (from old catalog), "The Jewish tabernacle and priesthood," 1874, https://commons.wikimedia.org/wiki/File:The_Jewish_tabernacle_and_priesthood_(1874)_(14758999626).jpg, By Internet Archive Book Images [No restrictions], via Wikimedia Commons.

translated in Greek as *hiereus,* ἱερεύς (Exodus 35:19). An important exception to this terminology, among a few others, is when Jesus is identified as a priest. When this occurs, Jesus is referred to as a ἀρχιερέα, as a high priest, a word that is based on the Greek word for priest, *hiereus,* ἱερεύς, which in turn is a translation in the Septuagint of the Hebrew word for priest, *cohen* (כֹּהֵן).

As time progressed, the Church used the term priest, *sacerdotes* in Latin and *hiereus,* ἱερεύς in Greek when referring to the ordained. By the fourth century, the practice of calling the ordained "priests" instead of using the New Testament terminology for the ordained was common, while not forgetting that there is only one New Testament priest (Hebrews 4:14) Jesus Christ. Jesus's one priesthood is participated in two different kinds, ministerially by ordained priests, and by the non-ordained by virtue of their baptism.[13] As the one priest, as the one mediator between God and human beings (sacerdos/ ἱερεύς hiereús) Jesus replaced the Old Testament priesthood, with its many priests, and in its place, comments Ronald D. Witherup, Jesus became the one priest that all are called by God to participate in.[14]

When the typological relationship of the Levitical priesthood to the New Testament priesthood is used to interpret the New Testament ministry, even when the term "priest" is not explicitly used by the New Testament for the reasons given above, difficult to interpret passages of Scripture become clearer. For example, as Pitre explains, James' request that Christians "confess your sins to one another (James 5:16

---

[13] John W. O'Malley, *A History of the Popes* (Lanham: Sheed & Ward, 2010), kindle locations 357-361.

[14] Ronald D. Witherup, "The Theology of Priesthood and Implications for Seminary Ministry," 13th Institute for Formators, Theological College, Washington, D.C. June 8th, Lecture Notes.

RSVCE)" may be interpreted in light of the New Testament's fulfillment of the Old Testament priesthood including the relationship of the Old Testament priesthood's relationship to the confession of sins. Leviticus 19:20-22 and Numbers 5:5-11 both describe confession of sins and restitution in relationship to priests (Numbers 5:5-11).[15]

The referred to passage from Leviticus brings out a dimension of the priesthood that is essential for understanding both Testaments' priesthood. Here it states that "the priest shall make atonement" for the sins committed and the sins "committed shall be forgiven to him (Leviticus 19:22 *RSVCE*). In describing priests as atoners of sin Leviticus also states, "it is a thing most holy and has been given to you [the Levitical priests] that you may bear the iniquity of the congregation, to make atonement for them before the Lord (Leviticus 10:17 *RSVCE*)."

The New Testament identifies Jesus as the high priest who perfectly atones for sin (Hebrews 10:12). The New Testament priesthood participates in this atoning ministry of Jesus by applying Jesus' perfect atonement to the mystical body as the Church traverses through time. Pitre points to the patron of diocesan priests, St. John Vianney, as one who deeply understood his participatory role in Christ's atoning sacrifice for sins. According to Abbe Trochu's account:

> When once Curé d'Ars had obtained from his penitents the indispensable signs of amendment, he showed himself exceedingly gentle in the application of the sacramental

---

[15] Brant Pitre, *Genesis and the Books of Moses: Unlocking the Mysteries of the Pentateuch*, MP 3 22.

penance. 'They reproach me with it,' he confided to Frere Athanase, 'but can I really be heard on people who come from so far, and who, in order to do so, have made so many sacrifices?' 'Were I to impose severer penances, I should discourage them,' he said another time. 'But how can we strike a happy middle course in this matter?' a brother priest inquired. 'My friend,' the saint replied, 'here is my receipt: I give them a small penance and the remainder I myself perform in their stead.'"[16]

The concept of a priest who sacrifices for the people's sins is present in the Old Testament rite of ordination of laying on of hands. In describing this rite, the book of Numbers states:

> When you present the Levites before the Lord, the sons of Israel shall lay their hands upon the Levites, and Aaron shall offer the Levites before the Lord as a wave offering from the sons of Israel, that it may be theirs to do the service of the Lord. Then the Levites shall lay their hands upon the heads of the bulls; and you shall offer one for a sin offering and the other for a burnt offering to the Lord, to make atonement for the Levites (Numbers 8:10-12 *RSVCE*; Cf. Numbers 27:18; Deuteronomy 34:9).

Pitre points out that the laying hands upon the heads of bulls

---

[16] Abbé François Trochu, *The Curé D'Ars St. Jean-Marie-Baptiste Vianney*, trans. Bertram Wolferstan (Charlotte: TAN Books, 2013), 316-317; Pitre, *Genesis and the Books of Moses*, MP 3, 19.

signified that the bull had been chosen to be sacrificed to God and, similarly, the laying hands upon a Levite during his ordination ceremony meant that the Levite was being sacrificed to God as a priest.[17] One way the Levitical priests sacrificed to God was by dying to the connection to the land of Israel, by not receiving an inheritance of land. According to Deuteronomy "the Lord set apart the Tribe of Levi to carry the ark of the covenant of the Lord, to stand before the Lord to minister to him…. Therefore, Levi has no portion or inheritance with his brothers; the Lord is his inheritance (10:8-9 *RSVCE*)."

As explained by Pitre, the Levites' inheritance of God himself demonstrates that the Israelites did not understand the Promised Land of Canaan as the highest good. Instead, God is the highest good. To believe otherwise would be to fall into the sin of idolatry, forbidden by the First Commandment. The Levites lack of a portion of the Promised Land served as a reminder to the Israelites that the Promised Land is only a sign of a greater world to come, not fully attainable in this life, the heavenly realm that the Holy of Holies in the Temple comes closest to representing.[18]

The Old Testament understanding of priest as victim, of priest as one who is called to sacrificially die, at least spiritually, intensified in the New Testament with the identification of Jesus as the "Lamb of God who takes away the sins of the world (John 1:29 *RSVCE*)." Ordination into the priesthood of Jesus Christ was passed on by laying on of hands, and this practice continues into today. The practice of perpetual celibacy and continence of Catholic priests is a way to

---

[17] Pitre, *Genesis and the Books of Moses*, MP 3 22.
[18] Pitre, *Genesis and the Books of Moses*, MP 3 23.

practically participate in the intensely sacrificial nature of the priesthood of Jesus Christ, who was a lifelong celibate and perfectly continent (Acts 13:3; 1 Timothy 5:22).

Jesus did not only fulfill the Old Testament priesthood by intensifying its demands but also fulfilled the Old Testament priesthood by instituting a non-Levitical priesthood, a priesthood that is not tribally based, not based upon physical birth. As the letter to the Hebrews states in reference to Christ, "You are a priest forever, according to the order of Melchizedek (Hebrews 5:6 *RSVCE*)." Hahn proposes that Luke subtly affirms Jesus's non-Levitical priesthood by the omission of any reference to Mary and Joseph paying the required redemption fee of five shekels to a Levite who replaces the firstborn son's service to God (Numbers 3:45-47; 8:15-16). According to Hahn, this may indicate "that Jesus is consecrated to the service of the Lord [according to the more ancient patriarchal priesthood of Melchizedek] instead of being 'bought back' by his parents."[19]

Even though Numbers describes the later, restricted, Levitical priesthood, all Israelites could be specially consecrated, set apart for God's service, by taking the Nazirite vow for a set number of days. This temporary or lifelong vow[20] consists of not eating or drinking anything made from grapes (including seeds, skins, pulp, juice, and wine), not cutting one's hair, and not going "near a dead body (Numbers 6:6 *RSVCE*)." The essence of these vows, identifies Hamilton, are that the "Nazirites are to be disciplined in their appetites, distinctive in their

---

[19] Hahn, *Catholic Bible Dictionary*, 728.

[20] Victor P. Hamilton, *Handbook on the Pentateuch, Second Edition* (Grand Rapids: Baker Academic, 2005), 312.

appearance, [and] discreet in their associations."[21] Men and women who take religious vows directly to God and diocesan priests a solemn promise of celibacy to God through their bishop are likewise to practice asceticism, be distinctive in their appearance, and practice discretion and prudence in whom they associate with while always keeping in mind Jesus's example and their participation in His life.

Numbers chapter six ends with Aaron priestly blessing through which God, not Aaron blesses the people. Aaron, remarks Hamilton, is only the "transmitter, not author"[22] of the priestly blessing.

The Aaronic Priestly Blessing

> The Lord bless you and keep you: The Lord make his face to shine upon you and be gracious to you: The Lord lift up his countenance upon you, and give you peace. (Numbers 6:24-26 RSVCE)

Section Questions

1. Compare and contrast the Levitical priesthood with the New Testament Priesthood of Jesus Christ. With specific reference to Scripture, include in your response the following: Kohathites, Gershonites, Merarites, cohen/hiereus, diakonos, presbyter, episkopos, casting lots, high priest.

2. Explain how two of the following are foreshadowed in the Old

---

[21] Hamilton, 313.
[22] Hamilton, 313.

Testament in a specific sense. Confessions of Sins to Priests, Priests Atone for Sins, Priests Sacrifice Goods of This World for God the Highest Good, Ordination by Laying on of Hands, Religious Vows

Rebellion

23

Resentment and envy of those who were chosen by God for priestly leadership occurred. Out of spiritual envy, Moses' brother, Aaron, and their sister, Miriam, complained, "Has the Lord indeed spoken only through Moses? Has he not spoken through us also (Numbers 12:2 *RSVCE*)?" In punishment, God turned Miriam into a snow-white leper. After Moses asks God to heal Miriam, God agrees but with the condition that Miriam is banished from the camp for

---

[23] James Tissot, "The Brazen Serpent, as in Numbers 21:9," c. 1903, https://commons.wikimedia.org/wiki/File:Tissot_The_Brazen_Serpent.jpg, James Tissot [Public domain], via Wikimedia Commons.

seven days (Numbers 12:1-16).

A similar, and more prominent, rebellion occurred in the revolt of Korah. This rebellion of 250 men was led by the Levite Korah, a cousin of Moses and Aaron (Numbers 16:21). They rejected the authority of Moses and Aaron by trying to cause all the other Israelites to resent and reject Moses and Aaron with the words, "You have gone too far! For all the congregation are holy, every one of them, and the Lord is among them; why then do you exalt yourselves above the assembly of the Lord (Numbers 16:3 *RSVCE*)?" God's response to the rebels was even severer than the punishment Miriam received. In confirmation of Moses' and Aaron's God given priestly authority, God split apart the ground below the rebels and they were swallowed up in a fiery chaos of earth and fire.

The punishment served as a "reminder to the sons of Israel, ... that no one who is not a priest, who is not of the descendants of Aaron, should draw near to burn incense before the Lord, lest be become as Ko'rah and as his company (Numbers 16:40 *RSVCE*)." It also may serve as a reminder for all time that God, comments Hamilton, grants different missions to different people.[24] We are all equal in the sense that we are all his adopted children, but we are not given the same blessings, responsibilities, missions and crosses, nor are we completely free to choose what these will be since these are portioned out according to God's divine plan.

In applying Korah's punishment in another way to our times, Pitre remarks that the divine punishment of physical death for rejecting authority appointed by God carries over into the New

---

[24] Victor P. Hamilton, *Handbook on the Pentateuch, Second Edition* (Grand Rapids: Baker Academic, 2005), 332.

Testament where spiritual death and not simply physical death is the punishment as the Letter of Jude indicates (Jude 8-13). [25]

The book of Numbers describes two times in which the Israelites as a whole rebelled against Moses' authority, and ultimately against God for bringing them out of Egypt into the desert. Numbers chapter fourteen describes "all the sons of Israel" murmuring "against Moses and Aaron (Numbers 14:2 *RSVCE*)." In complaining, the Israelites even question whether "it would not be better for us to go back to Egypt (Numbers 14:3 *RSVCE*)?" This questioning occurs after the Israelites are given a discouraging report by the majority of twelve Israelite spies sent into the Promised Land. According to the majority report, the inhabitants of the land, the Amalekites, will prevent the Israelites from taking up residence. In response to the Israelites doubt, God tells Moses that he will send a plague upon the Israelites and will disinherit them (Numbers 14:12). When Moses intercedes for his people, God lessens the punishment by stating that only Caleb and Joshua, will cross over into the Promised Land. (Caleb and Joshua were Israelites spies who did not support the majority report.) All other currently living Israelites, including Moses and Aaron, will die in the wilderness where they will wander about for forty years. God punishes them with their own fearful refusal to enter the Promised Land. As Hamilton points out, they are punished by God allowing them to experience what they desired. [26]

In applying the complaining Israelites to our own time, Pitre

---

[25] Brant Pitre, *Genesis and the Books of Moses: Unlocking the Mysteries of the Pentateuch*, MP 3.

[26] Victor P. Hamilton, *Handbook on the Pentateuch, Second Edition* (Grand Rapids: Baker Academic, 2005), 329.

convincingly demonstrates that in many ways we act like the Israelites did. We do so by harping on issues such as the moral disorder of our present generation is, the corruption of governments, the systemic destruction of the environment, poor quality public education, the lack of civility etc. Sometimes this complaining can be constructive but more often than not it becomes destructive and futile by causing people to expend their energy needlessly, to grow in resentment and rage at our present predicament, while, forgetting that God is with us as Emmanuel (עִמָּנוּאֵל)., which literally means in Hebrew the Lord is with us. God is with us even more than He was with the Israelites because we believe that he has taken on flesh in the person of Jesus Christ who by his Resurrection from the dead has conquered sin and death.

Jesus, as our new Joshua who leads us into the Promised Land of heaven does not want us to become depressed at the condition of the world. Instead, asserts Pitre, He demands, "In the world you have tribulation; but be of good cheer, I have overcome the world (John 16:33 *RSVCE*)." St. Paul repeats this teaching of Jesus with, "God loves a cheerful giver (2 Corinthians 9:7 *RSVCE*)." With joy, we are to face the trials and tribulations that this world offers because we believe that Jesus as Emmanuel is with us, has conquered sin, death, Satan, and offers us permanent citizenship to a heavenly kingdom. Growth in sadness and fear when facing our predicament in this world may serve as an indicator of an excessive attachment to earthly goods, of an excessive fear of suffering and of an excessive fear losing money, and prestige. This excessive attachment can lay camouflaged behind apparently pious complaints about the world's condition.

As just stated, sadness that appears holy may be caused not by

Godly reasons but rather by the very mundane reason that we love earthly politics, earthly wealth, and physical health, more than the promised heavenly homeland and a spiritualized life. Finally, Satan can trick us to become so enmeshed in fighting to improve our political, economic, and social context that we forget that, "we are not contending against flesh and blood, but against the principalities, against the powers, against the world rulers of this present darkness, against the spiritual hosts of wickedness in the heavenly places (Ephesians 6:12 *RSVCE*)." We are to fight against these fallen angelic beings who influence world politics, reminds Pitre, with cheerful confidence as we take up "the shield of faith, with which [we] can quench the flaming darts of the Evil One (Ephesians 6:16 *RSVCE*)."[27]

Numbers chapter twenty-one describes a second nation-wide rebellion of the Israelites. Once again they speak "against God and against Moses. 'Why have you brought us up out of Egypt to die in the wilderness? For there is no food and no water, and we loathe this worthless food'(Numbers 21:5 *RSVCE*)." God responds by sending deadly, venomous serpents that bite the people. Once again Moses intercedes for the people. He is instructed by God to make a serpent out of bronze and set it before the people. God promises that simply gazing upon the bronze serpent will heal those bitten by the deadly poisonous serpents.

The gospel of John compares the healing bronze serpent that was set before the Israelites with Jesus, "And as Moses lifted up the serpent in the wilderness, so must the Son of man be lifted up, that whoever believes in him may have eternal life (John 3:14-15 *RSVCE*)." Similar to the bronze serpent that God uses to restore physical life to the

---

[27] Pitre, *Genesis and the Books of Moses*, MP 3 22.

Israelites, Christ was lifted up on the cross to restore spiritual life that we had lost due to the poison of sin. A more hidden typological reference that Pitre identifies is a Eucharistic one. The food the Israelites reject as "worthless" is the manna that God sent down upon them. This manna points to the Eucharist, the true heavenly food that the Heavenly Father sent "in the fullness of time." Jesus makes this typological connection with, "Truly, truly, I say to you, it was not Moses who gave you the bread from heaven; my Father gives you the true bread from heaven…I am the bread of life (John 6:32, 35 *RSVCE*)." The food that nourishes us and gives us needed strength to persevere in our pilgrimage to the heavenly homelands is the Eucharist. May we not fall into a similar sin of the Israelites of taking for granted the nourishment that God provides for us and even rejecting it as "worthless."[28]

Section Questions

1. Why specifically did Korah rebel and, with respect to authority, vocations, and envy what does this rebellion teach us today?

2. Why specifically did the Israelites rebel in Numbers 14, and, with providence, hope, and criticism what does this rebellion teach us today?

3. Why specifically did the Israelites rebel in Numbers 22, and, how, in specific sense, did Jesus fulfill what Moses created for

---

[28] Pitre, *Genesis and the Books of Moses*, MP 3 23.

the Israelites to gaze at?

Faithlessness

[29]

In the previously described accounts of rebellion, Moses maintained faith in God while his fellow Israelites failed in faith and then rebelled. However, Moses himself also failed in faith. Numbers chapter twenty describes this faithlessness. Often, Pitre explains, this passage is confused with a similar account of a different event described in Exodus chapter seventeen.[30]

Exodus chapter seventeen describes the Israelites' shortly after their escape from Egypt, in place where they are camping, "at Reph'idim (Exodus 17:1 *RSVCE*)." At Reph'idim they complain to Moses that they are thirsty. "Why did you bring us up out of Egypt, to kill us and our children and our cattle with thirst (Exodus 17:3

---

[29] James Tissot, "Moses Strikes the Rock," between circa 1896 and circa 1902, https://commons.wikimedia.org/wiki/File:Tissot_Moses_Strikes_the_Rock.jpg, James Tissot [Public domain], via Wikimedia Commons.

[30] Pitre, *Genesis and the Books of Moses,* MP 3, 23.

RSVCE)?" they ask. After Moses cries out to God, God directs Moses to take his rod and strike "the rock at Horeb (Exodus 17:6 RSVCE)." Moses faithfully obeys exactly what the Lord had commanded him; he strikes the rock, water flows out, and the people's thirst is quenched. In memory of the rebellion, Moses calls the site Massah (מַסָּה) and Mer'ibah, (מְרִיבָה), place names that are derived from two corresponding words meaning test and contention.[31]

A similar episode of rebellion occurs in Numbers chapter twenty at Ka'desh, but this event takes place near the end of their journey through the desert to the Promised Land (Numbers 20:1). Out of thirst the people complain and rebel. Moses once again asks God for help and God tells him to "take the rod, and assemble the congregation…and tell the rock before their eyes to yield water (Numbers 20:8 RSVCE)." Notice that this time God does not command Moses to strike the rock. Instead, He only tells Moses to speak to the rock. Moses, though, decides to strike the rock as he had previously done, and not only once but twice. Although miraculously causing water to flow from the rock, God corrects Moses for not faithfully following his orders. God says, "Because you did not believe in me, to sanctify me in the eyes of the sons of Israel, therefore you shall not bring this assembly into the land which I have given them (Numbers 20:12 RSVCE)." With these words, Moses is not allowed to enter into the Promised Land. The place of Moses and the Israelites unfaithfulness is, like in Exodus chapter seventeen, also called a place of contention and is assigned the name Meri'bath-ka'desh

---

[31] "4532. Massah, Strong's Concordance," biblehub.com, http://biblehub.com/hebrew/4532.htm; "4809. Meribah, Strong's Concordance," biblehub.com, http://biblehub.com/hebrew/4809.htm.

(Deuteronomy 32:51).

Why Moses is singled out in Numbers chapter twenty as the one God punishes and not the people is, Hamilton explains, two-fold. First, Moses lacks a mediator because his role is to mediate between the people and God. Second, his role of mediator carries with it higher expectations, as Jesus, reflecting the Old Testament (Amos 3:2), taught, "Everyone to whom much is given, of him will much be required (Luke 12:48 *RSVCE*)".[32]

Pitre, in reference to the Church Fathers, provides a spiritual interpretation for why Moses was punished at Meri'bath-ka'desh. He does so by comparing the faith that God expected from Moses when standing before a rock with the faith God expects from Catholics when facing the great mystery of the Eucharist. In both cases a priest is only to say words and a miracle will occur. The Old Testament priest Moses was only commanded to speak to a rock so that water would miraculously flow forth. Similarly, New Testament priests are only to say the words of consecration so that bread and wine miraculously become the body and blood of Jesus.[33]

In support of this spiritual interpretation of Moses's "typological error"[34], of Moses error in failing to be a preparatory figure of Christ and the Catholic priesthood that will later be revealed in God's plan of salvation, Pitre refers to St. Paul's Letter to the Corinthians. Here, St. Paul explicitly refers to a "rock" that the Israelites drink from while in the desert and then states that "the Rock was Christ (1 Cor. 10:4 *RSVCE*)." In the celebration of the Mass, the "Rock" who is Christ

---

[32] Hamilton, 336.

[33] Pitre, *Genesis and the Books of Moses,* MP 3 23.

[34] Pitre, *Genesis and the Books of Moses,* MP 3 23.

appears under the accidents of bread and wine. Only words of consecration, explains Pitre, are spoken over the bread and wine by a priest in order for Christ's one perfect sacrifice at Calvary to be made present and its fruits applied to us.

Similarly, only words of the Trinity need to be said over the one being baptized with water for the fruits of Jesus' atoning sacrifice to be applied. Neither the water nor the bread and wine are struck for the Christ to act through them. This is because these Sacraments apply the fruits of Christ as the "Rock" in its fullest sense when He was struck at His passion. His passion is the only sacrifice that truly atones for sins, and that reconciles the world back to God. Upon being struck with a spear while hanging on the cross (John 19:34) blood and water flowed out of Jesus' pierced side (John 19:34). Traditionally, states the *Catechism*, "The blood and water that flowed from the pierced side of the crucified Jesus are types of Baptism and the Eucharist, the sacraments of new life."[35]

Priests in celebrating the Eucharist, and those who baptize, participate in Christ perfect atoning sacrifice, and do not add anything to its perfection. For this reason, they are only to speak words and refrain from adding anything else that is not contained in the sacred ritual. Doing so would be similar to Moses's lack of faith who mistakenly thought he had to add something else for the miracle to occur. May our faith, adds Pitre, be like the centurion whose words we repeat at every Mass "Lord, I am not worthy that you should enter

---

[35] "Catechism of the Catholic Church, 1225," vatican.va, http://www.vatican.va/archive/ccc_css/archive/catechism/p2s2c1a1.htm.

under my roof, but only say the word and my [soul] will be healed (Matthew 8:8)."[36]

Section Questions

1. Compare and contrast Moses' striking a rock in Exodus 17 with Moses striking a rock in Numbers 20. With specific reference to Scripture, include in your response the following: locations, time occurred, outcome, why Moses punished, typological explanation (1 Corinthians 10:4).

Infidelity

The chapters from Numbers that follow Moses's faithlessness at Meri'bath-ka'desh is on yet another type of infidelity, this time sexual infidelity of the Israelites at Moab. According to the Bible, the Moabites are descendants of the child, Moab, which means, according to ancient Jewish commentary, "from father" since Moab was the son of the incestuous relationship between Lot and his first-born daughter (Genesis 19:37).[37] Before reaching Moab, the Israelites defeat Sihon

---

[36] Pitre, *Genesis and the Books of Moses,* MP 3 23.

[37] "Rashi on Genesis 19:37," sefaria.org, https://www.sefaria.org/Rashi_on_Genesis.19.37.1?lang=bi. "מואב MOAB — This daughter who was immodest openly proclaimed that the son was born of her father (מֵאָב) but the younger named her child in a euphemistic fashion and was rewarded for this at the time of Moses, as it is said regarding the children of Ammon, (Deuteronomy 2:19) "Do not contend with them" — in any manner at all — whereas in reference to Moab it (Scripture) only forbade waging war against them but permitted them (the Israelites) to vex them (Genesis Rabbah 51:11)."

the King of the Amorites and Og the King of Bashan. Hearing of these defeats, the neighboring King of Moab, Balak, fears that his kingdom will also be defeated by the Israelites, so he sends elders to the pagan prophet, Balaam the son of Beor. The elders of Moab offer payment to Balaam if he will curse the Israelites (Numbers 22:6-7). Balaam accepts the payment and tries to fulfill the king's request by asking God to curse the Israelites, but God refuses to do so. "God said to Balaam…'…you shall not curse the people, for they are blessed.' (Numbers 22:12 *RSVCE*)"

Despite Balaam's resistance to the spirit of prophecy that is within him, and to the King of Moab, Balaam instead prophecies that Israel is blessed and will continue to be blessed by God. In addition, Israel will be blessed by increasing in numbers (Numbers 23:10), by being successful in battle (Numbers 23:24), and "a star shall come forth out of Jacob, and a scepter shall rise out of Israel; it shall crush the forehead

---

[38] James Tissot, "Balaam and the Ass, as in Numbers 22-24," 1896-1900, https://commons.wikimedia.org/wiki/File:Tissot_Balaam_and_the_Ass.jpg, James Tissot [Public domain], via Wikimedia Commons.

of Moab (Numbers 24:17 *RSVCE*)." According to John Chrysostom, this prophecy was "not merely about the people but also about the coming of the Savior" Jesus Christ.[39]

Although Balaam did what was right by speaking true prophecy, he greatly displeased God by, borrowing from T.S. Eliot's Murder in the Cathedral, doing "the right deed for the wrong reason" which "is the greatest treason." [40] This hidden offense of outwardly looking good but inwardly being corrupt has been named by Henri de Lubac as "spiritual worldliness." Quoting De Lubac, Pope Francis, writing as Cardinal Bergoglio, asserted that spiritual worldliness "is the greatest danger for the Church, for us, who are in the Church. 'It is worse,' says De Lubac, 'more disastrous than the infamous leprosy that disfigured the dearly beloved Bride at the time of the libertine popes.' Spiritual worldliness is putting oneself at the center. It is what Jesus saw going on among the Pharisees: 'You glorify yourselves. Who give glory to yourselves, the ones to the others.'"[41]

---

[39] Joseph T. Lienhard, Ancient Christian Commentary on Scripture, Old Testament III, Exodus, Leviticus, Numbers, Deuteronomy (Downers Grove: InterVarsity Press, 2001), 248. The following is cited, John Chrysostom, *Homilies on Genesis* 21.16.

[40] T.S. Eliot, *Murder in the Cathedral* (Orlando: Harcourt Brace & Company, 1963), 44. "The last temptation is the greatest treason. To do the right deed for the wrong reason."; cf. John Henry Newman, *Parochial and Plain Sermons*, Vol. IV, New Edition (Oxford: Rivingtons, 1868), sermon 2, 28.

[41] Sefania Falasca, "What I would have said at the Consistory: An Interview with Cardinal Jorge Mario Bergoglio, Archbishop of Buenos Aires," *30Days*, Issue no. 11 (2007), 30giorni.it, http://www.30giorni.it/articoli_id_16457_l3.htm; Henri de Lubac, *The Splendor of the Church*, trans. Michael Mason (San Francisco: Ignatius Press, 1999), Location 4075-4081 of 8029; "…the greatest danger we are to the

When not caught up the divine gift of prophecy, Balaam tries to prevent the Israelites from obtaining the blessings that he had prophesied about. He did so by encouraging Moabite and Midianite women to intermingle with Israelite men with the hope of seducing them into pagan, adulterous practices (Numbers 31:16; Revelation 2:14). These practices included worshipping idols and sexual intimacy, which may also have included ritual prostitution as a way of communing with a false god. "While Israel dwelt in Shittim the people began to play the harlot with the daughters of Moab. These invited the people to the sacrifices of their gods, and the people ate, and bowed down to their gods (Numbers 25:1-2 *RSVCE*)."

According to Hamilton, Numbers chapter twenty-two seems to indicate that one particularly egregious and shameless, sexual offense of pagan prostitution between the Israelite Zimri and the Midianite woman Cozbi took place by Israel's sacred tent "in the sight of Moses

---

Church, the most subversive temptation, the one that is ever and insidiously reborn when all the rest are overcome, and even strengthened by those victories, is what Abbot Vonier called the temptation to 'worldliness of the mind... the practical relinquishing of other-worldliness, so that moral and even spiritual standards should be based, not on the glory of the Lord, but on what is the profit of man; an entirely anthropocentric outlook would be exactly what we mean by worldliness. Even if men were filled with every spiritual perfection, but if such perfections were not referred to God (suppose this hypothesis to be possible) it would be unredeemed worldliness. If this spiritual worldliness were to invade the Church and set to work to corrupt her by attacking her very principle, it would be something infinitely more disastrous than any worldliness of the purely moral order-even worse than the hideous leprosy that at certain moments in history inflects so cruel a disfigurement on the Bride; when religious seems to set up the scandalous 'in the sanctuary itself....' Cf. Dom Anscar Vonier, *The Spirit and the Bride* (Assumption Press, 2013), Loc. 988, 1709.

and in the sight of the whole congregation of the sons of Israel, while they were weeping at the door of the tent of meeting (Numbers 25:6 *RSVCE*)."[42] Enraged at this offense, the priest Phinehas took up a spear and ran it through Zimri's and Cozbi's bodies (Numbers 25:8).

[43]

Hamilton points out that the Moabite woman Ruth who is distinguished by her exceptional fidelity and is part of Jesus genealogy (Matthew 1:5) is "a stunning contrast with the Moabite [and Midianite] women of Numbers 25."[44]

Section Questions

1. With respect to fidelity in a specific sense, contrast Ruth with Cozbi.

2. Who was Balaam and how, according to John Chrysostom, did Balaam prophecy the coming of Jesus Christ?

---

[42] Hamilton, 351.

[43] Unknown author / Public domain, "Zimri and Cozbi are slain by Phinehas," https://commons.wikimedia.org/wiki/File:Phinehas_and_Cozbi_are_slain.jpg.

[44] Hamilton, 350.

Deuteronomy

The final book in the Pentateuch is the book of Deuteronomy. This title comes from the Greek Septuagint and literally means second law in Greek. Hahn explains that the Septuagint took the title from its translation of Deuteronomy 17:18 which refers to a second kind of law with, "And when he [the king] sits on the throne of his kingdom, he shall write for himself in a book a copy of this law (Deuteronomy 17:18

[1] James Tissot, "The Ark Passes Over the Jordan," 1896-1902, https://commons.wikimedia.org/wiki/File:James_Jacques_Joseph_Tissot_-_The_Ark_Passes_Over_the_Jordan_-_Google_Art_Project.jpg, [Public domain], via Wikimedia Commons.

RSVCE)."[2]

The Second Law

[3]

Knowing how the law developed prior to Deuteronomy is essential to understanding why this book is called a "second" law. As Pitre explains, the Old Testament covenant went through three stages: Mosaic Covenant, Levitical Covenant, and Deuteronomic Covenant. In establishing the Deuteronomic Covenant God made concessions to the Israelites because of their sinfulness. In so doing, God tolerated lesser evils to avoid the greater evil of apostasy. Due to the concessionary nature of the Deuteronomic Covenant, which we will

---

[2] Scott Hahn, *Catholic Bible Dictionary* (New York: Doubleday, 2009), 214.

[3] James Tissot, "Moses Destroys the Tables of the Ten Commandments," c. 1896-1902, https://commons.wikimedia.org/wiki/File:Tissot_Moses_Destroys_the_Tables_of_the_Ten_Commandments.jpg, James Tissot [Public domain], via Wikimedia Commons.

discuss later, it is considered a second covenant in the sense of being of lesser quality than the preceding covenants.[4]

The very location in which these three covenants were made also indicate their status to one another, with the first one being the highest covenant and the remaining two being devolution of the first, comments Pitre. The sacred location chosen by God for the Mosaic Covenant, which took place prior to the idolatry of the golden calf (Exodus 32), was on the top of Mount Sinai (Exodus 24:12-13). Here, God gave Moses "two tables of the covenant, tables of stone, written with the finger of God (Exodus 31:18 *RSVCE*; cf. Deuteronomy 9:9-11)."

This covenant is followed by Moses breaking apart the first set of Ten Commandments. He does this after he comes down from the mountain top and sees the Israelites frolicking around a golden calf (Exodus 32:19). Moses then interceded before God on behalf of his sinful people. God responded by establishing the Levitical Covenant where the common priesthood of the Israelite fathers and first-born sons is replaced by the Levitical priesthood (Numbers 3:12). To signify the lower status of this covenant in relationship to the first one, God does not give Moses two tablets on the mountain top. Instead, God required Moses to cut two stone tablets at the base of the mountain and then go up the mountain where the covenant is re-established (Exodus 34:10; Deuteronomy 10:1).[5]

In contrast with the first two, the location of the Deuteronomic

---

[4] Brant Pitre, *The Old Testament-A Historical and Theological Journey through Jewish Scripture*, MP 9.

[5] Emil G. Hirsch, "Tables of the Law," jewishencyclopedia.com, http://jewishencyclopedia.com/articles/14189-tables-of-the-law.

Covenant is not even on or near the sacred place of Mount Sinai. Instead, this covenant takes place between Mount Ebal and Mount Gerizim (Deuteronomy 11:29). These two mountains are far away, points out Pitre, from the holy mountain top where both Melchizedek, the "priest of God Most High (Genesis 14:18 *RSVCE*)" of Salem, and the patriarch Abraham on Mount Moriah worshipped and offered sacrifice to God (Genesis 22:13, 22). Salem is an abbreviation for Jerusalem in a similar way that Zion is.[6] This word, according to Hebrews, comes from the Hebrew word peace (Shalom שָׁלוֹם). (Hebrews 7:2)

Psalm 76, points out Hahn, equates Salem with Zion with "His [God's] abode has been established in Salem, and his dwelling place in Zion (Psalm 76:2)."[7] Mount Moriah, the place where Abraham offered sacrifice, is likewise traditionally associated with Mount Zion. Second

---

[6] Mark O'Brien, *Restoring the Right Relationship: The Bible on Divine Righteousness* (Hindmarsh: ATF Theology, 2014), 178. According to O'Brien, the term Zion, especially in Isaiah, "is used variously to refer to the city/hill of Jerusalem (1:27; 2:3b; 4:3; 33:5, 20; 37:32; 20:9; 41:27, 52:1; 59:20; 60:14; 62:1); the temple mount itself ... a combination of the city and temple mount ...; the seat of the Davidic king ... and God's house/dwelling place ...."

[7] Scott Hahn, *Catholic Bible Dictionary* (New York: Doubleday, 2009), 429; Hahn also refers to who in his books Antiquities of the Jews wrote, "So Abram, when he had saved the captive Sodomites, who had been taken by the Assyrians, and Lot also, his kinsman, returned home in peace. Now the king of Sodom met him at a certain place, which they called The King's Dale, where Melchizedek, king of the city Salem, received him. That name signifies, the righteous king: and such he was, without dispute, insomuch that, on this account, he was made the priest of God: however, they afterward called Salem Jerusalem." Flavius Josephus, "Antiquities of the Jews, Book 1, Chapter 10, 2," sacred-texts.com, http://www.sacred-texts.com/jud/josephus/ant-1.htm.

Chronicles appears to confirm this identification since it states that Solomon built the first Temple on Mount Moriah: "Then Solomon began to build the house of the Lord in Jerusalem on Mount Mori'ah (2 Chronicles 3:1 *RSVCE*)."[8] Mount Moriah, adds Pitre, is the destination that God indicates the Israelites will arrive at after their long journey through the desert to the Promised Land. "You" sings Moses and Miriam "will bring them [the Israelites] in, and plant them on your own mountain, the place, O Lord, which you have made for your abode, the sanctuary, O Lord, which your hands have established (Exodus 15:17 *RSVCE*)."[9]

By sending the Israelites north of Mount Moriah to what is now northern Israel in the region of Samaria, God was sending them away from the promised holy "abode" and "sanctuary". Between these two Samaritan mountains God established the Deuteronomic Covenant and in so doing, argues Pitre, indicates that this covenant is not part of the original plan but rather a concessionary covenant, a "detour in salvation history"[10] from the intended destination of Jerusalem, i.e., Mount Moriah/Mount Zion.[11] Once the Israelites pass through the plains of Moab, and cross the Jordan River, God commands that a "blessing" is set on Mount Gerizim and "a curse" is placed on Mount Ebal (Deuteronomy 11:26-32 *RSVCE*).[12] Origin interpreted the cursed

---

[8] Scott Hahn, *Catholic Bible Dictionary*, 430.

[9] Pitre, *The Old Testament*, MP 14.

[10] Pitre, *The Old Testament*, MP 14.

[11] Pitre, *The Old Testament*, MP 14.

[12] "Behold, I set before you this day a blessing and a curse: the blessing, if you obey the commandments of the Lord your God, which I command you this day, and the curse, if you do not obey the commandments of the Lord your God, but turn aside from the way which I command you this

mountain of Ebal and the blessed mountain of Gerizim as representing two ways by which people are motivated by God. The people by the cursed mountain of Ebal represent those who "attain salvation by fear of evil things and dread of torments."[13] The people by the blessed mountain of Gerizim "indicate figuratively the ones who come to salvation not by fear of punishment but by desire of blessings and renewed promises."[14]

Before going to this sacred place between two mountains, Israel's tendency to pride is halted by God when he reminds them that He is blessing them not because of any merit on their part but simply because He has chosen them, chosen them for the sake of all nations, as becomes more evident in later passages of Scripture:

> [D]o not say to yourself, "It is because of my righteousness that the Lord has brought me in to occupy this land" .... It is not because of your righteousness or the uprightness of your heart

---

day, to go after other gods which you have not known. And when the Lord your God brings you into the land which you are entering to take possession of it, you shall set the blessing on Mount Geri'zim and the curse on Mount Ebal. Are they not beyond the Jordan, west of the road, toward the going down of the sun, in the land of the Canaanites who live in the Arabah, over against Gilgal, beside the oak of Moreh? For you are to pass over the Jordan to go in to take possession of the land which the Lord your God gives you; and when you possess it and live in it, you shall be careful to do all the statutes and the ordinances which I set before you this day. (Deuteronomy 11:26-32 RSVCE)

[13] John R. Franke, *Ancient Christian Commentary on Scripture: Old Testament IV, Joshua, Judges, Ruth, 1-2 Samuel* (Downers Grove: Intervarsity Press, 2014), 51.

[14] Franke, 51.

that you are going in to occupy their land .... Know, then, that the Lord your God is not giving you this good land to occupy because of your righteousness; for you are a stubborn people (Deuteronomy 9:4-6 *RSVCE*).

Besides the different locations as indicators of different covenants, the words of Scripture also affirm this distinction. In distinguishing the Mosaic and Levitical covenants from the Deuteronomic Covenant, Deuteronomy clearly states, "These are the words of the covenant which the Lord commanded Moses to make with the sons of Israel in the land of Moab, besides the covenant which he had made with them at Horeb (Deuteronomy 29:1 *RSVCE*)." Horeb is another name for Mount Sinai, explains Hahn.[15] The quoted verse from Deuteronomy distinguishes the covenant made at Horeb, in other words at Mount Sinai, with the Deuteronomic covenant Moses reminds the Israelites of in the "plains of Moab" at "Beth-peor (Deuteronomy 1:5; 3:29; 4:44–46)."

The time span between these two covenants is about forty years, the time that the Israelites were punished with by God for doubting that He would lead them safely into the Promised Land. The second of the two, the Deuteronomic Covenant, was made between God and the children of the Mosaic Covenant. It was established in the plains of Moab between Mounts Ebal and Gerizim, on the very site where the Israelites had sinned by cavorting with the woman of Moab and worshipping the Moabites' idols (Numbers 14:34-35, 32:13, 25:1-2).

Section Questions

---

[15] Hahn, *Catholic Bible Dictionary*, 853. Hahn provides the following Scripture references: "Exodus 33:6; Deuteronomy 1:6, 5:2; 1 Kings 8:9; etc."

1. Place the following stages of the Old Covenant in their proper chronological stages and then briefly distinguish each one: Levitical, Mosaic, Deuteronomic. In your response include the following: place where each covenant was made, Golden Calf incident, Patriarchal Priesthood, Levitical Priesthood, Concessionary Law

Not Good Laws

Deuteronomy contains laws that Christianity dismisses as "not good (Ezekiel 20:25 *RSVCE*)" and contains good laws that Jesus fulfills. We will first discuss the "not good laws" before touching upon those good aspects and good laws of Deuteronomy that are deepened and fulfilled by the New Testament. According to Ezekiel, God said, "I swore to them [the Israelites] in the wilderness that I would scatter them among the nations …. Moreover, I gave them statutes that were not good and ordinances by which they could not have life (Ezekiel 20:23-25 *RSVCE*)." Hahn explains that the reason for these "not good"

---

[16] James Tissot, "The Women of Midian Led Captive by the Hebrews James Tissot," c.1900, https://commons.wikimedia.org/wiki/File:Tissot_The_Women_of_Midian_Led_Captive_by_the_Hebrews.jpg, James Tissot [Public domain], via Wikimedia Commons.

laws was that God foresaw that if he retained the more demanding good laws a greater evil was likely to occur, apostasy. From the perspective of salvation history that gradually leads people from imperfection to perfection, these "not good" laws, as Aquinas teaches, are provisional, conditional, and perfect, not simply, but with respect to the "condition of time" that they were given. For example, laws that are suitable for a young child, are perfectly suited to the child state of growth. Although these laws may no longer be perfectly suitable with the child has matured into an adult.[17]

Therefore, ever respectful of our free will and mindful of our eternal destiny, God as the all wise, divine teacher yielded in an act of divine condescension by relaxing the laws demands and, in the process, permitting lesser evils than apostasy to be committed. Jesus explicitly states this reason with, "For your hardness of heart Moses allowed you to divorce your wives, but from the beginning it was not so (Matthew 19:8 RSVCE)." [18] In commentating on the divine pedagogy that Jesus is referring to, Aquinas states that the law was given and failures were permitted so that gradually people would realize that not by any human gift (intellectual, physical, emotional, volitional) can one fulfill what the law requires. Rather, the fulfillment

---

[17] Thomas Aquinas, "Summa Theologica," I-II, Q. 98 Art. 2, Reply to Objection 1, newadvent.org, http://www.newadvent.org/summa/2098.htm. "Nothing prevents a thing being not perfect simply, and yet perfect in respect of time: thus a boy is said to be perfect, not simply, but with regard to the condition of time. So, too, precepts that are given to children are perfect in comparison with the condition of those to whom they are given, although they are not perfect simply. Hence the Apostle says (Galatians 3:24): 'The law was our pedagogue in Christ.'"

[18] Hahn, *Catholic Bible Dictionary*, 216-217.

of the law can occur only by relying on grace, grace that Catholics believes comes through a relationship with the one mediator between God and humans, Jesus Christ.[19]

Among the lesser evils that was permitted and sanctioned by the lower Deuteronomic Covenant and its code of law was divorce and remarriage (Deuteronomy 24:1-4), wars of annihilation where a city and all the living and possession in it were completely destroyed (Deuteronomy 20:17), the permission of having a king despite that God alone is king (Deuteronomy 17:14-15, 33:5; 1 Samuel 8:7), and usury for foreigners despite being forbidden in Leviticus to foreigners or Israelites (Deuteronomy 23:20; Leviticus 25:36-37).[20]

In describing these additional, concessionary laws, comments Pitre, Deuteronomy explicitly represents them as a testimony to the wickedness of the Israelites:[21]

> When Moses had finished writing the words of this law in a book, to the very end, Moses commanded the Levites who carried the ark of the covenant of the Lord, "Take this book of the law, and put it by the side of the ark of the covenant of the Lord your God, that it may be there for a witness against

---

[19] Thomas Aquinas, "Summa Theologica," I-II, Question 98, Art. 2, Reply to Objection 3, newadvent.org, http://www.newadvent.org/summa/2098.htm. "As stated above (I-II:79:4), God sometimes permits certain ones to fall into sin, that they may thereby be humbled. So also did He wish to give such a law as men by their own forces could not fulfill, so that, while presuming on their own powers, they might find themselves to be sinners, and being humbled might have recourse to the help of grace."

[20] Hahn, *Catholic Bible Dictionary*, 216-217.

[21] Pitre, *The Old Testament*, MP3.

you. For I know how rebellious and stubborn you are; behold, while I am yet alive with you, today you have been rebellious against the Lord; how much more after my death! Assemble to me all the elders of your tribes, and your officers, that I may speak these words in their ears and call heaven and earth to witness against them. For I know that after my death you will surely act corruptly and turn aside from the way which I have commanded you; and in the days to come evil will befall you, because you will do what is evil in the sight of the Lord, provoking him to anger through the work of your hands." (Deuteronomy 31:24-29 *RSVCE*)

As the above passage indicates, the placement of the additional Deuteronomic laws outside of the ark and not inside the ark, which houses the Ten Commandments, is a sign of being "not good" laws. These "not good" laws, deliberately placed outside of the Ark argues Pitre, means that God does not intend them to bind as the Ten Commandments do and means that they are not permanent as the Ten Commandments are.[22] When Jesus came he returned us back to the original law, minus its concessions, without its exceptions and concessionary laws: "You have heard that it was said.... 'Whoever divorces his wife, let him give her a certificate of divorce.' But I say to you that everyone who divorces his wife, except on the ground of unchastity, makes her an adulteress; and whoever marries a divorced woman commits adultery (Matthew 5:27, 31-32 *RSVCE*)."

---

[22] Pitre, *The Old Testament*, MP3.

Section Questions

1. How does Pitre specifically relate Deuteronomy 31:24-29 with Ezekiel's "not good laws (Ezekiel 20:23-25)"?

2. List at least three not good Deuteronomic laws identified by Hahn and Pitre.

Good Laws

Mixed in with the Deuteronomic "not good laws," which Ezekiel identifies, are good laws. These laws deepen and flesh out the meaning of the Mosaic covenant. For example, the universal destination of all goods implied by Genesis which takes over personal property, as the

---

Catechism teaches,[24] and the relationship of this "primordial"[25] law to the Seventh Commandment of not stealing is clarified by, "If there is among you a poor man, one of your brethren, in any of your towns within your land which the Lord your God gives you, you shall not harden your heart or shut your hand against your poor brother, but you shall open your hand to him, and lend him sufficient for his need, whatever it may be (Deuteronomy 15:7-8 *RSVCE*)."

Pitre specifies that the Church's teaching on the "preferential option for the poor has its root" in these verses.[26] Reflecting this preference, the current Code of Canon Law obliges Catholics, "to promote social justice and, mindful of the precept of the Lord, to assist the poor from their own resources (*CCL* 222)."[27] Since Jesus identified himself with the poor, one way to encounter Jesus in a particularly intense manner is by serving the poor for Jesus said, "Truly, I say to you, as you did it to one of the least of these my brethren, you did it to me (Matthew 25:40 *RSVCE*)."

Pope John Paul II taught that this preference of Jesus for the least of the brethren refers to both spiritual and physical poverty. The

---

[24] "The *right to private property*, acquired or received in a just way, does not do away with the original gift of the earth to the whole of mankind. The *universal destination of goods* remains primordial, even if the promotion of the common good requires respect for the right to private property and its exercise." "Catechism of the Catholic Church, no. 2403," vatican.va, http://www.vatican.va/archive/ccc_css/archive/catechism/p3s2c2a7.htm.

[25] "Catechism of the Catholic Church, no. 2403," vatican.va, http://www.vatican.va/archive/ccc_css/archive/catechism/p3s2c2a7.htm.

[26] Brant Pitre, *Genesis and the Books of Moses: Unlocking the Mysteries of the Pentateuch*, MP 3, 20.

[27] "Code of Canon Law," canon 222, no. 2, vatican.va, http://www.vatican.va/archive/ENG1104/_PU.HTM.

Church's, he wrote, "preferential option for the poor… is never exclusive or discriminatory towards other groups. This option is not limited to material poverty, since it is well known that there are many other forms of poverty, especially in modern society—not only economic but cultural and spiritual poverty as well."[28]

In a certain sense, but with of course an important difference, what Canon Law is to the Church the book of Deuteronomy was to the Jewish people at the time of Jesus. For this reason, comments Pitre, Jesus repeatedly cites from Deuteronomy including when he dismissed the temptations of the devil while in the Judean desert prior to Jesus' public ministry. These two counters of Jesus to the devil come directly from Deuteronomy: "[M]an does not live by bread alone, but that man lives by everything that proceeds from the mouth of the Lord Deuteronomy 8:3 *RSVCE*"; "You shall not put the Lord your God to the test, as you tested him at Massah (Deuteronomy 6:16 *RSVCE*; cf. Matthew 4:1-11)."[29]

The Deuteronomic reference of man not living on bread alone but on the Heavenly Father's will was said in the desert by Jesus who perfectly fulfilled this verse, since, as Jesus said, "For I have come down from heaven, not to do my own will, but the will of him who sent me (John 6:38 *RSVCE*)." We are to identify both with the Israelites whom the quoted verse of Deuteronomy was first addressed and with Christ whom the verse was fulfilled in. We are like the Israelites, comments Pitre, in that our entire life on earth with its trials and tribulations

---

[28] "Centesimus Annus," no. 57, w2.vatican.va, http://w2.vatican.va/content/john-paul-ii/en/encyclicals/documents/hf_jp-ii_enc_01051991_centesimus-annus.html#%2410.

[29] Pitre, *The Old Testament*, MP 15, 16.

resembles the desert experience of the Israelites. God teaches us during these desert experiences we are to resist excessively hungering after the goods of this world which can never be ultimately satisfying, but rather to look to Jesus who desired to do only His Heavenly Father's will.[30]

Jesus not only cited Deuteronomy but also deepened what Deuteronomy taught, especially regarding the essence of the law as love of God and neighbor. The Greatest Commandment on love of God and neighbor comes directly from Deuteronomy and from Leviticus. Jesus taught this commandment upon being asked what is the greatest commandment. All three synoptic gospels provide slightly different versions of how Jesus responded. According to Mark's account, "Jesus answered, 'The first is, 'Hear, O Israel: The Lord our God, the Lord is one; and you shall love the Lord your God with all your heart, and with all your soul, and with all your mind, and with all your strength.' The second is this, 'You shall love your neighbor as yourself.' There is no other commandment greater than these (Mark 12:29-31 *RSVCE*)."

The first part of the Great Commandment comes directly from Deuteronomy's Shema prayer that devout Jews of the past and today pray daily.[31] (Deuteronomy 6:4-9) The prayer begins with affirming God of Israel "is one," (*echad* אֶחָד), thereby affirming God's one nature, or, depending on the translation points out Hamilton, is "the Lord alone" (יְהוָה אֶחָד the Lord *echad*), and in this case emphasizing Israel's unique bond with God alone.[32] When taken together these

---

[30] Pitre, *Genesis and the Books of Moses*, MP 3 24.

[31] Shema, the first word of the prayer, means hear (שָׁמַע).

[32] Victor P. Hamilton, *Handbook on the Pentateuch, Second Edition* (Grand Rapids: Baker Academic, 2005), 393.

translations, adds Hamilton, can be interpreted in an ethical manner. God is one and verification of his oneness is His unwavering faithful love to Israel.

Israel ought to have a relationship with this true, loving God since His love is true, his love is formed by truth defined as that which is consistent and "not fickle, capricious, or unpredictable".[33] Because God's love is consistently true and never wavers we in turn, no matter what historical period we are in, are called to respond with a similar love. For this reason, argues Hamilton, this verse on God's love is a call for an appropriate, similar response, loving God with all our "heart" "soul" and "might (Deuteronomy 6:5 *RSVCE*)."[34]

As pointed out earlier, Pitre points out an important difference in Jesus's version of this prayer. The difference that is present in all three synoptic accounts of the New Testament version is Jesus adds to the Shema prayer the Greek word for mind, a word that Biblical Hebrew lacks. In the New Testament version of the Shema prayer, we are to love God with all our "mind" and not just with what Deuteronomy lists: heart, soul, and might. By adding "mind" to the Shema prayer Jesus, through the Greek New Testament translation, explains Pitre, further interiorized the prayer and intensified its demands.[35] The second part of Jesus' Great Commandment on loving our neighbor as we love ourselves comes directly from Leviticus which states, "[Y]ou shall love your neighbor as yourself (Leviticus 19:18 *RSVCE*)."

Combining these two commandments into the most essential and greatest commandment and heightening the interior demands of the

---

[33] Hamilton, 395.

[34] Hamilton, 395.

[35] Pitre, *Genesis and the Books of Moses*, MP 3 24.

law is unique to Jesus and fulfills what Moses had told the Israelites: "[T]he Lord your God will circumcise your heart and the heart of your offspring, so that you will love the Lord your God with all your heart and with all your soul, that you may live (Deuteronomy 30:6 *RSVCE* cf. Deuteronomy 10:16)."

Catholics believe that the interiorization of the law that the Mosaic Law, especially Commandments Nine and Ten that prohibit coveting, and the interior requirements of the Deuteronomic Law are deepened and fulfilled in Jesus by the Holy Spirit in cooperation with human effort and not primarily because of force of will or intellectual ability.[36]

Section Questions

1. Name one way that the Deuteronomic laws deepen and further flesh out the goodness of the original Mosaic laws.

---

[36] Thomas Aquinas, "Summa Theologica," II-II, Q. 62, Art. 1, newadvent.org, http://www.newadvent.org/summa/3162.htm; Thomas Aquinas, "Summa Theologica," II-II, Q. 62, Art. 6, Ad. 3, newadvent.org, http://www.newadvent.org/summa/3162.htm; Thomas Aquinas, "Summa Theologica," I-II, Q. 98 Art. 6, Resp. newadvent.org, http://www.newadvent.org/summa/2098.htm.

Printed in Great Britain
by Amazon

42578423R00148